· THE ·
SACRED
PORTAL

In unserm Gemüt ist alles auf die eigenste
gefälligste und lebendigste Weise verknüpft.
Die fremdesten Dinge kommen durch einen Ort,
eine Zeit, eine seltsame Ähnlichkeit, einen
Irrtum, irgendeinen Zufall zusammen. So
entstehn wunderliche Einigkeiten und eigentümliche
Verknüpfungen—und eins erinnert an alles—wird
das Zeichen vieler und wird selbst von vielen
bezeichnet und herbeigerufen. Verstand und
Phantasie werden durch Zeit und Raum auf das
sonderbarste vereinigt, und man kann sagen,
dass jeder Gedanke, jede Erscheinung unsers
Gemüts das individuellste Glied eines durchaus
eigentümlichen Ganzen ist.

(In our soul everything is related in a most
particular, pleasant, and lively manner. The
most alien things are brought together by a
place, a time, a strange similarity, an error,
or by mere coincidence. Wondrous unions and
original relationships come into being, and
one thing recalls all things, becomes the symbol
of many other things, and is itself evoked by
them. Intellect and imagination are united by
time and space in the most peculiar way, so that
one can say that every thought, every aspect of
our soul is a most individual part of a
thoroughly characteristic whole.)

Fragment 1369 from *Die Enzyklopädie*
of Novalis (Wasmuth edition, 1957)

Wayne State University Press, Detroit, 1966

· THE ·
SACRED
PORTAL

A PRIMARY SYMBOL IN
ANCIENT JUDAIC ART

by Bernard Goldman
WAYNE STATE UNIVERSITY

Grateful acknowledgement is made to the American Council
of Learned Societies and to the Graduate Division of Wayne
State University for financial assistance in the research under-
taken for this book.

Grateful acknowledgement for financial assistance in pub-
lishing this book is made to the Morris and Emma Schaver
Publication Fund for Jewish Studies.

This manuscript was edited by Mary Garner, and the book
was designed by Richard Kinney. The text type face is Mergen-
thaler Linotype's Caledonia designed by W. A. Dwiggins, 1937.
The display face is Bernhard Modern Bold designed by Lucian
Bernhard, 1925.

The book is printed on Beckett Paper Company's Wayne
Text paper specially made for this book and bound in Columbia
Mills' Riverside Chambray cloth over boards. Manufactured in
the United States of America.

Bernard Goldman is associate professor of art history at
Wayne State University. He received his Ph.D. from the University of Michigan. A specialist in ancient near Eastern Art, he
writes The Sacred Portal from both field research and scholarship.

to my wife, Norma

· CONTENTS ·

· ILLUSTRATIONS ·

FIGURES

PHOTOGRAPHS

All photographs appear in numerical order at the back of the book

1. Beth Alpha: plan showing location of mosaics. (Drawing: Department of Archaeology, Hebrew University)

2. Beth Alpha: view of synagogue remains looking toward the wall niche. (Photograph: Department of Archaeology, Hebrew University)

3. Beth Alpha: view of synagogue remains looking from niche toward stone bema. (Photograph: Department of Archaeology, Hebrew University)

4. Beth Alpha mosaic: the Sacrifice of Isaac panel. (Photograph: Department of Archaeology, Hebrew University)

5. Beth Alpha mosaic: the zodiac panel. (Photograph: Department of Archaeology, Hebrew University)

Illustrations

27. Painted arcosolium in the Torlonia catacomb: drawn curtain reveals Torah cupboard flanked by Jewish ritual objects.

28. Jewish gold glass with "Temple of Solomon."

29. Solar deity between open doors with lion pivots on Akkadian cylinder sealing. (Boston, Museum of Fine Arts)

30. Sacred portal on Sumerian cylinder sealing. (Boston, Museum of Fine Arts)

31. Elamite bronze plaque of "High Place" dedicated by Shilhak-Inshushinak. (Louvre, Paris)

32. Shrine on Neo-Assyrian cylinder sealing. (from *Corpus,* no. 694; Collection of the Pierpont Morgan Library)

33. Achaemenian sealing showing *aedicula* formed by equestrians supporting winged disk; within, kneeling figure holds circle with portrait inside. (Tehran, Archaeological Museum)

34. Columnar figures of water-gods on façade of the Temple of Inanna at Erech. Cassite Period. (from Beek, *Atlas of Mesopotamia,* fig. 164)

35. *Kudurru* with altar shrines carrying symbols of the gods. 12th century B.C. (from Beek, *Atlas of Mesopotamia,* fig. 258)

36a. Terra-cotta shrine from Idalion, Cyprus (Paris: Louvre Museum)

36b. Altar-shrine with snakes and birds from Beisan (Beth-Shan). (Philadelphia, University Museum)

37. Etruscan cinerary urn. (Vatican, Museum; photography, Moscioni)

38. Ceramic ossuary with door posts from Azor. (Photo: J. Perrot, Mission archéologue française en Israel)

39. Copper "Crown" with representation of portal. (Israel, Department of Antiquities)

40. Ivory carving of Holy Sepulchre from early Christian casket, *circa* 400 A.D. (London, Trustees of the British Museum)

41. Stone tomb door from Kefer Yosef. (Paris, Louvre)

42. Stone tomb door from Ovalin. (Israel, Department of Antiquities)

43. Hamman-Lif mosaic: panel with Jewish cult objects. (Brooklyn, Museum)

44. Ceramic seven-cup container from Nahariyah. (Israel, Department of Antiquities)

45. Mosaic pavement from building near Hulda with standard Jewish cult objects. 6th century A.D. (Israel, Department of Antiquities)

46. Stone tomb portal from Kefar Tamra, near Shefar 'am. 5th-6th century A.D. (Haifa, Municipal Museum of Ancient Art)

47. Ceramic lamp with eight nozzles and portal enclosing lozenge. (from *Sym.* III, fig. 282)

48. Gabled lid with antefixes from sarcophagus at Beth She'arim.

49. Jewish ossuary with portal and rosettes. (Photograph: N. Avigad, Department of Archaeology, Hebrew University)

50. Columnar sarcophagus from Beth She'arim. (Photograph: N. Avigad, Department of Archaeology, Hebrew University)

Illustrations

51. Stone relief from Dura-Europos of deity on camelback before horned altar. (Photograph: Dura-Europos Publications)

52. Decorated sarcophagus from Beth She'arim. (Photograph: Israel Exploration Society)

53. Dipinto from Dura-Europos with eagle mounted on horned altar within a niche. (Photograph: Dura-Europos Publications)

54. Coin of Macrinus: betyl on horned altar in temple enclosure. (from Ronzevalle, "Venus lugens et Adonis byblius," pl. xxii, no. 7)

55. Altar of *Alexandros Amrou* from Khirbet-et-Tannur: winged goddess in niche. (Photograph: N. Glueck, Hebrew Union College)

56. Altar of *Alexandros Amrou* from Khirbet-et-Tannur: Zeus-Baal in niche. (Photograph: N. Glueck, Hebrew Union College)

57. Glass chalice with Cross in sacred portal. (Washington, Dumbarton-Oaks Collection)

58. Coptic wool textile fragment from Antinoë, Egypt. (New York, Metropolitan Museum of Art, Rogers Fund, 1931)

59. Hamman-Lif mosaic: head of Amazon in synagogue pavement. (Brooklyn, Museum)

60. Hamman-Lif mosaic: head of young shepherd in synagogue pavement. (Brooklyn, Museum)

· PREFACE ·

T HIS STUDY IS concerned with one aspect of the broad field of ancient Near Eastern art history: the examination of some of the most important thematic motifs that dominate the art of the ancient Jews. Its focal point is the mosaic pavement of the Beth Alpha synagogue that stood, some 1500 years ago, in the Lower Galilee of ancient Palestine. The crowning design in the decorative scheme of that synagogue is a pedimented portal, elaborately worked out in the mosaic cubes by the artists, Marianos and Ḥanina, father and son, which forms the backbone of this study and provides its title, *The Sacred Portal*.

The problems opened here are those properly within the purview of the art historian: What gave this work of art its particular character? Why does it carry this particular set of motifs? What are the sources of the symbols? How are the symbols used? And what external factors shaped style and content in the work and account for its appearance at this time and place in history?

The field of ancient Near Eastern art is seldom given more than a brief chapter in the general study of art history, for it is usually relegated to archaeology. The art of the ancient Jews is still more exotic. Except for the passing reference that is now almost always made to the murals of the Dura-Europos synagogue, the teacher of art history seldom brings his students into contact with the literature and monuments of the early Jews. Hence, it seemed best to provide this study with brief definitions, explanations, and bibliographies of the primary Jewish documents in the notes which the reader well-oriented in the field of Judaica can certainly omit. The bibliographical notes are not intended to be exhaustive, but rather to give the most important sources. Those books which catalog the Palestinian synagogues—Saller, Sukenik, Watzinger, and Hiram (see Bibliography)—are not listed in the basic bibliographies given in the notes on individual structures; the reader interested in any synagogue should, of course, begin with these volumes before going on to the more specialized studies noted.

Since the final draft of this study was completed before the publication of the three volume study of the Dura-Europos synagogue by Professor Goodenough and the general history of Jewish art edited by Cecil Roth, reference to these works is not included here. The excellent material they contain does not, however, alter my findings.

It is impossible to discuss religious art without becoming involved in the beliefs and concepts of the culture from which the works sprang and which they express. But the reader is asked to remember that the burden of this study, as well as the orientation of the writer, is art history. The history of religion is an extremely thorny field in which the casual traveler from a neighboring region can walk with only the greatest caution. The author can but hope that his errors of omission and commission in the remarks on the beliefs and practices of ancient Judaism are not of such magnitude that they affect the arguments and conclusions on the art of the Jewish communities.

Obligations are too many to list, but it would be an impertinence not to mention in gratitude some of the scholars without whose kindness this book would have been much the poorer. First, my colleagues at Wayne State University: Dr. Alfred Greenbaum of the University Libraries put his profound knowledge of Judaica and Semitic languages at my disposal; Dr. Ernst Scheyer and Dr. Sadayoshi Omoto (now at Michigan State University) of the Department of Art and Art History provided the necessary felicitous climate of scholarship and friendship; Dr. Harold Basilius went far beyond his official capacity as Director of the University Press in his help and guidance. In Israel: the staff of the Department of Antiquities, of the Ministry of Education and Culture, lent precious time and assistance in the museum and on visits to the sites being excavated under their jurisdiction; Mrs. Chaim Tadmor, of the Department of Antiquities, was particularly gracious; Dr. Shmuel Yeivin, ex-Director of the Department of Antiquities, saw to all my scholarly needs in Jerusalem; Dr. Asher Hiram freely gave of his commanding knowledge of synagogue architecture and in continuing friendship has kept me in touch with the latest synagogue discoveries so as to circumvent the usual time lag between excavation and publication; Dr. Michel Avi-Yonah generously took time from his professorial duties at Hebrew University to discuss my work and provide photographic material. Dr. Joseph Guttman, Director of the Museum of Hebrew Union College (Cincinnati), was most helpful in providing bibliographical material difficult to locate.

This book is offered as a small token of appreciation and respect to my teacher and friend, Professor Clark Hopkins, in his seventieth year.

B. G.

· I ·

INTRODUCTION

In the history of art, the first six centuries of the Christian Era are particularly important, comprising, as they do, a turbulent period which holds the last winter fruits of the Classical world as well as the spring flowers of the new world of Christianity. The regrouping of spiritual forces that took place at this time is signaled in sculpture and painting by a change from the representational art forms of pagan Classicism to the abstract forms of the early Medieval; from reliance on canons of physical form as media for expression of ideals *(physioplastic)* to emphasis on conceptual forms in order to express the transcendental *(ideoplastic)*.

Christian art was not born new, without antecedent, nor was it reborn, phoenix-like, in the aesthetic ashes of the ancient world: history is seldom so dramatic. Rather, in those first centuries, the old world of art was gradually transformed to carry the new message, the spiritual burden of the mystery religions. Indeed, Classical art during the last decades of Rome's hegemony appears, in retrospect, already to have been groping for a mode of expression that uniquely suited the pathos, the drama, and the ineluctable inner brilliance that the Christian soul demanded. Pagan art forms proved to be far more durable than the society that engendered them; they were carried into the Middle Ages, and beyond, down to our own times. Inevitably, freighted as they were with vital new content, Graeco-Roman art forms changed, but they maintained a genetic strain in later, Western Europe, which was never to be transmuted beyond

[18]

recognition. East Christian art, that of the Byzantines, took one course while the art of Western Europe took another; both, however, adopted pagan art and adapted it to serve its new master.

It is true that the art and architecture of the first centuries of the Christian Era lack that grandeur, sense of completeness, and display of technical virtuosity characteristic of Greek and Roman, on one side, and of Western Medieval and Byzantine art on the other. But art historians are long past that time when the first half-dozen centuries of the Christian Era were considered to be a barbaric, primitive wasteland of art. These years form a transition period between two great epochs that is difficult to evaluate because of the temptation (more often indulged in than resisted) to judge it in terms of that which had been so glorious before, and that which was so splendidly to follow. It is false, of course, to view the styles of Classicism and the Middle Ages as static, for they too were restless and ever-changing, reflections of the continuing dynamics of human history. The two great art traditions are not monoliths linked together by an era of anarchy, decay, and barbarization. Rather, Graeco-Roman art flowed out, uniting with other streams to form the tradition of Western Christian art. It is with one of these other streams that we are here particularly concerned.

Not many decades ago, though the scope and nature of the Oriental contribution are still but roughly calculated, scholars began to recognize the important legacy of the vast reservoir of ancient Near Eastern art to Western tradition. But progress in archaeology, with recovery of an astonishing variety of art works, offers an ever-increasing body of material to be evaluated, and greater discriminations can now be made.

One relatively new avenue for the investigation of Oriental and Classical contributions to Western art and culture leads to the Jews of the Near East whose art is of unusual significance. They were a people who, themselves Easterners with roots deeply bedded in the ancient Oriental scene, continued as a cultural entity through the first centuries after the birth of Christ, long after such great Eastern powers as Assyria, Babylonia, or Persia, had perished. Moreover, those later Jews of the

East were not an untouched Oriental group on the fringe of Western civilization; they had collided with the West and well knew its pervasive influence. Thus, first of all, the art of the Jews provides us opportunity to witness an amalgam of two distinct and ancient approaches to the artistic problems of style and symbol. And second, early Judaic art must surely yield significant data on the meanings of Christian art in its formative stages: profound familial bonds of cult, religion, and ritual are clearly stated in the arts of Jew and Christian in the early centuries. Judaic art is, then, a welcome gauge for measuring the continuation and constancy of ancient Near Eastern art traditions in a world that is modern yet maintains unbroken contact with the old and new movements of the West.

No single Jewish monument tells the whole story, but one complex work of art can provide an important index. The mosaic floor in the synagogue at Beth Alpha is well suited to serve as a case study of the style and form of Judaic art in the middle of the first millennium A.D. Not only is the mosaic in an excellent state of preservation, but it is also signed with the names of the artists and can be fairly closely dated within the sixth century A.D. And its contents are rich: the standard Jewish motifs and symbols of its time as well as a pictorial scene of the sacrifice of Isaac, which, at the present, is unique in ancient mosaics. The Beth Alpha floor is an important cultural and historical document, but more than that it is also a moving work of art.

In recent years a large number of synagogue mosaics of the Byzantine period have been uncovered in the old Palestinian soil. While the study of this material is still in its infancy, it is already obvious that the mosaics fall into a general pattern, one of the finest examples of which is that of Beth Alpha. Despite personal contributions of the mosaicists who made it this mosaic floor is a typical model of Jewish pictorial design within a religious setting. We can gain some insight into both the vast problems of Judaic pictorial art and its themes and symbols through a careful analysis of this one mosaic as an artistic document, as an expression of the religion it served, and as an integral part of the building that housed it.

When we come to an art object, we first ask its dominant theme, the central idea that formed the composition, gave it purpose and direction. At Beth Alpha the controlling theme is a tangible, symbolic expression at the head of the mosaic. Picked out there, in the bright ornamental cubes, is a portal closed with two doorleaves, a portal that is the crucial, formulating symbol in the Beth Alpha mosaic and must dominate the discussion of the entire work. The portal was used extensively by the ancient Jews in their pictorial compositions, but it is not simply a native Jewish motif, for it has a long history complexly involved with the Near East. In our process of clarifying the role of this motif in both its Jewish and non-Jewish contexts, we shall be laying bare the complicated foundation upon which Judaic art was raised.

By evaluating the forces and influences that guided the hands of the mosaicists at Beth Alpha we also help give definition to that relatively modest branch of ancient art that is called Jewish. But the outer structure and style of art works do not alone distinguish an art form; the thematic content is perhaps even more critical to its definition. Thus, for example, while the early Christians continued to use the old forms and solutions of the Graeco-Roman world, their art forms a distinctly new style, because they had filled the old vessel with a new, vital content. This study will, then, define visual symbols in ever-developing meanings.

There are but few metaphors in the arts that have a more persistent vigor than that of the portal. The portal stands as the ubiquitous symbol of transformation. It is the icon of metamorphosis and revelation. The inviting door holds forth the promise of fateful experience, the moment of rebirth and regeneration. Passage through it speaks of the primary act of generation. On the far side of its threshold lies hope of perfect understanding, transfiguration, and eternity, or despair in the grimmer regions of infernal darkness and the non-existence of death. It is to be approached with longing and with dread, for the doorleaves open on an unknown which yet holds promise of relief from the unknowable. To pass beneath the lintel is an act of consecration, a symbol of metamorphosis from which there is no turning back. Only the most sublime figures of literature have been allowed to return through it with their heavy burden of knowledge. In the East the passage back from the far side of the gate was allowed to the great goddesses Inanna and Ishtar, the Egyptian lord, Osiris, the melancholy hero Gilgamesh, and the victorious Jesus.

As with most profound images, the portal has been used as a symbol for the sacred and the profane, but the simple fact of its persistence is testimony to its unyielding power. Behind the multiplicity of specific meanings attributed to the door, the portal remains as the symbol of transformation and translation. It is an image that helps make life liveable, because it is the perpetual symbol of hope. And so was it used over and over again in the ancient world.

Ancient man's need for concrete, material images took the door motif out of the metaphorical and gave it physical form. The Jews of Galilee walked away from the rock-carved tombs in which they had laid their dead, closing behind them the stone doorleaves that effectively separated the living from the dead, the here-and-now from the eternal beyond. The catacomb door stood at the border of these two regions, and hence, carved upon its face were the symbols that speak of the cosmos. The sepulcher door was more than a barrier to scavaging animals and men. The congregation of Beth Alpha, as they turned in their prayers to face the Holy City, looked to the equally significant door picked out in the mosaic. Here they did not face death, but rather the fullness of life dedicated to the Law.

Finally, this study based on a single monument has two additional aims beyond the more general ones outlined above. First, it attempts to explain the use of the portal as a dominating symbol, and through it to obtain insight into the complex composition contained in the Beth Alpha mosaic. Second, it attempts to bring into sharp relief some of the essential facts of a very little known chapter in ancient history, that of Jewish pictorial representation.

· II ·

Marianos and Ḥanina
The Artists and the Synagogue

WHAT FRAGMENTARY REMAINS we have of Judaic art before the opening of the Christian Era are shrouded in anonymity.[1] Neither the name nor personality of its Jewish artist can be associated with any extant monument or art work of those early years of Jewish history. Such an identification cannot be made until long after the rise and fall of Israel's kingdoms, until after the cataclysmic disruptions of the Diasporas, until after the successive yokes of Persian satraps, Hellenistic kings, and Roman procurators, and until after the cherished hope of a reborn Jewish nation had all but lost its substantive basis. In the early centuries of the Christian Era there begin to appear, on tombs and synagogues, inscriptions mentioning the names of those who made all or part of the monuments.[2] Most of these inscriptions refer not to the artist or architect, but to the donor or administrator who supported the work or under whose administration the work was accomplished. Some the inscriptions detail exactly how many feet of a mosaic floor were "made" by each donor.[3] But a few inscriptions, proudly carved on the lintel of the synagogue, clearly refer to the artist. Thus, "I, Jose, son of Levi the Levite, the craftsman who made . . ." is inscribed on a lintel that probably came from a third century A.D. Galilean synagogue, Alma, near Safad, in the Upper Galilee.[4] We probably have more work from the hand of the same artisan in the synagogue of Kefar Barʻam, located to the north in the same district.[5] The craftsman signs, "Jose the Levite, son of Levi, made this lintel."

We must wait until the sixth century A.D. to meet in ancient

Palestine the name of a Jewish artist connected with a well-preserved and major example of his work. This artist is a provincial Galilean who, with the help of his son, made mosaic floors. Picked out in the tesserae of the mosaic floor of the Beth Alpha synagogue is the attribution in Greek: "May the craftsmen who carried out this work, Marianos and his son Ḥanina, be held in remembrance"[6] (Photo 7). The latter part of the inscription is a formula commonly found in tombs and synagogues after the names of donors and owners, but the first part assures us that we have here the names of the artists themselves. Recently, there has come to light a Samaritan synagogue at Beth Shean, a short distance east of Beth Alpha, which also carries in its historiated mosaic the names of Marianos and Ḥanina.[7] As yet, history makes no other reference to these artists; chance has preserved only two examples of their work. Yet, if their reputation had to rest on but a single work, that of the Beth Alpha synagogue, they would still be assured an important place in the history of ancient art. Marianos and Ḥanina are also qualified to stand as representatives for their many fellow artists who have been lost in the obscurity of time.

The synagogue of Beth Alpha is located in the plain of Esdraelon. Unlike the parched, stony landscape of neighboring regions, here is a fertile agricultural area extensively cultivated today. Some of the ancient synagogues are known from literary sources (such as the recovered synagogue of Capernaum, just north of the Sea of Galilee, which is mentioned in the Bible), but this building which was discovered by the modern community of Beth Alpha is known only through the excavations which were first made by E. L. Sukenik of Hebrew University. The ruins of the walls, preserved to little more than one and one-half meters, form a long, rectangular building, the basilica type, of limestone construction. (Photo 1) The main hall is roughly square, divided into three aisles by a double row of basalt pillars that supported the roof beams. Tentative reconstructions of the synagogue basilicas of this period show a single roof over nave and aisles. There is no evidence for the use of a clerestory, but galleries (for women?) may have been run over the aisles.* The prayer hall is entered through a courtyard and vestibule on the north side; the southern wall, oriented on the Holy City, contains a semi-circular niche, or apse, with a raised floor. (Photo 2) Benches were originally built along three walls of the prayer hall; later, a row of benches was added to the remaining, north wall on either side of the entrance. The niche in the south wall must have been used to hold the Ark or container of the Torah scrolls. Except for the mosaic floor, very little remains of the architectural decoration that the building once boasted. A square, stone capital gives hardly any indication of the decorative program. The excavator noted, but unfortunately made no further reference to, a modest floral decoration painted on plaster on the interior of the limestone walls. Some such smooth-plastered and painted walls would have nicely complemented the richly patterned and historiated floors.

Alterations in the ancient building indicate a certain degree of growth and prosperity in the community that supported the synagogue. On the basis of pottery fragments found imbedded in the wall and a deposit of coins that had been placed under the floor of the apse, Professor Sukenik dated the original building of the synagogue to the fifth century A.D.[8] Perhaps it was then that the earlier, first mosaic floor was laid. Only a few fragments of this flooring have been recovered, sufficient to indicate that it was composed, in part at least, of decorative patterns common to mosaics in the East, and possibly of some animal motifs.[9] The synagogue had served a healthy community that decided, some time between 518-527 A.D., to support a program of extensive renovation. The old mosaic floor had probably seen extensive use by then, perhaps, the floor had settled in spots; the mortar holding the tesserae had deteriorated, and large patches of mosaic had broken loose. Contemporary synagogues and churches tell just such a story, with whole sections of

* Some indication of the difficulty involved in the hypothetical reconstruction of the superstructure of ancient synagogues is provided by the ruins of Nirim. On the basis of the same evidence, Hiram and Dunayevsky reconstruct two totally different types of buildings: *Bull Rab*, III (1960), 6-40.

mosaic flooring reset, usually by a far more clumsy hand than that which created the original. But the Beth Alpha floor must have been too worn for thrifty patching. The fact that additional benches were placed in the building suggests that the community was financially healthy, and this made possible the expenditure of a considerable sum on an entirely new floor.

Marianos was called in to lay the new floor over the old fragments. He responded with a traditional, but elaborate scheme of religious decoration. Still later, after the mosaicists had finished their project, the additional row of benches was added along the north wall without apparent regard for the section of the mosaic the stonework covered. A stone reading-platform (*bema*) was also erected, probably replacing its wooden antecedent, against the pillar in the southeast part of the prayer hall, covering another, even more important section of the mosaic. (Photo 3) Thus, the synagogue grew over the years, a reflection of the community it served, a living symbol of the piety that found pictorial expression in Marianos' iconographically complex mosaic.

The dates of these successive changes in the structure and its interior decoration cannot be determined with accuracy. We can guess, however, that the expense of a new floor would have deterred the community from sponsoring the project until such time as the old mosaic floor had seen long service and was beyond piecemeal repair. If we allow for a generation of use before Marianos was hired, then the first floor would date to the last quarter of the fifth century A.D. at the latest. It is quite unlikely that the congregation would soon erect permanent installations —benches and *bema*—on its new mosaic; hence, the synagogue must have remained in use for a number of years after Marianos worked there. These are rough guesses at best; only the mosaic work of Marianos and his son can be dated with a degree of accuracy.

An Aramean legend (Photo 7) worked into the mosaic just inside the door of the prayer hall, below the inscription bearing the names of the artists, tells that the floor was made during the reign of the Byzantine emperor, Justin. The exact date was recorded, but the floor is mutilated at that point and the date lost.* There were two Justins: Justin I reigned from 518 to 527 A.D.; the regnal years of Justin II were 565 to 578 A.D. It is the first Justin, he who persecuted such non-believers as pagan Hellenes, Jews, Samaritans, and Manichaeans, to whom reference is made here.[10] The importance of being able to date this mosaic is obvious, for it provides a much-needed fixed point in the history of early Judaic art; but caution must also be used, for the Beth Alpha mosaic is not necessarily typical of Judaic art of the early sixth century.[11] Still, as our examination documents, the mosaic is well within a "normative," late Near Eastern style.

Toward the end of the sixth century or in the early seventh century, sudden disaster must have overtaken the community whose synagogue was now destroyed, never to be rebuilt again. The excellent state of preservation of the mosaic argues against an extended period of vacancy and slow ruin, for had the floor not been quickly buried under debris and forgotten, weather and iconoclastic natives would have destroyed much of the design. Other synagogue floors bear such traces: in some, mosaics have crumbled away while, in others, the devout have carefully cut out the faces of the human images. But Beth Alpha joins the long list of monuments that, preserved from the cruel vicissitudes of nature ánd warring men, would have been lost under the more felicitous circumstances of prosperity and peace. Some sudden catastrophe allowed Marianos and Ḥanina to achieve immortality as artists.

But who were these two artists? Only their names remain to identify them. At first it was suspected that they did not come from the Galilee, but from abroad, from someplace where Greek was the common tongue. Sukenik arrived at this tentative conclusion on the basis of the inscriptions: the spelling out of the names of the artists was in carefully formed Greek characters, while the other inscription in Aramaic seemed to be by a hand not familiar with the script. This line of reasoning is, however, open to question, for others hold that the seemingly carefully

---

* B. Kanael, in *Die Kunst der antiken Synagoge* (Munich-Frankfurt, 1961), p. 79, accepts the date of the mosaic by Marianos as that of the synagogue itself, but the appearance of a mosaic floor underneath the dated floor makes that impossible.

formed Greek letters betray rote copying.[12] That the mosaicists should use the Greek alphabet to sign their names is not in itself significant; Greek was in common use in the synagogue and funerary inscriptions.

The name Marianos is gentile, although Marinos (or Marinus) is very common among the early Jews. It is doubtful that the Greek *Marianos* spelling is a transliteration of the Hebrew *Marinos*, for one would expect the *aleph* (*a*) to appear after the *yod* (*i*) in the Hebrew.* The name Ḥanina, on the other hand, is clearly Jewish; quite common among Palestinian sages, it is used for at least two place names, Beth Ḥanina and Kefar Ḥanania.[13] Perhaps the name Marianos indicates that we are dealing with the son of a Hellenized Jewish family who, in his turn, shunned pagan influences and gave his son a name associated with the Jewish sages. At the least, then, the names and format of the inscriptions do not provide good reason for considering the artists as other than local craftsmen.

Whatever insight may be gained into the training and artistic heritage of the two artists by an examination of this single work must be tempered with the knowledge that the mosaicists had to fulfill certain foreordained, prescriptive requirements. The mosaic could not be a freely conceived work of art only generally conforming to its religious setting. It must be in harmony with the religious necessities of the synagogue institution, be obedient, in format and iconography, to the function of the prayer hall and the congregation it served, and be within the aesthetic tradition of the community. These several dicta need to be outlined. But, even within such strictures, the artist has some latitude as the variety of decoration in ancient synagogues testifies. Despite the wealth of comparative material that can be

* A possible restoration of a Greek inscription from a Jewish tomb at Carthage names an "Asiatikos, son of Marinus, of Tiberiade," possibly indicating the use of the name Marinus in or about Asiatic Tiberius: J. Ferron, "Inscriptions juives de Carthage," *Cahiers de Byrsa* 1 (1950), 181. For an inscription BR MRYN, "Son of our Lords," see H. Ingholt, "Parthian Sculptures from Hatra," *Memoirs of the Connecticut Academy of Arts and Sciences*, XII (1954), 28. There is the amusing coincidence of a Marinus who was a court painter to Justin I. For the rabbinical name, cf. W. Bacher, *Die Agada der babylonischen Amoräer* (Frankfurt, 1913); L. Zunz, *Namen der Juden* (Leipzig, 1837).

brought to bear on the Beth Alpha mosaic, there remain unique characteristics that are the personal signatures of Marianos and Ḥanina as artists. The mosaic reflects both the artistic idiosyncrasies of the two artists and the pervasive art forces that forged the stylistic idiom of the late antique in the East. The archaeological recovery of an ever-increasing amount of early Judaic art has considerably reduced the shock and surprise commentators once felt, less than a hundred years ago, over the discovery that Jews used art in their synagogues, as well as in their tombs.[14]

Mosaic flooring originally covered all three sections of the Beth Alpha synagogue, the forecourt, the vestibule, and the prayer hall (Photo 1). The floors contain a variety of geometrical designs; it was the center aisle of the prayer hall alone that was reserved for a more elaborate composition containing plant and animal motifs as well as human figures and archetypal Jewish symbols. The patterns between the piers and in the two aisles of the prayer hall are space fillers, the fairly insignificant decorative schemes common to mosaic art of the early Christian centuries in pagan buildings, church and synagogue. This center aisle received the full and individual attention of the artists quite properly, for here was the focus of the religious institution. The artistic personalities of the artists, then, are to be found in this central, three part mosaic.

Faced with the commission to set an appropriate design in the center of the building, Marianos and his son followed the example of other synagogue floors, but with one interesting change which, as yet, is without parallel in Jewish synagogue mosaics. Near the entrance is the panel depicting the story of the Sacrifice of Abraham (the *Akedah*): as Abraham raises his knife to slay his only son at God's command, divine intervention in the shape of a sky-borne hand saves the youth and presents the substitute offering of a ram (Photo 4). Next, the middle panel shows the sun, personified as Helios, in his quadriga within the circle of the zodiac (Photo 5.) The four seasons with their attributes complete the zodiac motif. The last panel, just before the niche of the Torah shrine, is composed of symmetrically arranged elements intimately connected with Jewish belief and ritual (Photo 6). A miniature building façade forms the axis of the composition. Actually, it is less a façade than a triangular pediment supported on twin columns enclosing a double-leaved door; that is, it is no more than a portal. Curtains drawn up to either side reveal candelabra, birds, lions, and ritual equipment.

The three part format and the individual panels have antecedents. The zodiacal and symbolic panels are found in mosaic work. The sacrifice scene is not, as yet at least, known in Jewish mosaics, but is found in other materials, in Christian art in particular. Until another *Akedah* is recovered in a mosaic setting, we must attribute this particular element and its introduction into the standard three part composition to the creative talents of Marianos and Ḥanina. If these two artists are indeed responsible for the combination of these three panels into one unit, then we have here men capable of symbolic planning, of integrating significant religious exposition on several levels. They are gifted artists, not mere artisans. But if they are talented artists, how then can we explain their seemingly naive technique, the "folk" character of their work?[15] We shall question first, however, whether their work is indeed naive or is representative of a basic, Oriental style that had gradually developed over the years. But even before that we must see in what manner the religious setting of the mosaic—the synagogue—formed one of the determinants of artistic expression.

We do not know to what extent the religious requisites and artistic desires of the congregation that hired Marianos were crystallized. But even if the community did not prescribe the specific format and iconography that was to be set in the Beth Alpha mosaic, the synagogue as building and as institution made fairly rigid demands on the artist. Although there are aspects of the mosaic wherein the meaning—the symbolic and religious content—is not above question, there is no doubt that the mosaic was formulated within the context of a Jewish prayer hall, that it now stands as an expression of the function of the synagogue in the religious life of the community. For this reason it is necessary to state briefly the role of the synagogue; without such definition the mosaic becomes a pure *objet d'art,* which it was never intended to be, and loses the vitality and meaning that make it an important human document. The portal, that motif which is the capstone of the Beth Alpha mosaic, is rich in meaning, but its synagogue setting provides an additional dimension to its iconography.

The ancient synagogue was a religious institution in the same sense as its neighboring Christian church and pagan temple: a spiritual nodal point from which the religious as well as social activities of the community flowed.* But the origin, function, and religious meaning of the synagogue were also quite different from those of church and temple. The Jews had two different religious structures which are sometimes confused with each other in popular thought, and these must be kept individual as well as distinguished from their counterparts in other religions.†

The holy sanctuary of the Jews, the Temple of Jerusalem that was planned by David, built by Solomon, and then rebuilt, no doubt followed the pagan Oriental tradition. The Oriental temple was a holy place, housing the divine noumenon that was manifest in its cult image. The temple was the mundane counterpart of the heavenly residence of the god, his regal palace-shrine on earth where his retainers, priests and acolytes attended his needs, clothed and fed him, administered his estate, and established the order of his divine, ineluctable will. The priests were the bailiffs of his palace, and he in turn ruled not only as a spiritual but also as a real king.‡

As a royal residence, the palace-shrine did not accommo-

---

* The term *synagogue* is sometimes used to indicate the congregation as well as the structure itself; here, we refer only to the physical building. For use of the term, see H. J. Leon, *The Jews of Ancient Rome* (Philadelphia, 1960), p. 139 and n. 2.

† For example, the recently discovered synagogue at Ostia, near Rome, was immediately reported in the press as "Temple ruins" (New York *Times*, Sept. 29, 1961, Sec. C, p. 11). By the following month, accuracy caught up with reporting (new York *Herald Tribune* [Paris ed.], Oct. 13, 1961, p. 5).

‡ "Thus the Mesopotamian gods symbolized not only the divine powers which man recognized but also the communities themselves. How else can we explain the fact that the god owned the land and its produce, that high and low willingly undertook the annual work on his fields, dikes, and canals, and that the most moving account of the destruction of a city takes the form of a lament by the city-goddess?" (H. Frankfort, *Kingship and the Gods* [Chicago, 1948], 221.)

date an ecclesia within its walls; the ritual pageantry and festival rites were witnessed by the people outside the sanctuaries. Within was sheltered the vessel of the theophany, the cult image —either in anthropomorphic or aniconic form—unapproachable in the holy-of-holies except by the anointed few. Hence, the portal of the temple assumed extreme importance, for from it issued the divine will as well as the actual god himself when his statue was brought out to the people.

In addition to the sanctuary proper, the palace-shrine complex contained storerooms to hold the lord's property and quarters for the god's retinue, the clergy.

An impressive temple complex, to cite a single ancient Oriental example, located on the Mesopotamian site of Khafaje, illustrates the power and splendor of a deity's mundane palace. Its sanctuary stood high upon a raised terrace girdled by a double circuit of massive walls, and built around this enclosure, or *temenos*, were the various auxiliary buildings.[16] The temple was sealed off from the city by its high walls, but the streets of the city, planned in acknowledgment of the temple's civil and religious authority, converged on the sacred precincts (as medieval European cities were also planned). Because nothing remains of the Temple of Jerusalem beyond the Biblical account, we must look to this kind of comparative material in order to visualize its majestic role in the city. However, the Temple of Jerusalem had its structural prototypes in Canaanite architecture, so that its physical appearance cannot be compared to the great Oval Temple of Khafaje.

There are many reasons for establishing Canaanite architecture as the source for the Israelite sacred building in the tenth century B.C. It is most likely that the early Israelite monarchy was completely dependent upon the arts of the Syrians and Phoenicians. The newly won and unified state, lacking a secure art tradition of its own, can well be imagined adopting that of the land which it had captured, as well as that of its more northern neighbors. The struggling kingdom must have welcomed the cloak of cultural respectability that could be bought ready-made in the highly skilled studios of Phoenicia. There is a reflection of the *nouveau riche* in the artistic pretensions of David and Solomon.[17a] The Israelites turned to the King of Tyre for masons and craftsmen, for architects, sculptors, and smiths.* Solomon purchased his chariots and other goods from the Egyptians, Syrians, and Hittites. It requires no stretch of the imagination to see the artists of these several states moving into the expanding markets of the new state. The combination of several factors—the geographical and political position of the Israelite monarchy, correspondences with pagan religion, ritual, and literature, and descriptive material in the Bible—provide the reasonable impression that Israelite art and architecture of the tenth century B.C. did not differ from that of the other people of the Palestinian littoral.

The Temple of Solomon can be reconstructed along broad lines despite the lack of physical remains. Standing within a precinct was a rectangular building with its entrance at the east end of the long axis and its holy-of-holies at the other. A flight of stairs led up to the massive portal which was flanked by two mighty columns named Jachim and Boaz.[17b] Behind the porch was the main hall which stood before a raised sanctuary containing the gorgeously veiled holy Ark supported and guarded by the winged cherubim. The walls of the Temple were paneled; the roof was of cedar. The building was surrounded by storerooms. What is described in detail is basically a typical Canaanite building erected by a Tyrian. The "long room" plan (*i.e.* a rectangular building with entrance and shrine at either end of the main axis) is an old Oriental type of building.[18] The second millennium B.C. Canaanite temple found at Hazor (in northeast Israel above Lake Tiberias) has a porch with columns on either side of the entrance that opens into a wide vestibule which stands before the main sanctuary. It has the "long room" orientation.[19] The temples at Canaanite Beth-Shan (located east of Beth Alpha in Israel) have two columns in the main chamber, rather than at the portal, and the buildings are squarer in plan

---

* The artist Hiram, son of a Phoenician metalsmith and a Jewess from the tribe of Naphtali (I Kings 7:14). II Chron. 2:14 says that Huram's mother came from Dan.

[33]

than that of Area H at Hazor. But they too are oriented on a long axis with a raised sanctuary partitioned off from the main room, with small chambers (storerooms?) built against the walls.[20] The elaborate descriptions in I Kings and II Chronicles of the Temple furnishings, while in need of interpretation, convey not only a sense of lavish splendor in YHWH's house, but also a clear picture of Canaanite decoration.[21] There is no question but that this Canaanite program of temple architecture was current during the days of Solomon's kingdom, for it was still vital *circa* 800 B.C. in a Phoenician temple at Tell Tainat. This small building has the twin free-standing columns at the entrance that leads into the central chamber and an isolated holy-of-holies at the far end.[22]

In one respect the Temple of Solomon differed from current Canaanite temples, and in the study of the history of religion this difference is more meaningful than what is implied by all the architectural similarities: the Israelite holy-of-holies contained no cult image. The central cult image, the reason for the existence of the shrine, was without form in the Solomonic Temple. It hardly need be mentioned that its absence springs from religious concepts and not from the simple prohibition against figural representation. The description of the furnishings of the Temple document that the period of the Kings was not without figural art, but the representation of YHWH was unknown. Yet the spirit of the Israelite God was present in his palace-shrine (I Kings 8:11-13) with a priestly class serving, offering up the necessary sacrifice at His altar. It is here that we find the essential and significant difference between the Temple at Jerusalem and the synagogue: the synagogue is in no sense a divine residence, it houses no holy covenant made between God and His people, has no officiating priestly group, and, consequently, does not incorporate the rites that can be performed only by the priests, those centered on the sacrificial offering.

It has been conjectured that the synagogue (named from the Greek *synagōgē*, assembly or coming together) came into being as a result of the destruction of the Temple, a local substitution for the lost central shrine, a temporary expedient until the day of its restoration.[23] This disaster was no doubt influential in the formation of the institution of the synagogue, but the matter is far more complex. Although the idea of the synagogue may date back to the seventh century B.C., extant remains of synagogue buildings do not antedate the first centuries of the Christian Era.[24] The remains of earlier synagogues may still be discovered. Or the curious loss of earlier structures may be due to the wholesale destruction of Palestinian synagogues by the Roman legions during the Jewish uprisings. In any event, we are completely ignorant of the art and architecture of the synagogue until the Christian centuries. Not only is the Old Testament silent on the matter of synagogue buildings and their furnishings, but it does not even mention the *synagogue* as such. It speaks only of a hall the name of which *(proseuche)** may have a meaning similar to synagogue.[25]

The specific impetuses that brought the institution of the synagogue into the Jewish communities are largely a matter of conjecture, although that argument which has received much favor in modern studies finds the origin in the needs of the dispersed Jews for a place to gather when the Temple of Jerusalem was no longer accessible to them. The destruction of the Temple and the Diaspora of the sixth century B.C. would then provide the stimuli and time for the inauguration of the synagogue. Until the dispersed Jewry, in exile from its homeland, could return, its members needed local places of assembly. The small Jewish enclaves in an alien world needed a focus for their socio-religious structure, a place in which to gather to read the Law, to offer up their prayers, to instruct their young, to manage their social and economic affairs, to provide a rostrum for the explication of the sacred books by the elders and visiting sages and prophets. Thus, the first synagogues in the second half of the first millennium B.C. would probably have been no more than rooms in private dwellings that were given over to the business of the synagogue at specified times of the week and year. As the displaced Jewish communities gained economic prestige and a degree of stability as well as social acceptability, they probably converted entire dwellings into synagogues, and, eventually, built struc-

* Some modern versions of the Bible translate the word, synagogues (Psalms 74:8); Ezek. 11:16 mentions a small sanctuary.

tures expressly for that purpose. This line of suggested development is important in regard to Judaic art, for it would imply that synagogue art and architecture did not exist as such in the pre-Christian Era, and were not developed until such time as all hope of ingathering, of returning triumphant to the Holy Land and restored Temple, was gone. For until then the synagogue may have been viewed as a temporary measure, a stopgap that made no demands for a distinctive mode of symbolic decoration and architectural design. The final destruction of Jewish nationalism at Roman hands may then have made the synagogue into a permanent institution in the Jewish mind, so that it became a focus for the community, requiring its own specific form and format.[26]

Such a tentative reconstruction has the advantage of explaining why extant synagogue remains are of such late date, for it would imply that the synagogues of the pre-Christian centuries are indistinguishable from domestic architecture and not liable to identification now. To some extent the history of the synagogue at Dura-Europos, although dating from the third century A.D., illustrates this thesis. This synagogue began as a room in a private dwelling on a side street next to the walls of the fortified town. It was later remodeled and expanded to include the entire structure, and was then decorated in a suitable manner.

A somewhat different point of view would envisage the seeds of the synagogue as germinating in the secular, rather than in the religious needs of the community, and having no necessary connection with the events of the Diaspora. One can picture the elders of village and hamlet gathering at regular times to deal with the legal, political, commercial, and social business of their communities. A prayer or short reading from Scriptures may have at first been appended to the business meeting which gradually developed into a fixed program that combined prayer, readings, and secular duties. Eventually the assembly may have become institutionalized, requiring separate quarters with designated officials to care for them and to conduct the program of the services. A proposed program of development that followed this line of reasoning would, once again, make early synagogue architecture and decoration indistinguishable from domestic.[27]

As may be suspected, the origin of the synagogue has been much discussed, but it is not necessary here to review all the many theories and their nuances.[28] The two theories briefly outlined above have much to speak for them, and give some idea as to the direction such reconstructions take. One further suggested origin, however, should be noted, for its conclusions, if correct, would have a strong impact on the formation of synagogue decoration and Judaic art in general. It has been suggested that the synagogue developed out of the local shrine. The Israelites when they first came to the Holy Land may have fulfilled their cultic obligations at local sanctuaries. This custom may be reflected in Ezekiel (20:27-31) when he inveighs against Israelite sacrifices being held at every tree and on every high hill. Sacrifice and worship, except at the one and only sanctuary, the Temple, were subsequently forbidden by the Deuteronomic Reformation of 621 B.C. But the Israelites may have continued to use their local shrines for prayer; the scattered rural communities could not continually travel to Jerusalem in order to satisfy their religious duties. The services offered in the many shrines would have been drastically altered, but the habit of attendance would have been maintained to perform what was to become the synagogue program. The focal point of the shrine, the sacrificial altar, would have been replaced by the reading desk, the lectern.[29] If this thesis has merit, then we must visualize the early synagogue as utilizing an architectural and decorative program derived from the small sanctuary, probably the Canaanite sanctuary with its ivory and metal embellishments, floral and figural motifs, horned altar, and cult niche. Or, if these rural shrines were simply composed of a horned altar (and sacred tree?) in an open place (the "high place"), then there would need to be an intermediate step between shrine and synagogue. That place would have been filled by adaption of the Roman basilica to Jewish purposes.

What these several arguments serve to point out for the

study of Judaic art is that the almost complete absence of works in the pre-Christian years may be due to the conservative and rigorous following of the mandate against figural representation, but another factor may be of equal importance. That is, a Jewish religious art may be lacking partly because there was no institutional vehicle to carry it.

Mystery surrounds the origin of the synagogue largely because that institution is unique. As a focal point for the religious activities of the group it differs from all others of the ancient world in four major ways: 1) the building housed no cult object, no divine form or symbol of a god; 2) the building did not act as a divine residence or hold the promise of a theophany; 3) it incorporated no ritual based on sacrifice; 4) its services and welfare were not supervised or ministered to by a clergy. Here the unnameable and concealed YHWH could have no earthly form, no physical concretion, no image. The sacred writings of the Pentateuch (the Torah) took the place of the cult image of the pagan world only in the sense that they were the spiritual focus of the synagogue and the service. The Temple of Jerusalem contained, not the cult image, but the Lord's throne carrying His covenant, the tablets of the Law. In the pagan world the cult statue had its own shrine or niche; so, also, the Torah was kept in its container (*aron* or ark) which, at least by the time of the Beth Alpha synagogue, was placed in its own specially constructed architectural niche. The Ark of the Law, the Bible relates, was carried into battle, much as the cult image pictured in Assyrian reliefs was carried with the troops. A remnant of the ancient tradition of parading the cult object is still preserved in present-day synagogue ritual by having the clergy and officials of the synagogue carry the sacred scrolls out into the congregation just as, in ancient Mesopotamian pageantry, the sacred images were carried through the city.* But if the Torah bears some echoes of the pagan cult image, it is more essential to remember the distinction between the two. The scrolls are sacred

---

* *E.g.* the parading of the god Anu in the city of Uruk at New Years. Description of the rites in I. Mendelsohn, ed., *Religions of the Ancient Near East* (New York, 1955), pp. 142ff.

writings; they are not the object of worship. The cult image, on the contrary, was the vessel of the divine spirit, the object of worship, the recipient of prayers.

A fairly clear picture of the administration and operation of the ancient Eastern synagogue can be drawn. In the first century A.D. a Hellenized Jew of Ophel, who claimed descent from an illustrious line of civic leaders, administered the building of a synagogue. This *archisynagogus*, Theodotus, had inscribed on the building that it was to serve for the reading of the Law and instruction in the precepts of Judaisms.* In addition, it was to house temporarily those who came into the city and had no other place to stay. As secular head of the synagogue, the *archisynagogus* presided over the congregation. A prayer leader was designated *(shlecha)*, and also a general supervisor *(chasen)* who took charge of the orderly progression of the service and the schooling of the young, as well as of the care of the building.†

With prayer, study, and sermon forming the core of the synagogue religious activity, the architectural necessities were few: a chest to hold the scrolls (apparently portable in the earliest synagogues) eventually required a permanent niche; benches had to be installed along the walls probably for the officials and elders; and a tribune or *bema* was needed for reading and instruction. The absence of any dramatic ceremony in the service—a sacrifice or offering up to a cult object, or the performance of a mystery ritual—suggests that the orientation of the congregation within the building was of no importance. There was no need to focus attention on an object or part of the hall, no need to establish an audience-actor relationship. By contrast, the Catholic Mass is a dramatic ritual; the visual as well as the spiritual focus of the congregation is on the altar where the profound mystery of the Eucharist is enacted. Thus, the Christian architect designed his building so that the assem-

* The inscription dates to either the very end of the first century B.C. or the first part of the first century A.D. Frey, *CII*, par. 1404; Ch. Clermont-Ganneau, "Découverte à Jérusalem d'une synagogue hérodienne," *Syria* 1 (1920), 193.

† Cf. the organization of the synagogue in the early Jewish community of Rome: Leon, *op. cit.*, pp. 171ff.

bly, as indeed the entire architectural program of the structure, focused on this critical spot where the heart of the liturgy was to be presented. The long axis of the synagogue certainly provided for such an orientation on the Torah shrine, but this building organization sprang not from ritual needs, but from the fact that the Jews adopted the Classical basilica form.

The location, management, and spiritual position of the synagogue became prescriptive. At least by the time of the writing of the Talmud* the synagogue had become a consecrated building. It had to be built on the highest part of the city so that no other structure might look down on it, or it had to be located by water. It could house no profane activities, nor could it serve even momentarily any purpose other than that for which it had been designated. One might not seek even temporary shelter from the rain under its roof, said the sages. Even the ruins of a synagogue were not to be profaned. Yet it seems clear, in these minutely detailed talmudic interdictions, that this pious regard for the structure did not spring from a concept of the innate sacredness of the building, but rather from the fact that the building became sacred by virtue of the religious activity it housed.

Scholars divide synagogue architecture of the first seven centuries of the Christian Era into two major phases. The earlier phase, in the first through third centuries, orients the building entrance on the Holy City, uses stone floors, and has no permanent arrangement for the Torah cupboard built into the walls. The early floorplans copy the long axis of the Roman basilica with interior colonnades. Gradually the long building widens,

* The Talmud (Learning) is a body of literature composed in sixty-three volumes, or tractates, containing the oral law of the Jews with rabbinical elucidations and commentaries. Each tractate is in two sections: the Mishnah, which states the pertinent passage of the code, followed by a commentary in Aramaic, the Gemara. Two texts have come down. The Jerusalem (Yerushalmi) Talmud, completed in the fifth century A.D., has the Gemara of the Palestinian sages; it has been translated in eleven volumes into French: M. Schwab (Paris, 1889). The other text, the Babylonian Talmud (completed in the sixth century A.D.), is more complete than the fragmentary Yerushalmi, and is considered authoritative; there are several translations in Western languages. The Hebrew Mishnah was compiled and edited by Jehudah ha-Nasi (R. Judah the Prince, or President of the Sanhedrin).

and the second phase of architecture opens with the fully developed square plan, or broadroom.* This later period, between
the fourth and seventh centuries, shows a gradual return to
the long plan, the Classical basilica which is also the prototype
for the early Syriac churches.[30] With the renewed use of the long
floorplan the tradition of constructing a niche for the scrolls
within the wall is firmly established. This niche develops into
a small apse extending outside the wall of the building proper.
The orientation of the building also changes in this later phase:
the Torah shrine is oriented on Jerusalem with the entrances at
the other end of the long axis. And now mosaic floors replace
the stone floors of the earlier phase. The Beth Alpha synagogue
construction is typical of the fully developed plan at the end of
the second phase.[31]

Although information on early Eastern synagogue architecture outside ancient Palestine is meager, remains have been
found in the Greek islands, Anatolia (Turkey), Jugoslavia,
Spain, and Italy.[32]

These remains generally show that synagogue architecture
followed the current building styles of the regions where they
are located: the Roman basilica in the Mediterranean and Hellenized East, the broadroom plan in Syria where Oriental building tradition was particularly strong, and the many aisled hall
of Egypt.[33] The most illustrious example is that of Dura-Europos.
Dura-Europos was a fortified military and caravan city on the
Middle Euphrates between Baghdad and Aleppo, founded by
the Seleucid dynasty and destroyed by the Persian Sasanians in
the mid-third century A.D. Among the many rich Dura-Europos
finds which have established this minor border town as one of the

---

* The synagogue at Dura-Europos is an early third century A.D. example
of the broadroom plan. Cf. the synagogue at Caesarea, tentatively dated first
half of the fourth century A.D., which has the broadroom orientation: M.
Schwabe, "The Synagogue of Caesarea and its Inscriptions," *Alexander Marx
Jubilee Volume* (New York, 1950) p. 433, in Hebrew; Sh. Yeivin, *A Decade of
Archaeology in Israel, 1948-1958* (Istanbul, 1960), p. 43; E. L. Sukenik, "The
Present State of Ancient Synagogue Studies," *Bull Rab*, I (1949), 17; "More
About the Ancient Synagogue of Caesarea," *Bull Rab*, II (1951), 28-30; M. Avi-
Yonah, "The Synagogue of Caesarea," *Bull Rab*, III (1960), 44-48; M. Avi-Yonah
and A. Negev, "Notes and News: Caesarea," *IEJ*, XIII (1963), 147-148.

most important sites in the study of the Hellenistic East is the synagogue with its amazingly well-preserved wall murals. It is these murals that have opened a completely unsuspected chapter in the history of Judaic art; indeed, with the exception of the painted chambers in the Jewish catacombs of Rome, they present the only large-scale positive evidence that the ancient Jews had developed a pictorial format for illustrating Biblical history.[34]

Such, then, is the synagogue tradition and environment in which Marianos and his son worked out the iconography of their mosaic floor. While the rabbis carefully set out rules governing the building of the synagogue and the manner of treating it, they were silent about its decoration. By the sixth century A.D., the synagogue was an architectural, religious, and social complex that had been fixed and standardized except in the matter of decoration, although this latter phase of synagogue architecture commonly accepted the use of mosaic floors with figural images. Did this use of images violate Judaic teaching? Certainly the Beth Alpha congregation knew the Biblical injunction: "Thou shalt not make unto thee a graven image, nor any manner of likeness, of any thing that is in heaven above, or that is in the earth beneath, or that is in the water under the earth" (Exod. 20:4; Lev. 26:1; Deut. 5:8). But Marianos was not apostate, nor was the Jewish community that employed him to decorate its prayer hall with lively figural designs violating the current attitudes of Judaism. Despite the rigid, all-inclusive injunction again imagizing, notwithstanding the horror expressed by such Hellenized writers as Josephus and Philo over the use of images in Jewish buildings, we can no longer be surprised to find early Jews violating the Law in painting, sculpture, and mosaic.

Synagogue walls, floors, and architectural elements carry a variety of plastic and pictorial images, human, animal, and floral. Walls of tombs are painted and carved with figures. Sarcophagi, coffins, and bone chests (ossuaries) flourish with pictorial representations. Even small, personal objects—finger rings, charms, lamps, glassware—carry images. It is difficult to avoid the conclusion that any sixth century Jew who could afford it, and not just the cosmopolitan, Hellenized Jew, brought figural art into his home.

All this physical evidence for the use of figural and decorative art offers assurance that the ancient Jew of this period was well aware of the visual arts and took a zestful pleasure in surrounding himself, even in death, with painted and plastic forms. The supposed deviation from the injunction against making "any manner of likeness" must be understood against the background of change during these early centuries of the Christian Era in the East. Even the most conservative element of society, that concerned with the preservation of the traditions and laws of the religious body, does not escape the flux of cultural change. The Second Commandment may have arisen partly out of a desire for exclusiveness, for keeping the Chosen People separate and distinct from their pagan, idol-worshipping neighbors, as well as from purely religious motives and a social environment that made, in effect, the injunction into a sumptuary law. But the Commandment was continually being read anew and reinterpreted with the changed perspective of different cultural milieux over the years.

The analyses, close reasoning, and apologetics in the Talmud provide a clear picture of the difficult re-evaluation of the injunction. There, the injunction and its interpretations are taken up in minute detail: hypothetical as well as real cases are examined and molded into precedent until, finally, specific instances are cited where both painting and mosaic images were allowed, even in prayer halls.[35] There are several passages in the *Jerusalem Talmud* that indicate rabbinical tolerance. We may cite, for example, the often-quoted statement that in the days of Rabbi Yohanan paintings were made on walls and he did not prohibit them. It is interesting to note that the first murals painted on the walls of the Dura-Europos synagogue date to *circa* 245 A.D. while Rabbi Yohanan was active *circa* 279 A.D. Rabbi Yohanan assured Rabbi Hiya bar Aba that a ladle (?) with a pagan image on it need not trouble him since water flowed over it,[36] and Rabbi Abun (middle of the fourth century) au-

[43]

thorized the use of mosaic designs.* What may appear to the casual reader, who is not concerned with the dialectics, as mere equivocation is a concrete example of changing attitudes: the Targum of Pseudo-Jonathan to Leviticus 26:1 (*i.e.* one of the vernacular translations of the Hebrew language text of Leviticus dating to *circa* the early part of the first century A.D.) permits the use of figural scenes in synagogues on the basis that they are not used for idolatrous purposes, but only for decoration.[37]

Obviously we do not need these literary assurances that the Jews used figural representations; we have the objects themselves. The importance of this literary material lies in the fact that it demonstrates that the art of rural synagogues in Palestine and the lands of the dispersions was accepted, in spite of many reservations, by the religious leaders. The Beth Alpha mosaic does not reflect the thinking of a dissident, "straying," Jewish community that had absorbed the pagan ways of the backwoods in which it was lost.

In the lower Galilee, a pleasant half-hour ride from modern Haifa, there has been under excavation and restoration for several years the settlement and burial grounds of Beth She'arim. A winding footpath in the softly rolling landscape brings the visitor into a valley which is honeycombed with tombs that are a treasure house for the study of early Judaic art. This Beth She'arim was an important burial ground to which Jewish dead were brought even from abroad. It became the seat of the patriarchate in the time of R. Judah ha Nassi, the compiler of the Mishnah. The town is mentioned in Talmudic literature, where is recorded the burial there of famous Jewish scholars.[38] In these grounds, sanctified by the presence of such holy remains,

---

* The Jewish sages ordained in Palestine were titled rabbi, those of Babylonia, Rab or Mar. The term rabbi does not imply an official who is paid; rabbis came from all strata of the Jewish community and practiced the several trades and occupations. Listing and dates of the rabbis: C. G. Montefiore and H. Louwe, *A Rabbinic Anthology* (London, 1938). Also, W. Bacher, *Die Agada der Tannaiten*, 2 vols. (Strasburg, 1890); W. Bacher, *Die Agada der babylonischen Amoräer* (Frankfurt -a-M., 1913). The Tanna'im (teachers) are the rabbis who developed the Mishnah; the 'Amora'im (originally meaning speakers) completed the Mishnah with the commentaries, i.e. the Gemara—which, combined, form the Talmud.

have been found stone sarcophagi and lead coffins elaborately decorated with animal, human, and symbolic images. Even the walls of the extensive catacombs are carved with images. Had there been strong rabbinical objections to such visual art, the tombs would hardly contain such "pagan" intrusions. Beth She'arim lays to rest the lingering ghost that religious Jews have always had a horror of visual art; pictorial art was official and customary in these centuries.*

The scarcity of Jewish remains enforces a rule of extreme caution when making generalizations based on the chance preservation and recovery of objects and the literary documents. Despite the wide dispersion of the Jews, there is little physical evidence to testify to the important Jewish communities in Asia Minor, the Balkans, the Mediterranean, North Africa, and the Palestinian littoral.[39] But with the necessary reservations, a generalization can be made that figural art and visual symbols suffered varying fortunes in Jewish history. The Solomonic period (tenth century B.C.) betrays an unselfconscious acceptance of figural art within the Canaanite-Phoenician tradition. Without a sequence of archaeological remains it is difficult to locate the later point at which this kind of art work was not only condemned but also excluded from the Jewish sphere. A logical time for the absolute enforcement of the ban on image-making is the period of the Deuteronomic reform (Deut. iv.15-19). The force of the exhortation, ". . . Take ye therefore good heed . . . lest ye corrupt yourselves and make you a graven image. . . ." may have slowly dissipated as the Jews came under the strong influence of the late Persian and Graeco-Roman cultures. But when the Jews needed once again to assert their identity, when there was a wave of ardent nationalism, and conservative forces—the keepers of remembered traditions of the great, lost past—had gained control, then the old laws began to be en-

* The city of Beth She'arim was destroyed in 351 A.D., which provides the terminal date for the catacombs. The earliest recorded burial is *circa* 217 A.D. The first extensive report in Hebrew is B. Maisler, *Excavations at Beth She'arim* (Jerusalem, 1940). Professor N. Avigad, Hebrew University, who has been directing the continuing excavations and restoration, provides a running series of preliminary reports of current work at the site in *IEJ* and in *Eretz-Israel* (in Hebrew).

forced with unusual vigor. The temple had to be cleansed of foreign accretions which were in no small part the cause for falling on evil times. The heroic, if suicidal, revolt against Rome, and the momentary re-establishment of a Jewish state in the first century A.D. may have occurred at a time like that, ripe to engender a spirit of complete iconoclasm.[40] It is instructive to note a parallel of nationalism in modern ex-colonial states: an emerging state's anxiety to remove all traces of foreign imperialism may bring to the forefront its most conservative cultural elements.

The collapse of the rebel Jewish state and its complete subjugation and annexation by Rome, symbolized in the destruction of the Temple in 70 A.D., may have marked the beginning of the slow return of figural representation. Art work was again accepted in religious and secular settings, accepted by the laity and the rabbinate. The return to image-making was no doubt grudgingly accepted by some, probably openly welcomed by the more urbane, Hellenized Jewry, and quite unnoticed by most. The discussions of the rabbis are testimony to the diversity of opinion. Cosmopolitan pockets of Jewry, and the outlying communities which were most removed from official, authoritative restraint, may have led the way in the return to the visual arts and the establishment of precedent.[41] It is unlikely that relief from strict obedience to the prohibition would have originated with the rabbis; weakening of religious discipline (and relaxation of the injunction must have been seen by many in that light) does not begin with the elders charged with the responsibility of guiding the religious life of the community.

However, on the primary issue of image-making the rabbis stood firm: the commandment against idolatry could not be broken. No Jewish images that may have had prayers addressed to them by the faithful have as yet been found, and there is no good a priori reason to expect that any shall be uncovered. It is true that the early Israelites may have defected at times to image worship, to anthropomorphic or aniconic forms of a deity; the repeated injunctions against such practice in the Bible would seem unnecessary unless there was deviation or real threat of it.[42] Figures of pagan lords that resembled in some respects the Israelite God and who assumed a similar role in the East, as for example Baal Shamin,[43] may have been made, and perhaps the Biblical Asherahs reflect a symbolic presentation.[44] By the time of Marianos and Ḥanina sacred and venerated figures and objects were allowed in art, Biblical history could be illustrated, and non-Jewish art could be adopted and adapted. If the representation of the Almighty was forbidden, then at least the divine hand of His activity could be shown.

Rabbinic writings, reinforced by preserved remains, provide another insight into the acceptance of art and artists in the Jewish communities. The sages discussed at length how, and under what circumstances, Jewish artisans might work for non-Jews, and they decided that if certain conditions obtained it was permitted.[45] On the walls of a *liwan* (a large room open at one end) in a house belonging to a Palmyrene at Dura-Europos is confirmation of the employment of Jewish artists by non-Jews in the second century A.D. The murals of the *liwan* portray a banqueting and hunting scene that is either dedicated to the memory of the owner or that records his funeral banquet.[46] A painted inscription in Palmyrene letters asks that the painters, Elahsams, son of Slt (Selat), and Thoma Benaiah who had accomplished the work, also be remembered. Because of his name, we must consider Thoma Benaiah as Jewish.[47] There is, of course, no way of even guessing how many unsigned works in non-Jewish surroundings may have come from the hands of Jews. We can only say with assurance that Oriental Jewish artists were employed outside their own Jewish community. At first it was suspected that the Dura-Europos synagogue and the Christian chapel, only a few blocks removed in the frontier town, bore sufficient common elements in their murals to lay the basis for deciding that a single artist was responsible for both.[48] Had this been so, as indeed their different styles assure it is not, we would have been hard put to know the religious affiliations of the artist.

The other side of the coin poses the question of whether there is evidence of non-Jewish artists working for Jews. The material is difficult to assess. Certainly there is no need to ask this question during the time of the Kings. Some of the archaeological remains of the early centuries of the Christian Era strongly suggest that non-Jewish shops produced for the Jewish art market. A number of lead caskets, of a type commonly used in the East, have been recovered in Jewish catacombs and are found to contain the distinctive Jewish symbols. Cast in sharp relief on their sides and lids are standardized patterns that are almost identical to those used on non-Jewish lead caskets. Some of the figural motifs on the non-Jewish caskets must have been considered inappropriate for the Jewish market and were not used on the Jewish lead caskets; the male and female nude, in particular, must have been too "Greek" for Jewish scruples.* But these individual, small motifs placed here and there on the lids and sides were made in separate dies so that they could be used interchangeably. The casket maker could add or delete or recombine the motifs to suit the taste and the religion of the customer. One illustration is sufficient to show that these lead caskets were made in shops for a common market, regardless of religion. Whether any particular shop was Jewish or non-Jewish we cannot know. A lead casket found at Beth She'arim in an individual grave, rather than in the rock-cut catacombs, has cast from a die on its narrow side the Jewish seven-branched candelabrum and other Jewish ritual objects within an arcade made of two columns supporting an arcuated lintel (Photo 13). The die marks of the emblems clearly show, so that we can see that the arch and its two columns were made with one die, and the candelabrum with its ritual objects were then inserted with a second rectangular die.[49] A lead casket that was originally in the collection of the University of Saint-Joseph in Beirut has on it the identical arch and columns. While it is difficult to be positive when examining photographs, minute details suggest that one and the same die was used for both.[50]

* For example, the Three Graces and a frontally presented nude on cast medallions on lead caskets: M. Chéhab, "Sarcophages en plomb du musée national libanais," *Syria*, XVI (1935), Nos. 27, 41.

On the latter emblem, in place of the candelabrum, the crafts-man has substituted a die portraying a mourning figure before an urn.

A similar situation existed in the manufacture of the elab-orately carved stone sarcophagi, of which some fine Judaeo-Hellenic examples come from Italy. These too are decorated with standard Classical motifs and patterns with the necessary minor alterations made to accommodate the religion of the deceased. So, for example, the usual motif on sarcophagi, a por-trait of the deceased enclosed in a wreath or ring, was altered for a Jewish buyer by replacing the portrait with the seven-branched candelabrum (menorah).[51] The Jews of the Roman West bought freely from the Roman stone carver, and some of the Jews, at least, did not demand that the nude be removed from their sarcophagi decoration.*

Christian sepulchral art presents the same picture, with Christian symbols being inserted in place of pagan emblems. There was probably a free interchange between Jews and Chris-tians. The designs on stone chancel screens from Jewish Ham-math-by-Gadara (El-Hammeh) and Ashdod (Photo 14),[52] and Christian churches are identical except that the first two have the menorah and the usual Jewish ritual objects framed by a wreath, while the others have a Christian cross in the wreath (Photo 15).[53]

It has been suggested that all such pagan decorated funer-ary material came from non-Jewish shops because Jews would not produce pagan designs. But this argument must rest on the prior hypothesis that Jews always and forever resisted pagan art; the Jewish material remains make this position untenable. Some of the synagogue mosaics are so similar to pagan and Chris-tian mosaics that the question must be asked whether artists

---

* Viz., a stone fragment with a nude (satyr?) from the Torlonia catacomb: H. W. Beyer and H. Lietzmann, Jüdische Denkmäler I. Die jüdische Katakombe der Villa Torlonia in Rom (Berlin, 1930), Taf. 24c. On the basis of inscriptional evidence, Leon, loc. cit. has attempted to divide the Roman catacombs between the more conservative and the more Hellenized Jews; he identifies the painted catacombs with paintings and the latter group.

crossed religious boundaries to work in churches and synagogues also. The synagogue mosaic of Nirim[*] is so close in design to that of the Christian mosaic of nearby Shellal[54] that it is tempting to infer the same mosaicist working at both. At the present state of our knowledge, we can do no more than keep the question open.

Hence, there is every indication that early pagan, Jewish, and Christian artists were not hermetically sealed within their separate religious environments, so that the carrying of compositions, symbols, and subjects from one context to the other may have come about not only by copying, but also by very intimate connections between artist and patron across religious lines. If this is so, then we have come a long way toward understanding the sometimes shocking use of pagan motifs in Jewish art, toward explaining why and how the art of Jewish communities in ancient Palestine and the lands of the dispersions assumed the forms it did. For, although the zodiac made by Marianos and Ḥanina is not a stranger to Judaism, it is initially surprising to find that the design and format ape Roman mosaics of the zodiac with Helios and the personified seasons. An interesting sidelight cast on the strength and longevity of a motif such as this, once it has been established, is the continuation of the circle-inscribed-square celestial pattern far to the East, in Hindu painting.[55] The symbol of the portal in ancient art is more vigorous still.

The artistic heritage of the mosaicists of Beth Alpha is extremely complex. Although the artists may have been sheltered in a provincial setting with limited access to major art works, and may never have experienced the tutelage of a first-rate artist—pagan or Jewish—nevertheless their work clearly shows that they lived in that very troubled sea of Near Eastern art which had been subject for almost a thousand years to strong

---

[*] The synagogue of Nirim (Maʻon) was discovered and excavated in 1957 (continued in 1958). The site is located just off the northern corner of the Gaza Strip in Israel. Yeivin, *A Decade of Archaeology, op. cit.,* pp. 44-45; M. Avi-Yonah, "Ten Years of Archaeology in Israel," *IEJ,* VIII (1958), 62; Levy, Rahmani, Hiram, Dunayevsky, Avi-Yonah, Yeivin, "The Ancient Synagogue of Maʻon (Nirim)," *Bull Rab,* III (1960), 6-40.

cross-currents and mixed stylistic winds that had blown from the cardinal points of the compass. Waves of influence broke from the nomadic North as well as, later, from the fountainhead of Eastern Christianity to the north of the Bosphorus. Syrian, Mesopotamian, and Iranian tides mixed with those from the South—Egyptian and Arabian—while the western shore was washed by Mediterranean currents of Hellenism. Indigenous peoples of the Levantine coast—Canaanites and Phoenicians— further complicate the scene. There is no single source or simple combination of styles which shaped the artistic tradition of the Jews. In the attempt to read order and meaning into this picture, one's experience is similar to Jung's in his struggle with a case history: when the amplifications "come to be worked out they take up an incredible amount of space, which is why expositions of case histories are such an arduous task. But that is only to be expected: the deeper you go, the broader the base becomes. It certainly does not become narrower, and it never by any chance ends in a point . . . ."[56]

· III ·

The Akedah and the Heavenly Circle
in the Beth Alpha Mosaic

THE MOSAIC "RUG" thrown over the center hall floor of the Beth Alpha synagogue has a broad border of textile-like designs reduced to their simplest terms. Their more elaborate antecedents are all found in Graeco-Roman decoration. Early Christian art picked up these framing patterns in the East and transmitted them to Christian Europe before the opening of the Middle Ages.[1] Along two sides of the Beth Alpha mosaic is a running pattern of lozenges and diamonds enclosing geometrical motifs, bits of fruit, charming sketches of chicks clustered about the mother hen, open-mouthed fish, and others (Photo 12). Roman pavements betray similar small animal vignettes; lozenge and diamond patterns are composed by Roman artists into complicated perspectival illusions, but they also employ the flat patterning found at Beth Alpha.[2] The interlaced vines of the third side, with triple leaf and berry clusters, frame small animals, a basket, and the bust of a person carrying a bird (Photos 9, 10, 11).

While these patterns are Classical, they are also completely at home in the Hellenized East. Jewish artists freely adopted this decorative idiom without significant change. That these border patterns were copied because of their charm and common currency in mosaics, textiles, and paintings, is certainly true. But they are also appropriate to the synagogue, speaking of the good things of the devout life, of its fruitfulness and abundance, of the homely virtues of husbandry and nature's gifts. Even the mother hen with her brood is not without pre-

[53]

cept at Beth Alpha; she teaches, just as she did later in the idyllic
farm settings of the Barbizon painters in nineteenth century
France. Portrayed in the mosaic of the Ma'on synagogue are
just such touching domestic vignettes encircled by the fruitful
vine: a hen with her newly laid egg is perched in a bowl, a caged
bird looks at her feeding dish.[3]

The fourth side of the mosaic frame, the one at the entrance
to the prayer hall, contains the handled tablets (*tabulae ansatae*),
with their inscriptions (Photo 7) flanked by guardian figures,
bull (Photo 8) and lion. The posing of antithetical figures on
either side of an inscription, portrait, or emblem is so well-used
a motif in ancient art that it defies brief documentation, but the
particular combination of animals is not accidental, for it occurs
elsewhere in this pattern.[4] The bull and lion have a lengthy history in the Ancient East as symbols of opposing forces in combat.
Their association is more peaceful in the Hellenized representations of the Oriental god, Hadad, and his consort Atargatis. The
bull of Hadad and the lion of Atargatis (their animal symbols)
are part of the double thrones of the seated gods. It is interesting
to notice in these tablets how the artists of Beth Alpha adjusted
their design to the logic of the mosaic floor. The letters of the
inscriptions are placed so that they can be read as one enters
the hall, while the animals are reversed, facing in the opposite
direction as part of the border design.

The border pattern is, of course, only incidental to the
significant three panel rectangle it frames. The symbolic content of these three panels is not above argument, but their orientation within the synagogue is easily intelligible. It is fitting
that the Jew entering the prayer hall should first be met by a
scene of Abraham's Sacrifice (Photo 4), the symbol in the Bible
of man's absolute obedience to the divine will. On one side are
depicted the two man servants of the patriarch. One youth holds
a goad and the reins of the ass; beside him stands the other lad,
perhaps about to unsaddle the beast. ("And Abraham said unto
his young men: 'Abide ye here with the ass, and I and the lad
will go yonder; and we will worship, and come back to you.'")
The animal's bridle, pack saddle, and bell are carefully, if arbi-

trarily, picked out. The center of the panel contains the sacrificial ram, not caught but neatly tied to a small stump that sprouts leafy branches ("and behold behind him [Abraham] a ram caught in the thicket by his horns"). The interpretation of the ram tied rather than caught comes from a targumic paraphrase, that is, from the Aramaic version of the Hebrew text. The ram is similarly represented in the third century A.D. synagogue mural of Dura-Europos[5] (Photo 16). The difference is important for it probably signifies that Jewish artists were not dependent upon Scripture for their text. But it also has another important aspect: if the source for the illustrations found in the mosaics and at Dura-Europos had been illuminated manuscripts of the Bible, as some authors have suggested, then we should expect closer adherence to the Biblical account.

Dominating the panel is the large figure of Abraham with the sacrificial knife in his left hand. Suspended, as if by some occult power, on the extended finger tips of the father is the small, frightened figure of his son Isaac. The boy's arms are crossed and tied in accordance with tradition: Isaac said, "Father, I am a young man and am afraid that my hands may tremble through fear of the knife and I will grieve thee, whereby the slaughter may be rendered unfit and this will not count as real sacrifice; therefore bind me very firmly."[*] Closing the composition is the high, rectangular altar with fire ablaze. Twig-like bits of vegetation are scattered over the scene to signify its woodland setting.

In the figure of the patriarch we may see indicated the covenant aspect of Judaism—the covenant between man and God that is made manifest, recalled by the Jew in his prayers, in the prayer hall. The binding of Isaac can stand for Israel in its

---

[*] Midrash Rabbah LVI, 8. "Midrash," from the root "darash": to examine, weigh, interpret. The midrashim were formulated in the first centuries of the Christian Era, although some of the material they contain may embody earlier exposition. The gathering and editing of the texts may have occurred in the sixth century. The format of the midrashim ties the exegetical material to the narration of the Scriptures, quoting text and then giving the rabbinical opinion on the meaning of the passage. Unlike the Talmud, which is organized on the basis of subject matter, the Midrash forms a continuous, explanatory, running commentary on Scriptures.

bondage, but as the Sacrifice of Abraham (the Akedah) would remind the devout, the redemptive hand of the Lord is ever-present to save those who are bound to him when the test of devotion has been passed. And Isaac is also the Jew in bondage to other nations. Hence, the divine hand of salvation reaches down into the scene of the Akedah. Further, in Jewish lore the site of Abraham's sacrifice was given profound significance. The Palestinian Aramaic version of the Hebrew Bible text (Targum Yerushalmi*) on Genesis 8:20 identified the same site as holding the altars built by Adam and Noah. The sages continued the identification: Abraham went to the altar upon which Adam had sacrificed, upon which Cain and Abel had sacrificed, upon which Noah and his sons had sacrificed.[6] The sanctity of the location was even further multiplied, for it was the ground upon which the Temple of Solomon was to rest![7] The rabbis recognized an intrinsic relationship among these important moments of sacrifice: "The ox which Adam offered up and the bullock which Noah offered up and the ram which Abraham our father offered on the altar in place of his son—all of them had horns extending beyond their hoofs . . . ."[8]

Hence, the congregation of Beth Alpha on entering the synagogue, may have been reminded not only of the Sacrifice of Abraham, but also of the consistent tradition of sacrifice in Judaism as well as the alignment of the Akedah with the promised site for the most holy of all buildings, the Temple of Jerusalem. In this manner, the flaming altar of the scene could well be taken as a sign of the Temple which was unique in that it contained the high altar of sacrifice. Written in the Midrashim, the rabbinical exegetical literature on Scriptures,[9] is the spiritual significance of the Akedah: the fate of Israel is symbolized by the story of Abraham's Sacrifice. The congregation in the house of prayer would have been aware that the Midrash on the Akedah taught that "Everything happened as a reward for worshipping. Abraham returned in peace from Mount Moriah only

---

* The earliest written Targum perhaps dates to *circa* third century B.C.; the complete version of the Palestinian Targum seems to be of *circa* the seventh century A.D. at the earliest.

as a reward for worshipping . . . . The Torah was given only as a reward for worshipping."[10]

Thus some of the basic patterns woven into Jewish religious life met the eyes of the Jew as he entered the Beth Alpha synagogue: the covenant between God and Israel, the theme of obedience to divine will, the political bondage of Israel, the redemptive powers of the Lord, the obligation of prayer, and the heavy stone that lay on all Israel's breast—the destroyed Temple. It is necessary, in this regard, to recall the distinction made earlier between Temple and synagogue. The Temple was the nodal point, the center from which Jewish religious life sprang and toward which all eyes turned; as such, it became the symbol of the unity of the Jews. As the Temple was destroyed, so was the Jewish nation dispersed and made impotent; the rebuilding of the Temple would mark the rebuilding of the Nation. The Temple was not simply the physical center of the religion, but also, and more important, it was the symbol of the ardent political aspirations of the Jews. The Temple was the seat of God.*

The importance of the scene of Abraham's Sacrifice in ancient Judaic art cannot be estimated by extant remains, for its only other appearance in large scale is on the synagogue wall of Dura-Europos. There, it is placed in that important position next to the Torah niche (Photo 16a). Immediately above the niche is a portal façade; the place opposite the Akedah holds the seven-branched candelabrum, whose prototype stood in the Temple. Thus, at Dura the Akedah dominates and, by its location on the façade of the sacred niche, once again implies the connection between the Sacrifice and the Temple. We may expect the Akedah to have been a well-used motif in Jewish circles if its popularity in early Christian art can be used as an index. The Church Fathers had adopted the theme and placed it in a Christological context. In the substitution of the ram for Isaac they saw the symbolic presentation of the passion of Christ: as the

---

* Exod. 25:17-22. The Hebrew "kapporeth" is sometimes translated as "ark cover" and "mercy seat." M. Haran, "The Ark and the Cherubim: Their Symbolic Significance in Biblical Ritual," *IEJ*, IX (1959), 30-38, 89-94; R. de Vaux, "Les Chérubins et l'arche d'alliance," *Mélanges de l'université Saint Joseph*, XXXVII (1960-61), 91-124.

ram was sent by divine will to be a substitute offering for Isaac, so was Christ sacrificed in place of all mankind.[11] It is highly probable that early Christian art developed this motif mainly because it had already been invested with a deep symbolic meaning by the Jews.

The Christian artist portrayed the Sacrifice in several different arrangements. In the Christian catacombs Abraham and Isaac are sometimes shown approaching the altar, or standing in the *orant* position, or with Isaac kneeling or standing about to be slain.[12] A Coptic painting portrays with dramatic realism the father grasping the hair of his bound son, his sword-like knife held ready.[13] Again, this scene, carved on a sarcophagus, takes on a rocky backdrop; Isaac kneels with hands tied behind him[14] (Photo 16b). An ivory box (*pyxis*) of the fourth century A.D. places the horned altar on a high dais; Isaac, held by the hair, poses on the bottom step.[15] A Coptic textile shows the naked youth on a low, decorated altar (Photo 17).[16] A fine glass plate has etched on its outer side a youthful, beardless Abraham drawing his knife from its scabbard (Photo 18). An adult Isaac (he was 37 years old at the time of the Sacrifice*) stands opposite his father. The two men glance modestly at each other over the small, flaming altar.[17]

The divine, arresting hand, which usually appears in the Akedah portrayals, at Beth Alpha bursts forth from a radiant dark cloud. The power of the hand is an ancient, as well as modern motif in the East. An obelisk of the twelfth century B.C., to select one early example, bears the prototype upon which the interceding hand of Judaic and Christian art is based: the hands of a solar divinity (probably Assur) reach out of a radiant sun disk.[18] In the reign of the Egyptian heretic pharaoh, Amenhotep IV, the all-powerful solar disk has life-bestowing hands flowing from it.[19] The location of the divine hand in the Beth Alpha panel is most significant; it is placed on the boundary line of the scene of sacrifice, while the dark cloud from which it issues is partly in the scene and partly in the narrow panel of formal palm

---

* So, the Midrash Rabbah, LV, 4: "But lo, I am now thirty-seven years old . . . ."

trees above. The meaning is clear: the divine gesture is made in the worldly sphere, but it issues from the heavens above. Thus, the hand reaches through the imagined borderline that separates heaven and earth. An evenly spaced line of palms in alternating colors presents the heavenly zone with puritanical simplicity. In this fashion the artists have provided by simple technical devices two distinctive and telling landscapes. The idyllic region of heaven is composed of formalized, stereotyped trees, while the natural world is enlivened with organically composed vegetation loosely scattered about. The contrast between the ideal, unchanging, abstract heaven, and the mutable world of nature could hardly be made clearer. As we shall see later, this distinction between heaven and earth is consistently formulated by the early Jewish, Christian, and pagan artists in this manner, contrasting the formal, static atmosphere of the supra-mundane with the temporal, naturalistic world. Such pictorial resolutions are the dim ancestors of the two regions depicted in Raphael's "Disputa," or El Greco's "Burial of Count Orgaz."

As one enters the prayer room, then, the eye is first caught by the worldly scene of the Akedah with its dramatic action suddenly arrested by divine intercession. Next comes the narrow band of heaven which is a prelude to the full statement of the heavens that holds the center of the floor mosaic: the wheel of the zodiac, the cycle of the months and seasons, the solar chariot that marks out the days. This center panel (Photo 5) takes us out of the Jewish enclave of the Akedah in both theme and format, bringing us into the pan-symbolism of the pagan world.

The Jews, like their neighbors, were enmeshed in the complicated web of astronomical "science" and astrological lore.[20] The lunar path in the sky that was marked out in Babylonian literature contained seventeen stars which were, much later, reduced to the twelve part solar path.[21] The signs of the zodiac apparently are of Babylonian origin, and then were adopted without significant change in names by the Classical world.[22] The Jews felt the controlling influence of the stars; even the zodiacal signs received Jewish sanction.[23] However, the rabbis would also argue that Israel, unlike other nations, was not under the sway of the astral powers.[24] It is interesting that the sages who inveighed against the idolatrous images in the public baths of the Romans should have permitted the representation of the zodiac in the synagogue, for just such zodiac wheels must have been depicted in those baths.[25] As is to be expected, the twelve signs of the zodiac were aligned with the twelve loaves of shewbread, the twelve bulls of the "Brazen Sea" in the Temple, the twelve stones set into the dress of the high priest, the twelve tribes of Israel, and other groups of twelve.*

The badly preserved mosaic floor of the synagogue at Yafia[26] contains an animal circle, similar to that of Beth Alpha, but it is not clear whether it represents the zodiac or the Twelve Tribes. The synagogue of 'Ain Douq (Na'arah)[27] contains an elaborately decorated mosaic floor with the wheel of the zodiac holding the center of the tripartite panel, much as at Beth Alpha; but, at 'Ain Douq an interlocking pattern containing animal and floral vignettes replaces the Akedah. In 1930, another historiated synagogue mosaic containing the zodiac was uncovered on Mt. Carmel at the village of 'Isfiya ('Esfia).[28] Also, some of the relief decoration from the synagogue at Beth She'arim may have composed a zodiac design.[29] The most recently discovered zodiac floor mosaic is one near Tiberias[30] that also repeats the Beth Alpha format but, in style, is far closer to its Classical art source (Photo 19). Here the three part mosaic has, in place of the Akedah, Greek dedicatory inscriptions flanked by lions. There are several other probable references to the zodiac in synagogue architectural decoration; for example, it is found on a fragmentary carved screen from Kefar Bar'am, and the double fish (*pisces*) appears on a relief from er-Rafid.[31] There is no question but that future excavations will bring to light additional examples. The frequency with which the zodiac appears in synagogue floors indicates not simply the popularity of the theme, but also its importance in Jewish metaphysics and a glance at the ceremonial art of later European Jewry shows that the zodiac

---

* But, with the standardization of the solar zodiac to twelve, rather than seventeen, signs coming fairly late in the first millennium B.C. in Babylonia, such interpretations of Old Testament numbers must have come after the fact.

signs were accepted and widely used as important elements in more recent Jewish iconography.

The format of the zodiac wheel, solar chariot, and personi-fied seasons, as it appears in the synagogues, is taken directly from Classical sources.[32] Beyond its obvious astral associations, lies the zodiac's more generalized meaning in the arts as the symbol of the heavens. The artist transformed the starry path into a canopy, dome, arch, and frame to express the cosmic dimensions of the icon and ritual it enclosed. In the paintings and reliefs of the mystery religion, Mithraism, in the early cen-turies of the Christian era, the zodiac is stretched as a vault or arch resting on twin columns, framing the cultic ritual of the god, Mithra, slaying the divine bull (Photo 20a). The voussoirs of the arch contain the astral signs while the keystone holds the radiant bust of the solar god; thus, the starry path is trans-lated into an architectural canopy.[33] Mithra's cave, which had its counterpart in his temples, was also made as a heavenly vault. And, in addition, not only the sun god but any important figure may be introduced into the frame of the zodiac if the intent is to indicate that the person or the ritual he enacts resides in the heavens (Photo 20b). Hence, Jupiter as well as Mithra is pro-vided with the zodiac frame to indicate celestial residence.[34] The lesser gods, also, are enshrined in the zodiac canopy on the cult stelae. Semi-divine figures, such as Heracles, and worldly princes are represented as carried to the heavens in scenes of apotheosis by the symbolic wheel of the zodiac that frames them. Like the charioteer in the Beth Alpha mosaic, they are lifted in their horse-drawn vehicles. By the fourth century A.D. it became a common practice to indicate the celestial residence of the dead by placing their portraits within a wheel supported by the per-sonified Four Seasons.[35]

The funerary use of the zodiac wheel to frame the dead is an extension of a much older theme, that of placing a portrait of the deceased within a circle. In the tomb paintings of Palmyra, for example, such portraits are carried aloft by the figure of Victory, implying the devout wish for triumph in the final, fatal journey. This theme, with its overtones of immortality, enters the

Jewish sphere. The heavenly circle carried aloft is the central device on the thoroughly Classical sarcophagus from the Jewish burial at Vigna Randanini.[36] We may compare the scene on this fragmentary piece with that on the so-called Barberini sarcophagus where the format is the same except that the circle is interpreted as the wheel of the zodiac (Photo 21).[37] The two reliefs are alike in using the standardized elements of a central medallion, personified seasons, winged figures, harvesters with their grape arbor, and so on. But on the Jewish sarcophagus the winged figures carry, not the zodiac with its portrait of the dead, but the undecorated circle (*clipeus*) framing the seven-branched candlestick. Here we have a common substitution found in Judaic art: the *menorah* replacing the sacred image within a completely pagan format. Similarly, the Christian artist substituted Christological symbols within a pagan design. It is a moot question whether the Vigna Randanini sarcophagus was made by a Jewish carver or in a Roman shop that catered to Jewish trade. There are no substantial arguments on either side of the frequently raised question. The significance of the relief lies in the fact that Jews tolerated and accepted the heavenly circle as signifying the celestial realm of the symbolic *menorah*. In the Roman Jewish catacomb paintings this symbolism is still more manifest when the *menorah* in the wheel is placed overhead, on arches and domes that form the celestial canopy in the same manner as the zodiac canopies in the Mithra reliefs.[38] The Classical wheel of heaven as a ceiling design penetrated the East where its influence is found in the religious paintings of Afghanistan, India, and China.[39]

Substitution of the cult symbol (such as the *menorah* in Judaism) for representation of gods and figures translated into the heavens by means of the celestial wheel has pagan precedence. One indication of Egyptian influence on Greek astrological thought is found in a second century B.C. Greek papyrus where the Egyptian solar symbol, the scarab, is placed in the center of the zodiac.[40] On late Phoenician coins the wheel of the zodiac spins around a ceremonial cart associated with the cult of Astarte.[41] On the other hand, the personification of good fortune, a veiled woman wearing the battlemented city walls as a crown (*tyche*) looks out of the center of the wheel of the zodiac on a Nabataean relief (Photo 22a).[42] It is appropriate that she reigns in this celestial circle, for the fortunes of a man are determined by the zodiac signs dominant at the critical moments in his life. The moon-goddess Selene, portrayed against the starry canopy heaven, is enshrined in the zodiac circle (Photo 22b).

As may be guessed beforehand, Christian art contemporaneous with that of the synagogue utilized the zodiac theme in a similar manner. In one well-preserved zodiac mosaic, the hall floor of the sixth century monastery at Beth Shan, both sun and moon are personified in the hub of the wheel.[43] The elaborate radiating wheel of the sixth century church mosaic at Hanita (Photo 23) must have had a bust in its now destroyed center, for it follows almost exactly the plan of the Roman mosaic in Corinth (Photo 24).

There is yet one other aspect of the zodiac with its charioteer that forms the background for its inclusion in synagogue mosaics. While the concept of the solar god in his daily course through the heavens moved from the Mediterranean eastward, another association of charioteer and the zodiac was current in the Roman world. Here the form and format of the circus games were related to the cosmos: the twelve doors of the circus represent the signs of the zodiac; the quadriga, the four elements; the seven winning posts, the seven days of the week; and so forth. "Thus the mysteries of nature were represented in the colourful variety of the public games."[44] And so the victorious charioteer of the games becomes triumph incarnate in Roman art and lives on in Byzantine art (Photo 25).[45] A somewhat similar charioteer appears in Coptic art, and another (Photo 26, perhaps illustrating the apotheosis of Alexander the Great) rides a panther-drawn chariot in a fifth or sixth century A.D. textile from Egypt, while Alexander commanding a chariot pulled by griffins (who are solar beasts) is still depicted in the late Middle Ages at Saint Mark Cathedral.[46]

These various aspects of the supreme solar deity and the zodiac, of the circus charioteer, and of the chariot of apotheosis found in the Roman monuments, all have a common denominator, that of the final victory. The apotheosis and the ordered workings of the cosmos promise victory over death. It is probably fruitless to ask in what sense the synagogue artists conceived of their representations of the zodiac and the celestial charioteer. By the time the synagogue mosaics were laid in the sixth century, this complex of symbolic references had no doubt coalesced into a generalized theme of heavenly power triumphant. It is hardly possible that the simple equation Yahweh equals Helios, or Yahweh equals the divine charioteer, was made. While the Jewish artists may have adopted the motif directly from the Romans, it must be remembered that it was popular in Byzantine Christianity, and the concept of the victorious charioteer was current in the art of Sasanian Persia.[47] Sasanian art, and particularly Sasanian textiles, had a pronounced effect on that of Eastern Christendom; we may rightly look for evidence of its influence on the art of the Jews.

While some of the Jewish sages condemned the representation of celestial signs, the Talmud finds reason for their employment, and Judaism perpetuated them.[48] The tractate 'Abodah Zarah (Chapter 3) relates that the sage Gamaliel had a chart with celestial signs, seemingly in violation of the Commandment. But, to the delight of any pedagogue, it is found to be permissible, because, among other reasons, "when it is for the purpose of study the matter is different . . . thou mayest learn in order to understand and teach." Professor Goodenough, however, would see the representational aspect of heavenly signs at Beth Alpha carried still further. He does not hesitate to suspect that "Helios and the chariot symbolize the divine charioteer of Hellenized Judaism, God himself."[49]

As a symbol of the heavens and the constellations under whose aegis the destinies of nations and of men were ordered, the zodiac panel forms a fitting medallion for the center of the prayer hall. But it is also a preparatory panel for the next step. The panel just beyond the entrance of the prayer hall moves from the Biblical world of human events to the borders of heaven from which the intervening hand stretches forth; then the zodiac and the Seasons commit the devout to the heavenly sphere. The last panel, that before the cupboard that held the holy scrolls, takes us into the realm of the most holy symbols of Judaism, to the conceptual region that is above and aloof from the physical powers of the stars (Photo 6).

Marianos and Ḥanina purposefully designed the third panel of the mosaic at Beth Alpha to provide a sense of admission, entry into the most holy precincts whose only language is that of the symbol. The dramatic device employed is that of drawing back flower-strewn curtains to reveal the sanctuary of symbolic motifs. In the center of the symmetrical composition is the pedimented portal with its inlaid doorleaves. The door jambs are pilasters resting on rectangular bases with a center post (*trumeau*). The pilasters are without capitals, and support the thin line of a lintel on which stand three broad-mouthed vessels with curling handles. At the base angles of the stepped, triangular pediment are large, horn-like acroteria; drawn in the pediment are a shell motif and a hanging lamp. Animated birds with outstretched necks appear to be scampering up the steep pitch of the roof. Seven branch candelabra and roaring lions flank the shrine-like portal. Scattered in the field around the central design are a flowering branch and a dry twig, square incense shovels with slender handles, two ram's horns (*shofar*), and a bundle of branches (*lulab*) with attached citrus fruit (*ethrog*).

The major elements of this panel are well within the standard repertoire of the early Judaic artists. The newly discovered mosaic at Tiberius (Photo 19), for example, uses the same design, with only the lions and birds omitted. The curtain motif is differently placed at Tiberius, hanging before the double portal rather than the entire scene. The curtains are reminiscent of the Temple where they were used to screen the innermost sanctuary from its outer chamber.[50] We reserve discussion of the several motifs in this panel until we have examined its most crucial element, the double portal, but it should be remarked here that these designs are the primary, and hence most frequently encountered, iconographical elements in early Judaic art. They speak directly of the ceremonial and historical, and, as such, can be briefly identified. The lions can simply be seen as the lions of Judah; the candelabra represent the *menorah* of the Temple; the

[65]

shrine-like portal may first be taken for the cupboard to hold the scrolls; the bundle of branches, citrus fruit, and ram's horn are used in annual festival ceremonies; the incense shovel is part of Temple equipment. The wading birds and the two types of branches are not so easily identified.

Before investigating more fully the symbolic panel at the head of the mosaic, it may be helpful to summarize briefly the format of the nave mosaic as a whole. One may discern a programmatic unfolding in the ordering of the three panels. The congregation, on entering the prayer hall, first meets the narrative scene of Abraham's sacrifice with its implicit injunction to worship, to remember Israel's great sacrifices, and to keep ever in mind the Temple altar toward which the hopes and prayers of Judaism are directed. The radiant cloud on the border of the panel links the worldly scene with the sky above where the ordered and regulatory cosmos reigns over the destiny of man. And, finally, beyond the operative mechanism of the heavens appears the symbolic presentation of the metaphysical—the immutable, the unknowable. The apparatus of the heavens—constellations, sun, and seasons—can be transformed into signs; but only the language of symbols is capable of expressing the elemental concepts of a religion.

The organization and unity of these three panels is an intriguing problem which has not wanted for answers. There have been different solutions which seem to contradict each other, but they are not necessarily mutually exclusive. Professor Goodenough interprets the organization as developing a mystical passage from the Sacrifice, along the great ascent of the zodiac, to the curtains which open to reveal the true heavens, personified in the Torah Shrine.

> Mystics who follow the Perennial Philosophy have always tended to see three stages in mystical ascent, stages which have most generally been called purgation, illumination, and unification. The three stages here might well be given the names purgation, ascent, and arrival. No mystic would have objected to the change. Men who walked through this design to the earthly and material concomitants in the niche at the front had there by a constant reminder of the real significance of the ritual which they physically enacted.[51]

Another ingenious suggestion provides more specific referents for each of the panels. The three part mosaic is identified as representing the priesthood, the kingdom, and the Torah. The panel of Sacrifice would recall and stand for the priesthood, for it is the priestly class that is responsible for sacrifice. The ark (i.e. the pedimented portal) and its associated symbols would stand for the Torah, the life-blood of Judaism that flows from the Pentateuch. The zodiac would represent the Davidic kingdom of the Jews. The key to this attribution is found, in the eyes of its author, in the discrepancy in order of the zodiac signs at Beth Alpha in relation to the seasons. The reason for this subtle change was to make the ascendant zodiacal sign of Judaism rule over the sign of Rome by standing above it.[52]

Probably there is no single, correct answer to the order of the panels, because matters of iconography are not resolved into single, hermetic propositions. Professor Goodenough's sense of a dynamic—the progression from one plane of realization to another, from one stage of being to the next—is substantiated most clearly by the elements of the composition and their historical antecedents. The pedimented portal, focal point of the Beth Alpha mosaic, is also the capstone of its thematic composition.

What does this small, shrine-like structure represent? It and the seven branch candelabrum are the most frequently encountered motifs in early Judaic art. The double doors, as already suggested, bear some obvious attributions. First, the structure may be taken as a model of the lost and destroyed Temple of Jerusalem. It also may depict only the innermost sanctuary of the Temple, that which contains the ark of the covenant. Certainly the suggestion easiest to substantiate with comparable designs is that the portal represents the cupboard in which the sacred scrolls were kept, the Torah shrine. And, finally, it could stand for the synagogue structure. It is not necessary, of course, that every depiction of a portal in Judaic art need refer to the same specific structure.[53] On some Jewish gold glass, for example, the doors stand ajar to reveal shelves and the rolled ends of scrolls;[54] Jewish catacomb paintings in Rome use the same device (Photo 27). It would be difficult to argue that these are other than Torah shrines. A more elaborate portal is used on one bit of Jewish gold glass (Photo 28) and on Maccabean coins; it seems quite proper to recognize in this the columned portal of the Temple of Jerusalem, used in the latter cases as symbol par excellence of the militant political aspirations of the time. Over the Temple façade is placed the star of the Maccabees. These specific attributions of the portal, however, may also be seen as local uses, as particularized applications of a symbol heavily weighed with meanings that it accumulated over the years. In broadest terms, the portal design at Beth Alpha opens onto the realm of the Most High, whether it be in the nature of His shrine, His books, His covenant, His residence, or His prayer hall. The House of God manifest is deeply rooted in ancient Oriental tradition, and it is within this tradition that the pictorial sources for the Beth Alpha thematic material are to be found.

· IV ·

The Heavenly Portal's
Origin and Symbolism

FROM ANCIENT ORIENTAL times, the door motif bears an association with the personified power of the sun that ebbs and flows in one religious disguise or another through Oriental art history and on into the beginnings of Christian art. It is increasingly apparent that the ancient East developed a strong tradition of architectural symbolism. This important area of study has not been examined at length, no doubt partly because of the scarcity of corroborative literary documents. The study of Christian architectural symbolism, by contrast, has been intensive, for in that area the historian has the advantage of an abundance of Christian writings that develop the complex symbolism expressed in church architecture. The early Church Fathers, for example, provide rich descriptions of the symbolic contents of the architectural "vessel."[1] There are no such lengthy narratives from the Oriental pre-Christian periods, and, although there are references scattered through the literature which help to provide a skeleton for the reconstruction of architectural iconography, the richest source for the study of ancient symbols is to be found in the visual arts.

The solar god—in his abstract, anthropomorphic, and zoomorphic forms—has a pre-eminent role in Eastern iconography. The eagle, and sometimes the hawk, portrayed in the display position, have divine affinities. No doubt the bird served as the luminous manifestation of different sky gods in Asiatic pantheons, of celestial powers who rule in the heavenly precincts, but the connection between bird and solar power was early established. In the second millennium B.C. the heraldic eagle yields to a more abstract representation, the solar disk with wings. This pictorial device may be seen as a conflation of the eagle and the solar disk. The origin of the winged disk may lie in Egypt, and was carried from there to the Near East,[2] or it may have developed concurrently in Egypt and Asia.[3] But whatever the relationship between the solar disk of Egypt and that of the Orient, it is abundantly clear that they both deal with solar concepts under several guises: Amon-Re, Assur, Shamash, Ahura-Mazda, Nergal, Marduk, Ninurta, and the like. In the Near East, the solar disk hovers over gods, royalty, and scenes of presentation and of ritual. It presents in visual terms a meaning that is probably equivalent to the literary metaphors of Assyrian literature: the person or ceremonial act represented as under the aegis of the solar disk is invested with the power, the all-encompassing attributes (but not identity with) the sun.[4] In Assyrian art, and later in that of Persia, the sky power manifest in the winged solar disk is given additional anthropomorphic attributes: the god in human form rises from, or is framed by, the solar ring. By the second quarter of the first millennium B.C., the winged disk has assumed a variety of forms that combines human and animal features, a range of motifs that migrated from the Orient to the Mediterranean lands of antiquity.[5] The charioteer in the wheel of the zodiac at Beth Alpha is a direct descendant of this old tradition.

Akkadian art of Upper Mesopotamia in the early second millennium B.C. is characterized by a strong tendency toward realistic representation. Hence, when the solar deity is portrayed, he is shown as a virile, bearded man; his identifying symbols are a long mace with serrated, saw-like edge or blade and sets of three or four radiating lines that issue from his upper torso and arms.[6] Cylinder sealings, which provide one of the most abundant sources for the study of Akkadian art, show a deity with his solar attributes, standing between twin mountain peaks. He lifts one leg, placing his foot on the mountain peak as an unmistakable sign of the morning sun rising over the eastern hills, climbing above the horizon of the sky (Photo 29, Fig. 1).[7]

Sometimes the ascendant deity is portrayed alone with the twin mountain horns, but on many sealings he is shown on the eastern horizon framed between tall doorleaves that are held open by attendant deities.[8] Given the realistic pictorialism of

1. Solar god on eastern horizon between open doors with attendant keepers. From Akkadian cylinder sealing. (after: *Corpus*, no. 178)

Akkadian art, we are safe in interpreting the scene in a manner that finds confirmation in later texts. The sealings depict the "portals of the sky" thrown wide, announcing the new day, for it is Shamash "who openest the darkness" as he makes the "mighty mountain pregnant" with his glory.[9] Shamash, as well as Marduk who has solar affinities, stands in the great door of the sky from whence his thunderous voice calls out to his mundane overlords.[10] On some of the sealings, the deity with solar attributes is shown partly concealed by the mountainous horizon; sometimes he is enthroned. Perhaps these different positions indicate different times of the day which, in turn, would reflect the varying roles and aspects of the solar power. The seated representation may stand for the deity in his full power as ruler, dispenser of justice, and cruel overlord. The sun at its zenith is not a beneficent force. The solar force partly concealed by the horizon may be the evening, waning sun who becomes the god of the nether world.[11]

While such an anecdotal reconstruction of these miniature scenes seems to be too obvious to avoid, the doors that open before the deity have a further significance beyond the metaphor of the gates of heaven. The doors are also the entranceway of

[71]

the celestial palace of the god, his cosmic dwelling. A palace setting is indicated in some of the scenes that show the deity seated between incense holders, with the gate and its attendants standing before.[12] The incense burners, which help to indicate

2. Solar eagle on mountainous horizon. From Sumerian cylinder sealing. (after: von der Osten, *Ancient Oriental Seals in the Collection of Mr. E. T. Newell*, no. 55)

the palace-shrine setting, also appear in the scene of the morning sun revealed on the mountain horns between open door-leaves; gods and adorants make obeisance before their liege lord in his home sanctuary.[13]

The depiction of the morning sun on the eastern horizon is probably more ancient than its realistic portrayal in the Akkadian period. Mesopotamian cylinder sealings of the fourth millennium B.C. present the motif of a cross within a disk, which has been interpreted as a solar symbol, nestled in the depression of an undulating ribbon design.[14] The cross in a disk is sometimes replaced by the heraldic eagle, while the curving ribbon is made to rest on triangular mountain shapes (fig. 2).[15] At first glance, these rather simple, abstract patterns appear to be only decorative flourishes. But they do indicate a landscape, as is well-illustrated on a sealing from Susa that has the undulating ribbon pattern with fish in it. In this case, the artist has used the ribbon motif as a sign for flowing waters with the swimming fish. The artist, of course, has not simply designed a landscape scene; the flowing waters teeming with fish have a cult significance. Certain deities are depicted holding vases from which streams of fish-laden waters flow.[16]

It is not of substantive importance whether the Akkadian

gem cutters had in mind the celestial palace of the morning sun or the architecture of the god's terrestrial house, the shrine that housed his cult image and received his noumenon, when they depicted the god within his portal. In so far as the shrine or temple of a god is a temporal reflection of his sky home, no clear-cut distinction need have been made.[17] Gudea, the priest-king of Lagash, received divine instructions from the god Ningirsu on the construction of his temple.[18] Such architectural guidance from on high is not unusual in religious literature; we may note in passing that a similar motif is recorded in the Old Testament when Yahweh directs Solomon to build His house in Jerusalem, and when He directs Moses concerning the building of the Tabernacle.[19] On the other hand, the details of the celestial palace built for the Canaanite Baal, preserved in the Ugaritic tablets of Ras Shamra, probably reflect the construction of his worldly shrine or chapel.[20]

The portals of these buildings, as literary references repeatedly demonstrate, received special attention. Esarhaddon speaks of work done under his regime with Assyrian pride: "Door-leaves of cypress, whose odor is pleasant, I bound with a band of gold and silver and hung them in their doors."[21] The earlier annals of Gudea report that for his temple he made such gates with lions and panthers at the top of the leaves to serve as pivots. The doors represented on Akkadian sealings show just such details.[22] These doors, then, are more than metaphors for the gates of the morning sun; their primary function is as that of the literary synecdoche: they stand for the palace-shrine of the deity. Throughout ancient art the portal is stressed above that of any other architectural feature, for it is through the portal that divine, and by analogy, royal, figures emerge, and it is between the doorleaves that the epiphany is to be beheld. When the doors of the palace-shrine are thrown wide at the appropriate moment, the theophany is made manifest.[23]

The various elements of the door—leaves, frame, and post —are understandably important elements in art where they serve as the symbols for the palace-shrine of the deity, as well as for the supramundane precincts. The significance of the door

[73]

in the cultic reference is augmented by the fact that the ancient mind not only personified the door of the shrine, as Henri Frankfort pointed out in his ground-breaking treatise on the relationship between kings and their gods in antiquity, but it also endowed the personification with the qualities of the divine, in the form of minor deities (see below for the divine doorkeepers).[24] The seal-engravers also used the door motif without accompanying figures, and while it is difficult to interpret its meaning in such instances, it seems obvious from the context in which they appear that they are meaningful symbols (Photo 30).

One enigmatic design that frequently occurs on the sealings shows a portal with closed doorleaves mounted on the back of a recumbent bull. We are accustomed to the motif of gods standing on the backs of animals which become their vehicles, or avatars, and come to represent the power of the divine. Some goddesses are so mounted, standing within a rectangular shrine or aedicule.[25] The doorframes without the god present may serve as substitutes for the deity, or perhaps they indicate his cosmic dwelling. Wings, or perhaps they are rays of light, emanate from the doorposts.[26] It can only be suggested that these doors are the heavenly gates, perhaps closed before the awakening sun whose divine radiance breaks over the horizon with his first stirrings.[27]

While Akkadian glyptic art depicts in a realistic manner the solar god manifest on the threshold of his palace-shrine, earlier Mesopotamian art presents a similar theme in a shorthand style with zoomorphic motifs. At ancient Ur, for example, doorposts with looped tops frame a single doorleaf; the heraldic eagle, previously mentioned as hovering between the horns of the mountainous horizon on early sealings, is shown perched over the door between the tall doorposts.[28] These are related pictorial themes: the eagle on the horizon line, the eagle perched over the door between the posts, and the deity standing between twin mountain horns framed by the door posts. The mountainous horizon line that rises in twin peaks, and its architectural counterpart—the doorposts—probably share a common meaning: they are the borders of the sky, the ends of the heavens. They symbolize, using the part for the whole, the sky itself.

That the doorway with heraldic eagle poised on the lintel represents a shrine is proved by a scene that shows libation being

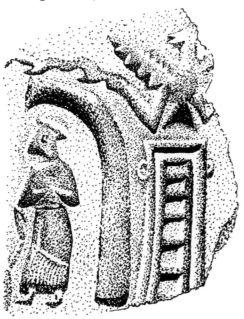

3. Deity in palace-shrine with eagle over portal. From Early Dynastic cylinder sealing. (after: *Cyl* S, pl. xv, e)

made by a nude priest to a god (or his image) standing under a baldachin; behind the baldachin is the paneled doorleaf with the eagle (Fig. 3).[29] The scene follows the standard Oriental format for representing building interiors, of priest and icon *within* a shrine denoted by the door.[30] The baldachin may be taken as another sky sign, for there is mention in the texts, concerning the New Year's festival rites held at Babylon, of a Golden Heaven from the treasury or sanctuary of the god Marduk. The Golden Heaven may refer to the canopy that covered the cult image.[31] A variant setting shows the god standing within the rectangular portal; the Akkadian doorleaves are omitted, but the keepers of the doors are present, holding the doorposts instead of the doors.[32] Or, a water deity, for example, sits within a rectangle— an ideographic bird's-eye view of the precinct or shrine[33]—with the gatekeepers holding the heavenly doorposts on either side.[34] These few examples must serve as a slight indication of a widespread use of the door and doorpost motifs in ancient glyptic iconography.

Unfortunately, large-scale representations of the complicated iconography presented in miniature in the cylinder sealings are relatively rare in ancient art. Three-dimensional "scenes" are all but nonexistent. The exception is a fine sculptured bronze plaque from the time of the Elamite king, Shilhak-Inshushinak (1165—1151 B.C.) (Photo 31).[35] It is a vital document in the study of Oriental cult practices and of the architectural settings. The plaque, uncovered at Susa, is sculptured in the round: a rectangular platform holds two crouching men who are engaged in the cult ritual, surrounded by ceremonial equipment. While it is difficult to identify some of the cult objects, there is clearly represented a three-stepped altar that dominates the setting. The inscription on the plaque dedicates it to the *Rising Sun*.[36] The plaque, it would seem quite likely, represents one of those ritual *high places*, the elevated, open air sanctuaries, with the priests engaged in a ceremonial. It may be an early Iranian example of the type of *high place*, the Bâmāh,* that is mentioned in the Old Testament.[37]

Before the horned and staged altar stands a low offering table; flanking the table are two short columns with worked tops that cannot be deciphered with any degree of assurance. The nude figures facing each other in front of the table and altar must be priests, for nudity is uncommon in Oriental art except in representations of priests and, in selected instances, of gods. It has been argued that the two columns are solar pillars, or perhaps the thrones of deity.[38] The representations of the cosmic palace-shrine in glyptic art make clear that this plaque provides a three-dimensional model of the same motif. The stepped altar

* Of the Hebrew meaning, Albright says: "the etymological picture is now sufficiently clear to enable us to set up a basic meaning 'projecting mass of rock, mountain ridge, stone burial cairn' for Heb. bâmāh, 'high place'." W. F. Albright, "The High Place in Ancient Palestine," *Vetus Testamentum, Supplement* IV (1957), 257.

is the mountain horn that the solar god ascends and which marks his home; the pillars are the gateposts of his palace. There are many examples on cylinder sealings of the deity ascending just such a stepped structure, instead of a mountain. On one sealing, for example, the god mounts the rectangular altar that has door-posts at one end; behind him is the cosmic portal with door-leaves thrown open.[39] Another sealing shows the god climbing a stepped altar that is crowned with an offering table; the four stages of the altar are inscribed with triangles to indicate that the altar is a symbol of the mountains.[40] A similar type of ziggurat altar is represented on a sealing from the Mesopotamian site of Uruk-Warka, with the difference that the doorposts are mounted on top of, rather than before, the altar, probably to emphasize the close association of the two symbols.[41] Also related to the bronze plaque is an archaic sealing, also from Susa, with the figure of a squatting adorant before the portal and high door-post.[42]

The plaque from Susa is the only reliable model we have of the appearance of an outdoor shrine dedicated to the sun god. With its aid, we can envisage the ancient holy place, the broad open area dominated by the high altar. The *high place* is the seat of the god, his palace, and so entrance must be made between the doorposts that signify the structure, his celestial house on earth. To pass between these posts is to enter his palace. The staged altar to which the deity descends to receive his sacrifice is, of course, a form of ziggurat, a man-made mountain.

Some Proto-Elamite sealings provide another graphic illus-tration of heavenly mountains: triangular mountain shapes, with trees between, are supported and raised aloft on the forelegs of erect lions.[43] The concept of the mountain as the residence of the gods is deeply bedded in religions the world over. Olympus of the Greek myths immediately comes to mind, as does Sinai to which Yahweh descended, the Capitoline of Jupiter, and Sumeru of the Buddhist-Hindu gods. There is considerable question as to the various symbolic ramifications of the Oriental ziggurat, but, in general, it served a cosmic function as the sky mountain of the gods;* its several stages were probably connected with the planets.[44] The ziggurats not only had small shrines built on their topmost stage and in front at a lower level, but also the door through which the god made his entrance could be located within the ziggurat, once again symbolizing the emergence of the deity from his celestial chambers formulated as the sky mountain.[45]

It is necessary to return to the double-leaved doors portrayed on the sealings in order to mention briefly the important figures of the doorkeepers. As keepers of the palace door, those wardens who guard the entrance, they assume several identities. E. D. Van Buren has collected literary evidence for at least six pairs of guardians of the heavenly doors, not the least famous of whom are those epic comrades-in-arms, Gilgamesh and Enkidu.[46] The literature refers to these keepers as major-domos who regulated the flow of petitioners to the gods. In the fourteenth century B.C. tale of Adapa, to select one example, the divine Tammuz and Gizzida are the doorkeepers who carefully question the petitioners that come to the gods.† The idea has common currency. Homer tells that the Gates of Heaven "are kept by the hours, the wardens of the broad sky and of Olympus, whose task it is to close the entrance or to roll away the heavy cloud."[47] It is St. Peter who stands at the doors of the Christian heaven.

In Mesopotamia the doorleaves are personified and identified with their keepers. Ninshubur, one of the doorkeepers for the great god Anu, also bears the name Ig-galla—"the great doorleaf."[48] Thus, door and doorkeeper are not separate and distinct entities, which explains the variations in the glyptic representations of the portal: doorkeepers are portrayed holding the heavenly door, or they can stand alone without the door, or the

---

* Cf. Th. A. Busink, "La Zikurrat de Dûr-Sarrukîn," *Compte rendu de la troisième rencontre assyriologique internationale* (Leiden, 1954), 119, that the origin of the ziggurat is due primarily to 1) need for providing a safe shelter for the house of god, and 2) to raise the house above those houses of men and lesser deities.

† The story of Adapa is an Akkadian epic, the earliest written account of which dates to the fourteenth century B.C.: *ANET*, 101 ff.

doors can be shown without their keepers. This anthropomorphism of doorleaves is not restricted to that one architectural element, but is extended to other parts of the portal.

> In the late Assyrian An-Anum list in which Ig-galla, "the great doorleaf," appears as a name of Anu's vizier, we find that the latter has a son called Hedu. This word simply means "lintel, arch," or possibly "doorframe." This part of the door, then, was also felt to be charged with divine power and to be a separate entity: the connection with the doorleaf was considered to be that of son with father.[49]

In Sumerian texts, divinities such as Baba and Ningirsu are personifications of the door.[50] Such symbolic traditions did not die with antiquity; a Dominican Sisters' convent in Detroit bears the name, "Our Lady, Gate of Heaven."

The door was a potent symbol in the ancient Orient, as well as in the modern West. It stands for the divine residence—for both the sky house and, by extension, the sky itself—and for the mundane reflection that is the palace-shrine on earth. The parts of the door are vital entities and even take on familial relationships. The keepers of the door are its extensions. The doorposts, which are almost ubiquitous in ancient Oriental art, are aniconic, then, representing a pair of deities as well as being an architectural synecdoche for the heavenly precincts. Hence, the supramundane is pictorially conceived as concrete, palpable. In Genesis the world is dealt with in terms of abstractions: earth without form, light divided from darkness, and so on. The comparable story of creation in Babylonia puts flesh on these abstract bones. The great hero Marduk slays monstrous Tiamat.

> He slit her in two like a fish of the drying yards,
> The one half he positioned and secured as the sky . . . .
>
> .   .   .   .
>
> The great (sun-)gates he opened in both sides of her ribs,
> Made strong the lock-fastening to left and right . . . .[51]

But also in the Bible there is found the more concrete imagery of the ancient East. Jacob set up a pillar which was to house the Lord (Gen. 28:22). On his way to the house of Laban he remarks

"How awesome is this place! This is none other than the abode of God, and that is the gateway to heaven" (Gen. 28:17).

In the first millennium B.C. a new motif becomes extremely popular, an image based upon the concept of the deity supported

4. Winged figures holding solar disk aloft to form aedicula. From Achaemenian cylinder sealing. (after: *Corpus*, no. 817)

by the mountain horns within his palace-shrine represented by the door. The winged solar disk, symbol of the god, is raised aloft on a columnar doorpost. Also in use is the format of two deities, descendants of the doorkeepers, holding the solar symbol over their heads on raised hands (Fig. 4). We should not be far wrong in seeing in these designs simplified versions of the older, realistic portrayal of the god's palace-shrine. Confirmation is found in the use of this latter device to frame a miniature shrine, much in the manner of the pillars that frame the altar on the bronze plaque from Susa (Fig. 5).[52] This framing device, then, is composed of the doorkeepers/doorposts who stand for the heavenly precinct, supporting the solar deity who is now displayed as the lintel of heaven. The artists seem to be saying that the sun is not only carried up in the heavens, but also, if one would pass through the door of heaven, he must do so by passing under the overarching wings of the sun.

Sometimes these anthropomorphic doorposts are shown holding long tendrils that issue from the solar disk they support; in like manner the doorkeepers on Akkadian and Assyrian sealings frequently hold the doorleaves by long cords (Photo 32).[53] These tendrils have been interpreted as possibly being the umbilici between the navel of the earth and the sky, for in this view, the "sacred tree" over which they frequently descend is given the role of omphalos.[54] The cords could also be taken as the emanations of the solar force. But the ancient artist inter-

5. Scorpion men and solar deity forming aedicula for shrine. From Assyrian cylinder sealings. (after: *AAAO*, pl. 119c)

preted them in still another manner; he turned the cords into a framing device to form an *aedicula*, or canopy, over the sacred object. A later, Persian interpretation of this framing device shows two armed guards holding their lances as if they were doorposts; the winged solar disk rests as a lintel on the points. The cords issuing from the disk touch the lances to form the *aedicula* that contains a winged, royal figure.[55] There are several different ways of forming this doorway that turns into an *aedicula*. One standard mode in Persian art of the Achaemenian period has winged genii with raised arms holding the solar disk as a lintel over a *clipeus* that contains the portrait of the god (Fig. 4).* A sealing found at Persepolis shows the same theme but with what is probably Greek influence: the ring with the portrait of Ahura-Mazda rests on the shoulders of an atlas figure over whom is spread the winged disk lintel supported on either

* *Corpus*, No. 817. The ring of the *clipeus* in these Persian examples has a swelling at the bottom, serving as lunar crescent and solar disk, a conflation of moon and sun. Cf. B. Segall, "Notes on the Iconography of Cosmic Kingship," *Art Bulletin* XXXVIII (1956), 77-78.

side by equestrians.[56] These supporting figures also become the personification of the atmosphere that stands between earth and sky.[57] As we shall note later, this concept of the winds holding up the sky is a familiar Egyptian device, where Shu, god of the atmosphere, is portrayed as supporting the sky goddess.

6. Cartouche of Mursili III (ca. 1282-1275). From Hittite stamp sealing. (after: Akurgal, *Art of the Hittites*, pl. 45)

The common denominator of these several representations is the establishment of a rectangular framing device around a sacred figure or object, a frame that must be derived from the motif of the heavenly door of the epiphany. Hence, the door symbol assumes another dimension; it is a pictograph for sacredness. Whatever appears framed in the door is thereby cloaked in sanctity. It is a small step, indeed, to translate the door frame into an *aedicula*, a shrine, or a sacred niche. The Babylonian cult niche is the door of epiphany (*Scheintür*).[58] Unlike our modern concept of heaven as a vast, open expanse, the sky of the ancients was conceived of as a solid substance; hence, the gods had need of a door through which they could pass.

If we move into a different cultural sphere in the Orient, northward into the land of the Hittites of Asia Minor, ancient Anatolia, we find a similar graphic use of the sacred door. A

Hittite hymn (that has Babylonian affinities) is dedicated to the sun-god Istanu: "The door of heaven they open for thee Istanu, and thou, well-established Istanu, passest through the gates of heaven."[59] The architectural character of this literary image ap-

7. Cartouche on rock relief of Yazili Kaya.
(after: Akurgal, *Art of the Hittites*, pl. 78)

pears to be graphically presented in the Hittite cartouches that are composed, in part, of winged disk supported by tall, triangular columns with scroll capitals (Fig. 6).[60] Professor Akurgal, the foremost Turkish authority on Hittite art, reminds us, however, that the Hittites never used the column and capital in their architecture. Therefore, he feels that these supposed "columns" and "capitals" on the cartouches, which have the hieroglyphic value of *king* and *great* respectively (i.e., forming the title "great king" in conjunction with the king's name), can have no architectural significance.[61] Yet, the Hittites were not necessarily ignorant of the post with scroll top (or at least the reed bundle with loops) used by their neighbors to the south, nor would they have hesitated to adopt and adapt a foreign iconographical element as their own. The cultural ties between Anatolia and Mesopotamia are many and well-documented. The close similarity between the Mesopotamian and Anatolian framing devices leaves little doubt that the cartouches present an architectural symbol.[62]

The extensive rock-reliefs of Yazilikaya, for example, show

the cartouche *aedicula* held aloft as if it were a miniature building (Fig. 7), identified by Professor Trell, of New York University, as one of the earliest examples of the *naophoros*—a shrine or church model carried by saint, patron, or priest—which persists

8. Monument at Eflatun Pinar.

as an important pictorial motif in Classical and Christian art.[63] A sickle-winged goddess stands inside a miniature sanctuary composed of a winged disk lintel resting on the pseudo-Ionic columns.[64] A carved ivory plaque, found at the Palestinian site of Megiddo, but which is the work of either a Hittite ivory-carver or a local artisan directly under Hittite influence, shows the shrine supported by Janus-head lion demons enclosing, and so sanctifying, a royal figure.[65] But the clearest representation of the palace-shrine door is the monument of the Eflatun Pinar (Fig. 8). This thirteenth century B.C. monument puts the architectural symbol of the door shrine back into a physical architectural form. It stands on a masonry foundation and is of ashlar construction, 6.83 meters by 3.85 meters. Akurgal suggests that it may have been a shrine dedicated to the sacred spring in whose waters it stands.[66] The face of the monument is composed of supporting figures carved on piers that physically support the lintel carrying the winged solar disk. Within the palace-shrine formed by these elements, stands a royal pair or, perhaps, the deified personifications of *earth* and *water*,* Estan and Wurusemu.[67]

* For the opposite opinion, that the solar disk is not connected in the Hittite sphere with divine form: E. Laroche, "Eflatun Pinar," *Anatolia*, III (1958), 43-47. That the triple disk on this monument is apotropaic and has no solar meaning: Pering, *op. cit.*, 282.

The shrine of Eflatun Pinar, with its heavenly portal, calls to mind a wealth of supporting material from Egypt. Harold Nelson summarizes the cosmic aspect of the Egyptian temple: "The two pylon towers are the hills of the horizon between which the

9. Winged solar disk enthroned on stool. From Middle Assyrian cylinder sealing. (after: *Corpus*, no. 598)

sun-god rises,* and the platform above the gate between the two towers where the sun first penetrates into the temple each morning is frequently decorated with reliefs of the morning and evening solar barks. . . ."[68] The horizon from which the sun rises is the boundary of the heavens as well as the edge of the earth.** The portal of the Egyptian chapel is of first importance; elaborate attention is paid to its decoration. Gates and temples are built "like the horizon of heaven, wherein Re rises."[69] The sky is personified as the divine Nut. Her star-spangled body arches over the earth as a canopy; she rests her fingers and toes on the horizon line, while the boats of the morning and evening suns glide over her back.† The Egyptian ideograph for *sky*, the determina-

* Th. Dombart identifies the twin door towers as representing the hills of the eastern horizon, with the winged solar disk of the lintel as the ascending sun-god: "Der zweitürmige Tempel-Pylon altaegyptischer Baukunst und seine religiöse Symbolik," *Egyptian Religion* I (1933), 3, pp. 87ff.

** "The gods of the horizon," "resting place of the two horizons," "the boundaries of Egypt as far as the heavens on every side," *Anc. Rec E*, III.

† Similarly, for the concept in Mesopotamia of the morning sun rising on the horn of the eastern mountain and the evening sun setting on the western: P. Gordon, *L'Image du monde dans l'antiquité* (Paris, 1949), p. 59. R. Anthes summarizes four concepts of the sky held by the Egyptians—as cow, as ocean, as the goddess Nut, and as roof. The picture of the sky, depicted as the wings of a vulture supported by two of the heavenly pillars, originated about 2900 B.C.: R. Anthes, "Mythology in Ancient Egypt," in S. N. Kramer, ed., *Mythologies of the Ancient World* (Garden City, 1961), pp. 20-21.

tive in the name of the sky-goddess, takes the shape of a low stool. Relative to the solar door, it is interesting to note that this hieroglyph is connected with the earlier signs for *gateway*,[70] particularly since the sky ideograph is used to form a portal,

10. Air-god Shu (?) supporting the sky. From North Syrian scarab sealing. (after: von der Osten, *Ancient Oriental Seals in the Collection of Mr. E. T. Newell*, no. 534)

supported on the raised hands of two royal figures.[71] The design appears in somewhat the same manner in the Orient: a stool, decorated with astral rosettes, is held up by supporting genii; enthroned on the stool is the winged solar disk (Fig. 9).

The door motif occurs in another related form in Egypt when the cow-goddess, Hathor, is assimilated with Nut. As the star-studded celestial cow, her four legs are referred to as the four pillars of heaven, and the pharaoh is to be found standing within the portal of her forelegs. Shu, lord of the air, kneels under the canopy of the arching body of Nut; he raises her and supports her on lifted arms.[72] A North Syrian scarab reveals its Egyptian affinities, but more important for the purpose here, it demonstrates the currency of the theme of supporting the personified sky (Fig. 10). On it, the body of Nut is replaced by the solar disk with down-curving wings which frame a winged, uraeus-wearing, kneeling figure who bears the sky symbol on his raised hands.[73] He probably is the god Shu, but no matter what his identification, he serves in the role of supporter of the sky.

Hence, there is a quantity of evidence to demonstrate a general theme current in ancient art of the Near East and Egypt: symbols of the cosmos—sky, astral bodies, and sun—are conceived as lintels that are carried by architectural elements or their personified counterparts. It remains, then, to see this pictorial imagery transformed into clearly architectural terms, and, indeed, this happens. The solar disk with drooping wings (an Egyptian trait, in contrast to the straight or up-turning sickle wings of the East) is utilized graphically as an arcade over Egyptian scenes. This celestial canopy is carried over from Egyptian into Phoenician art, where it appears on stelae and on the shallow bronze bowls that have been found in numbers in the East and in the Aegean basin. But it is the Egyptian solar disk with straight wings that becomes the architectural lintel, supported on columns and pilasters, making up the shrines of the Phoenician cults. These shrines, which also serve as altars, are made in several designs, but with a common formula. The deity is portrayed within the doorway of his shrine under the celestial lintel.[74] Some of the altar-shrines carry an animal-decorated seat of the god within the *aedicula*.[75] The western Phoenician goddess, Tanit, is present in these small chapels,* as is also her eastern counterpart, Astarte. These monuments, with their Egyptian architectural details and Phoenician deities, were current in the fifth and fourth centuries B.C.†

We are then prepared by the background sketched above to interpret the architectural imagery of the Phoenician altar-shrines as a rendering of the heavens, the celestial abode of the deity enshrined, her palace-shrine. The columns framing the goddess are doorposts, the "pillars of heaven,"[76] the borders of the sky; they represent the horizon on which rests the primary sky symbol—a winged sun—as lintel. The Egyptian doorposts,

* Tanit seated in her Aeolic-type *naos* surmounted by the Egyptian entablature of winged disk and uraei: D. Harden, *The Phoenicians* (London, 1962), 306, pl. 34.

† Viz., *naos* from Saïda which shows the standard format, a row of cobra heads bearing solar disks, above the uraeus and lintel of alternating lotus buds and flowers, and palmette-decorated jambs: M. Dunand, "Notes sur quelques objets provenant de Saïda," *Syria*, VII (1926), Pl. xxxiii, 2.

like those of the Orient, are conceived anthropomorphically; in one such shrine motif, placed as a crown on the head of Hathor, the top of each doorpost is itself a head of that goddess.[77] It is worth noting that Hathor, a goddess intimately connected with fertility beliefs, should assume the role of doorpost, for, in the Orient, the great mother-goddess herself assumes an aniconic form. There are reasonable arguments for identifying her in the looped reed bundles that frame doors in Sumerian art.[*]

The establishment of the cosmic door motif in Phoenician art has several important aspects. Its appearance there indicates the historical continuity of the symbolism down into the last centuries of the pre-Christian era. That such continuity should occur is not surprising in view of the complex heritage of Phoenician art in general. Phoenician art forms one of the great eclectic styles of the ancient world, combining and continuing the diverse styles of Egypt, Mesopotamia, Syria, and Anatolia. The geographical location of the rich Phoenician cities on the Palestinian littoral, one of the most hotly contested regions of antiquity, accounts in no small part for this mixed heritage. But if Phoenicia was a gatherer of diverse cultural elements, it was also one of the chief vehicles for the exportation of Oriental art into the Classical lands of the Mediterranean. (The Western adoption of the Phoenician alphabet is symptomatic of the important Oriental cultural influence on the West.) There are a dozen roads along which one small motif, such as the celestial portal, could travel from East to West. One modest instance can be cited. A "Phoenician" bowl, of the type mentioned above, found its way to Olympia, in Greece. Among the designs engraved upon it is that of a nude goddess (one aspect of the Ishtar-Hathor fertility cult figure) standing inside her celestial sanctuary, composed of two slender columns carrying the winged solar disk lintel.[78] This goddess in the doorway is a direct descendant of the nude fertility goddess who appears within the portal in the cylinder sealings, mounted on the back of a bull.[79] On some

* The cosmic aspect of the doorposts suggests, also, that more is involved in these cult presentations; perhaps they function as a symbol of the celestial corral that holds the horned animals of the gods. See: G. R. Levy, *Gates of Horn* (London, 1948), 99-100.

sealings the doorframe of the goddess is winged, final proof of its aerial location.[80]

We may anticipate, then, that the cosmic architectural iconography of the portal would be carried over into the Graeco-Roman sphere where it was adapted to the Classical architectural *koine* of a triangular pediment on columns. The transition into the Classical world can be witnessed if we follow the enshrined nude goddess. In the Romano-Egyptian art circle, the nude goddess is shown standing on a throne of lions, framed within lotus-bud columns topped by a triangular pediment.[81] The composition is Egyptian, the lion throne is Near Eastern, but the triangular pediment with *acroteria* is a Western substitution for the sun disk lintel.

Twin cosmic pillars, sometimes conceived in human form, make their appearance in the Mediterranean. The evidence is sufficiently strong to have led Cook (in his monumental work on Classical myth and religion) to the conclusion that the Greek sky-god was pictured as resting upon a "tangible pillar, his vehicle and support."[82] Cook also envisions a connection between the pillar and the Milky Way. Thus, the Classical supporting column is a celestial sign much in the manner of the supporting column of the solar disk in the East, as a symbol of the heavens whose burden is the god. Ovid's Palace of the Sun *(Regia Solis)* "stood high on lofty columns, bright with glittering gold and bronze that shone like fire." Under the ivory-encrusted gables swung the magnificently sculptured double doors of the portal.[83] In the Mithraeum of the Seven Spheres at Ostia, each planet is symbolized by a portal. Another Mithraeum in the same port town has, depicted in mosaic, the seven gates, standing for the seven planets.[84] Once again we are reminded of the "gateway to heaven" in Genesis (28:17).

Returning now to the Orient, we must take note of a further development of the celestial doorposts when they stand alone without accompanying architectural motifs.* On the altar

---

* For the doorpost symbol as an intermediate stage in the line of development beginning with a bundle of reeds with looped top and ending in the conventionalized "sacred tree": W. Andrae, *Die ionische Säule* (Berlin, 1933), particularly pp. 53-55.

of the king, Tukulti-Inurta, twin, bearded deities, who are crowned with spoked wheels, hold posts that support other wheels.[85] The figures are familiar as the doorkeepers of the sealings. These on the altar hold the heavenly pillars that carry the solar wheel, which can be readily identified as such by its frequent appearance in glyptic art as disk or spoked wheel on top of a pillar.[86] The single column, then, may be used to represent the support of the sky, a development of the old mountain motif that held the solar god. In the annals of the Assyrian Sargon, the mountain shape is likened to that of a pillar,[87] while we meet the literary image of the "four pillars of heaven" in Egypt.[88] The pillar of cloud and the pillar of fire are heavenly enbodiments in the Old Testament (Num. 14:10).

Although it is difficult to maintain the distinction, mainly because the two symbols appear to have been used interchangeably, the heavenly pillar and the "sacred tree" probably carried different meanings. Interpretations of the "sacred tree" are almost as numerous as its appearance in the ancient East, where it is almost everpresent in one form or another.[89] The "sacred tree" is pictured in a realistic manner as a tree, or as a stylized combination of plant shapes, or as a column composed of alternating patterns of circles and disks.[90] Taking into consideration the uncertainty of the meaning, for our purposes here it is sufficient to notice that the single pillar and decorated column can act as the heavenly support for the solar disk. Hence, we are prepared to find the pillar located, architecturally, in the upper regions, within the triangular pediment. In the West it stands over the Lion Gate at Mycenae, and in the East it maintains its popularity in the pediments of late Anatolian (Phrygian) portals to shrines and tombs. This architectural symbol is found in the most sacred of Israelite buildings, the Temple of Jerusalem.

In our examination of the Temple of Solomon, we pointed out that the building was patterned on the architectural models current in the tenth century B.C. On the whole, it followed contemporary Phoenician building practices. The Temple had been planned on a long axis, containing an inner sanctuary, fore-chamber, peripheral chambers, porch, and twin free-standing columns before the main portal. Something of the cosmic symbolism of Oriental architecture is carried into the Israelite building; the Bible continues the concept of the heavenly city and temple as prototypes for the mundane. While W. F. Albright dismisses the argument that holds the extreme view that "solar myth and ritual were to the front in Solomon's Temple . . ." and that "in the popular estimation there was an almost complete identification of the cult of the sun with that of Jahweh . . . ,"[91] he, as well as others, recognizes both heavenly significance and solar orientation in the Temple.[92]

The image of "a tabernacle for the sun / Which is as a bridegroom coming out of his chamber" (Ps. 19:4-5) strikes a familiar chord. The sanctuary itself is spoken of in the rabbinic literature as reflecting heaven.[*] The importance of the eastern orientation of the Temple portal, so that the rising sun of the solstice would shine through it, is specifically stated in the Jerusalem Talmud.[93] The Jewish historian and apologist, Josephus, mentions that the first gate had no doors, "symbolizing thus the vast inexclusible expanse of heaven."[94] In Ezekiel (43:4-7), the solar imagery is manifest in the "glory of the Lord" coming into the Temple through the east gate where it "filled the house" that held the "place of my throne and the place of the soles of my feet." As in Egyptian literature,[95] there appears in the Old Testament the metaphorical association of heaven and pillar (Job 25:11). The twenty-fourth Psalm presents an image of the Divine entering the sacred portal: "Lift up your heads, O ye gates; and be ye lifted up, ye everlasting doors; and the King of glory shall come in."

Hence, there is good reason for placing the free-standing pillars—named Jachin and Boaz[96]—within the cosmic framework of the heavenly doors of the palace-shrine. Columns flanking the portal of the pagan temples are a well-documented arch-

---

[*] *Viz.*, by Rabbi Pinhas ben Jair (*circa* 165-200 A.D.), one of the Tanna'im, Teachers who lived during the time of the codification of the Mishnah. See W. Bacher, *Die Agada der Tannaiten*, II (Strassburg, 1890), 495-499.

itectural feature, found in the sacred buildings, a Byblos, Schechem, Si', Khorsabad, and Tainat.* The etymology and significance of the names, Jachin and Boaz, have received much attention, of course,[97] but important here is the fact that the personification of doorposts and columns is an integral part of the old Oriental pattern in palace-shrines. As described above, the doorkeepers of the palace-shrines had specific identities, just as in Egypt where the keepers of the portal were likened to Isis and Nephthis, daughter of the sky goddess Nut, in their role as bearers of the solar disk in the Pyramid texts. The ideal moral qualities which have been suggested as the meaning behind the names of Jachin and Boaz are similarly found embodied in the Mesopotamian solar doorkeepers who stand for righteousness and justice.[98] Another interesting connection is the attribution of these celestial major-domos as fire-gods, sometimes symbolized as torch and lamp.[99] Professor Albright has put his authority behind the view that the Solomonic pillars were also giant cressets.[100] But it should be kept in mind that there existed in the ancient East the tradition of incorporating tall, columnar figures in the walls of buildings. The water-gods portrayed on the façade of the Temple of Inanna at Erech may provide an example of the early anthropomorphic column type from which the pillars of Solomon's Temple indirectly derived (Photo 34).

The recent excavations at Canaanite Hazor provide evidence for envisaging the sun-god's palace-shrine of the Levant as following a format much like that described above. The Late Bronze Age II shrine of Hazor, that contained cult objects pertinent to a solar shrine, is very close in plan to the later Israelite temple, as one of its excavators has noted. It also has twin pillars erected before the main hall, on axis with the inner sanctuary.[101] A life-size lion orthostat which formed part of the door jamb is

---

* The free-standing pillars before the Temple of Melquart, described by Herodotus (II, 44), are probably represented on a carved stone slab from Niniveh: R. D. Barnett, "Phoenicia and the Ivory Trade," *Archaeology* 9 (1956), 91, fig. 9; Harden, *op. cit.*, fig. 50. The usual reconstruction of the two pillars before the Solomonic Temple shows them as not having an architectural function, that is, they do not carry a lintel or cross beam. But it is also argued that they were part of the portico, carrying the architrave: J. L. Myres, "King Solomon's Temple and Other Buildings and Works of Art," *PEQ* (1948), 28-29.

within the tradition of the Anatolian and Mesopotamian lion gates, but it also may be related to the lions of the solar doors mentioned in the texts and depicted on the sealings. The combined evidence of Akkadian, Assyrian, Egyptian, and Hittite solar portals makes a compelling argument for placing the portal of the Solomonic Temple within the framework of the Oriental, celestial palace-shrine tradition and for seeing it as an Israelite adoption of Oriental iconography.*

By reason of its central role in Judaism, the Temple of Jerusalem may well be reflected in, and be the source of, the portrayal of the pedimented double doors in the Beth Alpha mosaic. But, if the design refers directly to the Temple, it then has a more general significance as the celestial home, as the symbol of the heavens. We indicated earlier that the Beth Alpha panel of the Sacrifice of Abraham recalled the Temple because of its sacrificial theme and the altar. There is in the Orient an intimate bond between altar and sacred dwelling, for the two are combined into one unit in miniature altar-shrines.

Stepped altars made in the shape of small shrines have an extended history which goes back, on the evidence of pictorial representations, to 3000 B.C. Ceramic altars, uncovered in the sanctuary of the Ishtar Temple at Assur, are made in imitation of buildings of half-timber construction (Fig. 11). The walls are composed of vertical and horizontal "beams," framing panels that are pierced with door and window openings. The detailing of these altars must be authentic reproductions of contemporary architecture. The altars are made in the shape of two story buildings; the second floor covers only part of the lower story, following in appearance the shape of the ancient stepped altars (Fig. 12).[102] Above the doors are square or triangular windows. These altars probably served in the cult of Ishtar as stands for the offerings and incense; the serpents that crawl over the sides of one of the altars are appropriate consorts to Ishtar in her chthonic aspect. There has been some question as to whether

---

* Albright takes the point of view that Canaanite symbolism as well as architectural program influenced the Solomonic Temple: W. F. Albright, *Archaeology and the Religion of Israel* (Baltimore, 1953), 147-148.

these and some related altars (see below) represent sacred or domestic buildings. This issue, however, does not deserve much attention, for a miniature altar-shrine in the cult room of the great goddess is quite appropriate; the same can hardly be said

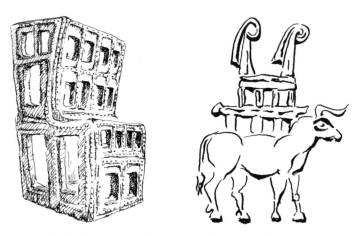

11. *Left.* Ceramic altar-shrine from the Ishtar Temple at Assur. (after: *Gotteshaus,* pl. ivb)

12. *Right.* Stepped altar surmounted with door posts. From Sumerian cylinder sealing. (after: von der Osten, *Ancient Oriental Seals in the Collection of Mr. E. T. Newell,* no. 22.)

for placing a model of a domestic structure (complete with serpents!) in the shrine. Sufficient proof that we are indeed dealing with model altar-shrines is found on the cylinder sealings,[103] where these two-staged structures are portrayed in their ceremonial role with the offering vessels placed upon them (Fig. 13).*

Triangular windows above the portal also appear on the representations of the palace-shrine doors. Ceramic altar-shrines, such as the burner from Ay (Fig. 14), provide the earliest examples of the incorporation of miniature, model, sacred buildings in temple furnishings. They are humble, but none the less instructive ancestors of the goldsmith's art—reliquaries and containers in the form of buildings—of church and synagogue.

* E. D. Van Buren favors the idea that the stepped altar is the exclusive property of the goddess Ishtar in her many aspects: "Akkadian Stepped Altars," *Numen,* I (1954), 228-234.

There is the possible extension of the iconography of these two-staged altars into the seat or throne of the deity, the cathedra. Oriental deities, when not standing, are usually seated on backless thrones, low stools, that do not have architectural fea-

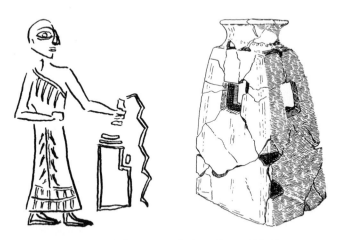

13. *Left*. Priest before stepped altar. From Akkadian
cylinder sealing. (after: *Corpus*, no. 220)

14. *Right*. Ceramic incense burner in form of a shrine. Found in the
sanctuary area of Ay. Circa end of 3rd millennium. (after:
Marquet-Krause, "La Deuxième campagne de fouilles à Ay," pl. lv)

tures. The throne is sometimes placed on a low dais with a separate footstool, or the deity's animal symbol placed under his feet. Chair thrones appear somewhat later in Assyrian art. However, there are a few interesting exceptions which indicate that the shrine as the seat of the deity was explicitly stated. An Akkadian deity sits upon a throne that conforms in shape to the two-staged altar (Fig. 15). One cannot be certain as to its construction because of the miniature scale of the sealing design of which it is a part, but it does seem to be composed of the long bricks of Mesopotamian building.[104] Other pictures of two-staged altars have the mountain symbol—rows of triangles—drawn on the sides, indicating that they are also the sky mountain that houses the god. It would be appropriate to interpret the mountain palace into a clay brick counterpart, much in the manner of the artificial mountain, the ziggurat, which was made of bricks.

Altars, which combine the features of altar with the deity's palace-shrine, are also simply made as rectangles with a door on the side. Symbols of the gods to whom the altars are dedicated are placed on top of the structures.[105] We may speak of a well-established Oriental tradition of altars that serve as palace-

15. Deity seated on altar-shrine. From Akkadian cylinder sealing. (after: *Cyl S*, pl. xx-k)

shrines of the gods, as well as their thrones. In addition, these examples form the basis for a tradition of placing doors in altars.

A few fortunately-preserved model altar-shrines represent the tradition on the Palestinian coast. A small, rectangular ceramic altar-shrine from Megiddo (Middle Iron Age: early first millennium B.C.) betrays its architectural prototype in its use of doors, windows, and cornice. The roofline of the model is supported on the backs of composite beasts—lion bodies with human heads.[106] The motif used here is the architectural expression of the old solar palace-shrine, which has composite figures holding aloft the winged disk lintel. A conical stand from Beisan (Beth Shan) has triangular windows and plastic animals (Photo 36). An incense altar stand from Tell Tanaach (located just south of Megiddo in the Lower Galilee) is pyramidal in shape; lions and sphinxes modelled in relief, one on top of the other, are ready to bear the weight of the offering bowl that would have been placed on top.[107] Another tall altar in the architectural tradition, decorated with plastic figures of beasts, men, and eagle, was recently found at Tell Chuera.[108] There is also evidence of this altar format in the Mediterranean, but with a less extravagant use of figural decoration. A tall, circular stand from Gournia, Crete, is pierced with two tiers of rectangular openings which may be interpreted as windows. The top of this stand is edged with the bull-horn motif, the dominant if still undeciphered sacred symbol of Minoan Crete.[109] These horns were ranged along the roofline of some of the buildings at Cretan Cnossos, which would indicate that the Cretan stand, like that of Tell Tanaach, is based on architectural elements.

Roughly contemporaneous with these forms of altar-shrines is another, slightly different type, where the incense, or other offering, is placed inside the shrine through its wide portal.[110] In these altar-shrines we once again meet the motif of a portal with flanking columns, in a sacred context, in the land of the Canaanites and Phoenicians. One altar-shrine is made in the shape of a semi-circular hut with dome roof. The front of the "hut" is straight, composed almost completely of a door flanked by semi-detached pillars crowned with double, volute capitals.[111] A lintel decorated with a plastic bird in display position completes the small porch before the building. This type of altar is also found in Egypt.[112] Another altar-shrine, that belongs to this category, was found at Tell Fara (west of the Dead Sea). It has the flanking columns with volute capitals and an enigmatic emblem composed of incised lines and circles over a horn-like pattern in the center of the lintel (Fig. 16).[113] If it were needed, there is still additional proof that these ceramic "huts" are model shrines. A ceramic model with pillared portico was found in Cyprus, but it is within the Canaanite art tradition (Photo 36a). It is the same type of structure as that from Megiddo, but the Cypriote model's door is open, not to receive the offering, but to reveal the sphinx-like beast within; heads of other figures peer out through the side windows (cf. Beisan stand, Photo 36b).[114] Here, the model shrine holds the noumenon.

Similar model "huts" with domed roofs are used as model shrines for a female deity in the Aegean. A model from Crete (from the Late Minoan IIIb period) has painted decoration in imitation of the upright beams that support the roof. Two clay lugs, pierced to take the rod that fastens the door in place, are placed on either side of the rectangular door opening, which discloses inside a nude figure.[115] These model shrines with their sanctified inhabitants were still in use in the first millennium B.C.,[116] and while they belong within the circle of the miniature

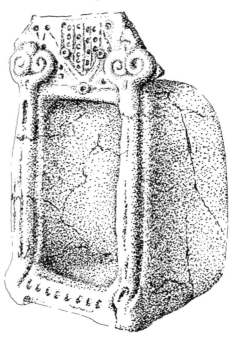

16. Model shrine from Tell Fara. (after: Jirku, *Die Welt der Bibel*, Taf. 87)

palace-shrine, there is a question as to whether they are related to similarly fashioned building models that were used for funerary purposes in the second and first millennia B.C.

Many forms of ceramic containers have been used as burial receptacles for bones and ashes, but the ones relevant to this discussion are those that obviously imitate a building. What manner of building are they modelled after? The round hut with domical or raftered roof is found in Europe in the first millennium B.C. (Photo 37).[117] The standard format is that of the Cretan shrines: the "hut" is dominated by a large rectangular door with paired lugs to take the door fastening. Human figures, birds, and geometrical devices are placed over the door and along the cornice line. The Italian models are sometimes oval, sometimes rectangular, and sometimes round in plan. A small window

may be cut over the doorway. These model structures are highly descriptive of contemporary wood architecture, even to such
details as the arrangement of the rafters on the double-sloped
roof, the post and beams, and the door frames. It has been argued
that these are models of domestic buildings—a man's mortal
remains are placed in a copy of his lifetime dwelling—but the
substantiating evidence is weak.* On the other hand, the sacred
shrine models in the East, and the model "hut" urns and shrines
of Crete strongly suggest that the Italic urns are within the shrine
category, that is, that they signify not the domestic dwelling
of the deceased, but the sacred precinct of the dead where the
gods of the shades reside and rule; the dead, in burial, are translated into the celestial realm of the gods.[118] If this is true, then
the door of the funerary urn is iconographically tied to the heavenly portal.

Are we justified, however, in attributing to Villanovan-
Etruscan Italy, symbolic ideas that were current in the Orient?
As already mentioned, there was an intrusion of Oriental ideas
and art into the Mediterranean in the first half of the first millennium B.C., and we may see in the development of the model
funerary "huts" another instance of the relationship between
East and West. Some of the earliest examples of funerary urns
in the shape of model buildings come from a cemetery located
five kilometers southeast of Tel Aviv, at the village of Azor
(Yazor). These ossuaries date from the closing centuries of the
third millennium B.C. They are models of rectangular buildings
with high façades and sloped roofs, and sometimes they are
placed on short stilts.[119] The doorways are flanked by doorposts
and beam ends in precisely the same manner of construction as is
pictured on the sanctuary portals of contemporary cylinder seals
of Mesopotamia (Photo 38).[120] Even the free-standing doorposts
of the Mesopotamian palace-shrine are probably represented
on one of the Azor ossuaries.[121] Guaranteeing the sacred character of these building models is the deformation of the gable

* *Viz.*, R. Bloch, *The Origins of Rome* (New York, 1960), 70-74. Bloch
compares the hut-urn plan with that of foundations uncovered on the Palatine.
He considers the Palatine remains as domestic architecture although little occupation material was found.

of the façade into a head with round eyes and beaked nose. And the significance of these ossuary façades, or portals, is further emphasized by their use without the model building behind. Some bronze cult objects recently discovered use this type of portal, and we can now identify this sacred portal in earliest Palestinian painting (Photo 39).[122] On the one hand, then, the Azor ossuaries bear an iconographical relationship with the Oriental sacred palace-shrine portal; on the other hand, they are related to the much later temple models and funerary urns of Greece and Italy.[123]

Hence, there is a very early development of the relationship between sacred architecture and the house of the dead. The portal of the ossuary received the deceased into the sanctified realm of the palace-shrine, the dwelling place of the gods. It is related in the epic of the hero Gilgamesh how, in his search for immortality, for the secret of everlasting life, he travels to the place beyond the grasp of death. He seeks the counsel of Utnapishtim (a "Noah" figure in Mesopotamian mythology), who was granted everlasting life. Gilgamesh, in his journey to the home of this immortal, finally comes to the twin-peaked mountain with its fearsome monsters that guard this gateway to the dwelling place of the sun. He persuades the keepers to open the mountain gates to him so that he may reach the immortal one he seeks. Is it a journey such as this that is signified by the portals of the ossuaries? Are they also related to the doors of the sun-god on his heavenly mountain peaks? At least there is reason to believe that in most ancient eschatology there existed the concept of the dead being translated into the supranatural regions of the gods, into the land of the sun where he reigns at night as chthonic deity of the underworld, or during the day as a celestial god. Gilgamesh had witnessed the death of his boon companion Enkidu; he had learned for the first time the tragic lesson of life, which is death. So he began the all-consuming search that has occupied man forever after, to give meaning to life by giving hope to the dead.

· V ·

The Portal of the Dead

OLD ORIENTAL AND CLASSICAL eschatological beliefs were far from comforting. Even though the doors of death did not close on existence, the promised "life" beyond them was vague and dreary; the good and the innocent, the just and the pious, shared the dismal underworld with the evil, the false, and the doer of wrong. The concept of reward after death, that the meritorious life shall enjoy release from spiritual pain, was developed fairly late. In ancient Mesopotamia the place of the dead had its cosmic aspects—the "great above" and the "great below,"—ruled by gods in their palaces. The sun, after lighting the world of the living, descended into the nether world to bring it day.[1] The Sumerian tale, "Inanna's Descent to the Nether World," and its later, Semitic, Akkadian counterpart, "Descent of Ishtar," provide the most extensive early Oriental accounts of that drab region of the "Land of no Return . . . the dark house . . . the house which none leave who have entered it . . . the house wherein the dwellers are bereft of light, where dust is their fare and clay their food."[2] The dead go down into the region of no hope; the great doors are unlocked by the infernal gatekeeper, Neti. The palace of death is likened to a lapis lazuli mountain ruled by the supreme goddess of the underworld, Ereshkigal, and the seven fearful judges whose word "tortures the spirit." The horrible demons, who carry off the living, lack the basic human perquisites. It is small wonder that Gilgamesh tried so mightily, but without avail, to avoid the common fate.

The Hebrew version of the nether world, a great underground cave, is hardly less gloomy. The fiery valley of Hinnom (Gehenna) was connected with Hell.[3] Greek Hades presents a picture somewhat similar to that of the Hebrew Sheol-Abaddon.* The suitors of Penelope, prematurely sent through the portal of death by the bow of her avenging husband, are led "down the dank ways, past the streams of Oceanus and the White Rock, past the gates of the Sun" (*Odyssey* xxiv, 1). Later, in Classical times a distinction is made between the souls of the good and those of the evil, for after a period of trial the good ascend to higher regions where there is cessation of care, pain, and the misery of time. Gradually, in the days of the Roman Empire, the separation of the good from the evil took on a vertical orientation; the evil souls were condemned to the underworld, while the apotheosis of the good was made into the higher cosmos.[4] In later Roman art, the pious dead are shown carried aloft, upward through the cosmic wheel of the zodiac into the realm of the divine.

The monuments and their decoration may picture the physical aspects of the world of the dead, but they cannot, of course, relate the contemporary attitudes held on death and the afterlife. Ritual formulae and religious format often survive skepticism, tolerant amusement, and outright disbelief. But the pictorial remains indicate that there was a formal continuation, at least, in the belief in a celestial region where the dead pursued an existence in one form or another, in the belief that the state of the dead could be altered by the actions and prayers of the living, and in the belief that the dead were translated into a sacred place. This much funerary art reveals; to go beyond these primary facts, we must look to the extrapolations made from social and religious documents by the historian of religion.

We should note here, however, that early rabbinic Judaism does not codify a clear, consistent attitude toward death: judgment, reward and punishment, the nature of death's kingdom, and the location of the Nether World, are spoken of in frequently

---

* The sources of Jewish, and by extension Christian, eschatological beliefs are variously argued and divided between the Greeks and Persians. Cf. for a recapitulation of present-day positions, T. F. Glasson, *Greek Influence in Jewish Eschatology* (London, 1961).

conflicting terms.[5] The Talmud relates (Berakoth 28b) that Rabban Jochanan ben Zakkai spoke on his deathbed of "two ways before me, one leading to Paradise and the other to Gehinnom." In the *Chapters of the Fathers,* the souls of the righteous are "in safekeeping under the throne of glory," while the "wicked go roving and roaming all over the universe not knowing on what to rest."[6] The Lord sits as judge, and the evil are promised "darkness and gloom . . . dust, worm, and maggot."[7] The grave takes in, and the grave gives up; the shades of the dead inhabit the cemetery, chatting and walking about in the world of the living. But the shades are also taken up into heaven, into the "Academy of the Sky."[8] The Roman Jews sent their dead on the journey to a celestial abode, to the heavenly home in the hereafter.[9]

The architectural symbol of the door as the celestial abode, as the residence of the divine power, and as the objective correlative of the cosmos is present in the sepulchral art of the Jews of the early Christian centuries. At least by the first century A.D. the Jewish religious shades are pictured as going up to heaven. The vertical ascent follows the same pattern as that expressed in the Classical pagan world. Professor Goodenough proposed that the Jewish rock-cut tomb entrance, with decorated triangular gable, was inspired by the temple pediment; and, "since temples were the abode of the gods," a temple suggested "the apotheosis of the person buried under it."[10] The present study suggests that the foundation for this hypothesis is very ancient, being based on the ossuaries and cinerary shrine-urns of the Near East and Europe. And, as we have attempted to demonstrate, it is not merely the temple as the house of the god but, more basically, the celestial region given architectural form, that finds expression in the pedimented doorway.

The Jewish tombs in the early centuries of the Christian Era used the temple front, but they were also closed by doors of stone and, probably, wood. Grave doors were in use in rock-cut pagan tombs at least by the first century B.C. and remained popular in Jewish cemeteries for the next several centuries.[11] The inner rooms of Jewish tombs were closed off with slabs of stone that carefully fit into the rabbeted doorways.[12] The millstone was also used as a closure, rolled in specially prepared channels across the tomb entrance. A few of the millstone doors have survived; the Herodian tomb, located just a few steps from the King David Hotel in Jerusalem, still holds its large stone.[13]

17. The tomb of Rabbi Shimeon and Rabbi Gamaliel at Beth She'arim.

At the extensive rock-cut cemetery of Beth She'arim, tomb closures carved to represent paneled doors were found *in situ* (Fig. 17). Some of the entrances are closed by double stone doors under a flat lintel, while other have a single slab that is sometimes carved to suggest the double doors.[14] These tombs at Beth She'arim span a period of a little less than 150 years, the earliest dating from approximately 217 A.D., and the last to *circa* 351 A.D.[15] The stone door frames of the tombs are rabbeted to take the closing slab, and carry sockets for the door pivots and closing bolts.[16]

Usually the stone slabs are made in imitation of wood-paneled doors with imitation coffering and panels. Elaborate nail bosses carved in the stone may indicate that the wooden prototypes were covered with metal. Such construction is used in the ancient East, as, for example, on the famous Assyrian wooden gates of Balawat that bore a heavily decorated bronze sheathing affixed to the wooden core with metal nails whose raised heads formed part of the decorative floral borders for the historiated panels. Probably just such metal-covered doors are indicated in the paintings of the Dura-Europos synagogue.[17]

It is highly probable that some Jewish tombs were closed with similarly decorated doors carrying figural reliefs. The recovered doors at Beth She'arim are only of the unornamented, panel type, but a stone tomb door from Neby Turfini has lion heads and bucrania in the panels. Another door, from Khirbet Semmaka on Mount Carmel, has a male figure standing in an arcuated niche.[18] It is true that neither of these doors can be identified positively as Jewish. But the only argument against their having come from Jewish tombs rests in the early assumption that Jews eschewed such pictorialism. The figural representations in the funerary art of Beth She'arim, and the decorated doors portrayed in the Dura synagogue murals rather suggest that these door panels come from Jewish cemeteries. Christian tombs used these historiated doors also. A delicate representation of the tomb of Christ, on an early Christian ivory, shows the paneled doors ajar, to indicate the empty tomb chamber (Photo 40). The two Marys, with the sleeping guards, complete the scene. The doors contain the conventional lion-head doorpulls, and the panels are illustrated with episodes from the miracles of Christ. The door motif is carried over to both pagan and Christian tombstones. It is depicted complete with pediment and *acroteria* on, for example, a long series of tombstones dating in the third and fourth centuries A.D. in Phrygia.[19]

Of unusual interest for our purposes, however, are two Jewish tomb doors that carry sacred symbols in their panels. One, completely preserved, was acquired by the Louvre Museum in 1902 from a chance find at Kefar Yasif (the Village of Joseph), located in the region of Mount Carmel, seven and one-half kilometers northeast of Saint-Jean d'Acre (Photo 41).[20] The doorleaf has a small pivot at the bottom and a tenon at the top to fit into the door frame; an iron handle was once attached to the front. The face of the doorleaf is divided into six rectangular panels with a vertical median strip. Three of the panels bear circles inscribed with, respectively, a petalled rosette, a six-lobed geometrical rosette, and a circle of swirling arcs. A fourth panel is composed of rectangular latticework. The remaining two panels hold a candelabrum with crescent-shaped objects, and a model shrine with shell pediment. The second door from Ovalin (Ibdlin, Galilee), of which only the lower portion is preserved, repeats some of the same motifs in its bottom two panels: the six-leaf geometrical rosette, the candelabrum, and the median strip (Photo 42).[21] These two doors are important documents, for they are the only funerary doors yet recovered that contain a complex of specific Jewish symbols.

The circle inscribed with a six-lobed rosette made by intersecting arcs of a compass is a design that comes into the Oriental decorative scheme fairly late, but it is well established in architectural decoration in the century before the beginning of the Christian Era.[22] It becomes a standard motif in early Christian church decoration, in Nabataean building, is particularly popular in Parthian art, and enters synagogue decoration. The importance of this simple design lies in the fact that it marks, in the Hellenized East, the introduction of an entirely new system of decorative treatment opposed to Classical decoration and is indicative of a resurgence of Oriental art after Hellenistic domination. The design is probably of Iranian origin and was carried by the Parthians in their march westward. It becomes a leitmotif in Judaic art on the stone ossuaries (Photo 49).[23] It is not only used on catacomb doors,[24] but is also used as a motif flanking the representations of doors, indicating that there is more than a casual relationship between the rosette and the portal. As a further indication of its importance in the Judaic decorative scheme, this design appears as the central motif on the stone chair, the so-called seat of Moses, from the synagogue of Khorazin. The circle with inscribed radiating arcs that form a whirling "sun" design is also well-known in the East and is particularly popular at the same time as is the geometrical rosette.

This fairly ubiquitous use of the circle and rosette designs by different cultures would seem to imply that they are devoid of iconographical content. But the manner in which these designs are employed in Judaic art indicates that they are meaningful. The inscribed circle is associated with the *menorah* and can be used in place of the *menorah*; candelabra or rosettes flank the sacred door and are placed upon the lintels of doorways.[25]

The two grave doors under discussion place the circle next to the candelabrum. The *menorah* is certainly not a meaningless item of decoration, and, hence, we may suspect that if the rosette can be substituted for the sacred symbol, then it must be considered in terms comparable to that symbol. The Kefar Yasif door displays this significant triad in Jewish iconography—candelabrum, rosette, and portal—on, it is important to remember, a tomb door.

The small portal-shrine carved on the Kefar Yasif doorleaf is made of two short columns on stepped bases surmounted by a tympanum in the form of the scallop shell. (Such shells are commonly used as the crowning feature of *aediculae*, and are taken over by the synagogue for the Torah shrine, as at Beth Alpha and Dura-Europos.[26] (They also appear on the portal-shrines carved on sarcophagi.) Enshrined in the miniature portal on this doorleaf is a square with inscribed lozenge; this could be merely a fill pattern, but it is found in the same setting on a Carthaginian stone.[27] The occurrence there could be a coincidence, but there was an active Jewish community at Carthage which could account for a borrowing of symbols.[28] The square and lozenge are used in other Jewish decorative work, and Professor Goodenough would see in it the female principle.[29] It well may be used in the pagan world as a symbol for the fertility goddess who, as we have noted, is placed within the sanctifying portal and is used in pagan funerary art as a sign of rebirth. While the goddess would have no place in Judaic art, the pagan abstract symbol that held the promise of everlasting life may well have been carried over into the Jewish sepulchre.

The candelabrum on the doors follows the Biblical injunction that the arms of the *menorah* shall be of equal height (Exod. 25:36). The bent leg tripod of the candelabrum is the form commonly used (Photo 43). The chief exception to this type of candlestand is the depiction of the Temple *menorah* on the arch of Titus in Rome.[30] The candelabrum on the Kefar Yasif door has the most unusual feature of nine, rather than seven branches. Is this deliberate or accidental? One of the first commentators on the stone door felt that "the absentmindedness of the craftsman gave it nine branches instead of seven."[31] Unfortunately, the door from Ovalin is fractured across the arms of the *menorah,* but what remains indicates that there were seven branches represented there. Perhaps the carver of the Kefar Yasif door was mindful of the Biblical clause that forbade making a candelabrum with the same number of arms as that of the Temple.[32] If this is the case, then we have here the work of an unusually scrupulous artisan. The candelabrum used for the festival of Chanukah has eight arms (for the eight days of the festival), but it is difficult at best to reconcile the festival lights with this funerary setting. Hence, although it is always best to seek the explanation for an anomaly in something other than a mistake or "distraction," perhaps in this instance such is the answer.

On either side of the candelabrum are two crescent-like designs with circles underneath. These are most unusual companions for the *menorah.* The Beth Alpha mosaic provides the complete list of symbols that are usually associated with the *menorah* in Judaic art: portal, branches, citrus, incense shovel, lion, and ram's horn. The crescent-shaped objects can be related to none of these. They may be bowls, perhaps containers for the oil of the lamps. The closest representation is found on the exotic relief (in Istanbul) of a man carrying on his head a crescent-shaped object on a pole. A thyrsus rises out of the bowl from which two small animals drink. A Beth She'arim relief pictures a *menorah* carried on the head of a man.[33] The crescent on a pole, a symbol of the lunar god, is found in the ancient Orient, and persists in later, Nabataean art where it crowns columns. The circle and crescent on the door could stand for the sun and moon, both of which appear in the hub of the zodiac wheel at Beth Alpha; the celestial character of the *menorah* would support this suggestion, but there is no firm confirmation.

The last panel on the Kefar Yasif door—a rectangle with geometric lattice-work—is somewhat anonymous. However, relative to the other designs on the stone, and the fact that this is a door, we may see in the lattice a symbol of the portal. A glass plate found in the catacombs of Beth She'arim has a lattice design held between two door posts (Fig. 18).[34] A Palmyrene medallion shows a pedimented portal with doorleaves that have a similar type of lattice in the upper half.[35]

The central, vertical strip has been mentioned as imitating the division between two doorleaves. The portal painted over

18. Glass plate with portals under arcade found in
Catacomb 15 at Beth She'arim. (after: Avigad,
"Excavations at Beth She'arim, 1954," fig. 12.

the Torah niche at Dura-Europos has such a median strip decorated with seven circles; the stone door has six circles. But the triangles at either end seem to make the band into something more than a divider. A vertical column of circles is employed as a specific symbol inside a portal-shrine, in East Roman iconography, on coinage of Caracalla and Severus Alexander from Hieropolis. On a Dolichenean bronze plaque, the column of circles stands in a shrine over a crescent. These motifs are mounted on poles, while the Kefar Yasif circles are raised on triangles.[36]

Do these stone doors present a chance assemblage of general duty designs whose ultimate purpose is decorative, or do they contain an internally consistent set of motifs that are significant in their funerary assignment? Doors of tombs, as the Christian ivory plaque in the British Museum shows (Photo 40), were vehicles for cult representations. The two stone doors are not just doors to close off a chamber, but rather stood at the

[109]

portal that separated the living from the dead. If the inscribed circles are to be seen as only decoration, certainly the same cannot be said of the *menorah* and the pillared miniature shrine. But, if the stone doors belong within the ancient theme of the celestial portal, then we are provided with a key to a coherent pattern of celestial symbols.

The circle and the circle inscribed with star and rosette patterns have a long history in the East that connects them with celestial bodies. It is this heavenly association that is indicated when the star appears in the pediment, the architectural representation of the sky.[37] The sepulchral rosette appears early in the Mediterranean world, and, in the centuries just prior to the beginning of the Christian Era, it becomes a standard motif on sarcophagi. In the Hellenistic period it may serve to denote the heavenly aspirations of the deceased, or it may more specifically refer to the flower of Adonis, who is the archetype of death and resurrection.[38] The variety of rosettes on the stone doors are related to the combinations of rosettes on Classical funerary monuments, but we may suggest that the rosettes on the doors refer to the celestial abode, the place beyond the door of the grave. A parallel motif is found on a Roman funerary relief that shows the deceased on his catafalque, covered by a star-studded canopy with the crescent moon.[39] There is no suggestion that the astral rosette of Jewish funerary monuments is related to that major symbol of later Judaism, the six-pointed star formed by two intersecting triangles. This hexagram, the "Star of David," is found first in the architectural carving of the third century A.D. synagogue at Capernaum; it is used there in place of a rosette within a rinceau. But the hexagram drops out of pictorial Judaic art as a significant element until it reappears in the seventeenth century.[40]

The heavenly setting suggested by the astral rosettes would then be reinforced by the latticework as representing the heavenly portal, and the pillared shrine with the shell pediment as the symbol of cosmic architecture. We noted that superimposed circles appear in the Hellenized Orient as a device inside a shrine. They have been convincingly argued by Professor Harald

Ingholt as being images of the Syrian goddess Semea, the *Heavens:* "The word *semeion* makes sense both in Aramaic and in Greek, meaning respectively, 'image of Heavens' and 'sign, *signum*'."[41] The circles represent planets; originally seven planets, the Pleiades, were portrayed, although fewer may be used. Seven circles are used on the Dura-Europos median band, six on the Kefar Yasif door. The similarity between the *semeion* in the shrine and the band in the Judaic examples may be coincidental, but it should not be summarily dismissed as such. The band of circles stands next to the *menorah,* whose lights Philo interpreted as symbols of the planets.*

The candelabrum, symbol par excellence of Judaism, is laden with many interpenetrating meanings, all of which make it an appropriate motif for the celestial door of grave and synagogue.[42] The sacred *menorah,* carefully described in the Old Testament, stood in the sanctuary of the Temple of Jerusalem whose innermost recesses were hidden behind a curtain of Babylonian manufacture, embroidered with "the whole vista of the heavens."[43] While the number seven is so ubiquitous in ancient magic and ritual that an attempt to define its significance in an isolated case runs the risk of being a display of ingenuity rather than of authority, the astral associations of the *menorah* argue well for the seven lamps having derived from the Babylonian planets.[44] But the Jerusalem Talmud ('Erubin 5:22c) also indicates an ancient relationship between the sun and this magical number in Judaism. Philo says, "For the sun, like the candlestick,

---

* Philo, *De Vita Mosis*, II, 12. Philo, a Hellenized Alexandrian Jew (b. *circa* 25 B.C.-d. *circa* 45/50 A.D.), is not regarded as a particularly reliable commentator on Judaism: "Yet the philosophical schools fascinated him apparently as much as, if not more than, the teachings of the Bible in their simple and literal form. And Philo was also deeply moved by the ideas behind the Mystery Religions which had poured into the hellenistic mixing bowl of Alexandria from all sides. To what extent he was influenced by them is just at present a highly controverted point, but, if his mystical language and terms be discounted at the very lowest rate, and thought to be only terms which Philo 'took from the air' without essential influence upon himself or his ideas, still there they are, staring at us from almost every page, and there can be no question that Philo's own religious experience was of a kind for which he found such a terminology expressive." (E. R. Goodenough, *An Introduction to Philo Judaeus*, [New Haven, 1940], pp. 11-12).

has the fourth place in the middle of the six and gives light to the three above and the three below it . . . ."[45] The construction of the Temple *menorah,* with its knops and buds, reflects the old "sacred trees," with their laterally branching arms and flower-like terminals that readily lend themselves to being interpreted as flames.[46] Clusters of seven cups have been found in second millennium B.C. sacred areas at the Palestinian sites of Nahariyah, Megiddo, and Byblos, probably providing the cultic background for the seven oil lamps of the candelabrum.[47] The funerary symbol of the *menorah,* then, stands not only as a celestial symbol, but may, through its association with the oil of the olive tree—the tree that was supposed to live to a very great age—and the Tree of Life in the Garden, have also acted as a symbol of perpetual life.[48]

The *menorah* does not enter the ensemble of pictorial devices used by Jewish artists until well into the first century B.C. It first appears on coins from the mint of Mattathias Antigonus, and in the Hasmonaean period is also scratched on the wall of a tomb.[49] After this hesitant beginning, the candelabrum dominates Jewish pictorial representations in the early centuries in tomb and synagogue.[50] In the Jewish catacombs of Rome it is inscribed in the wreath of victory, probably as a sign of triumph over death for near it are other symbols of enduring life, the pomegranate and the dolphin. The ram's horn (*shofar*), branches (*lulab*), citrus (*ethrog*), and incense shovel are appropriate companions of the *menorah* (Photo 45). The ram's horn signifies the Feast of the New Year (*Rosh Ha-Shanah*), and the branches and citrus represent the Feast of the Tabernacles: these holidays mark the periods during which the world is judged, when it is determined who shall live and who shall die. The Mishna describes the handled incense shovel used by the High Priest on the Day of Atonement (Yom Kippur: Yoma 4:4; 5:1), and the *shofar,* with its mouthpiece of gold or silver, sounded on New Year (Rosh Ha-Shanah: Rosh Ha-Shanah 3:2-5), for Israel ". . . will be ultimately redeemed by the ram's horn . . . ." (Midrash rabbah lvi, 9).

Returning to the Beth Alpha mosaic for a moment, we note

that it contains, besides the symbols of the festivals of the New Year, the Day of Atonement, and the Feast of the Tabernacles, some other motifs which may fit this pattern of judgment. The Mishna lists four times in the year when judgment occurs:

> At four times in the year is the world judged: at Passover, through grain; at Pentecost, through the fruits of the tree; on New Year's Day all that come into the world pass before him like legions of soldiers, for it is written, *He that fashioneth the hearts of them all, that considereth all their works;* and at the Feast [of Tabernacles] they are judged through water.

(Rosh Ha-Shanah 1:2)

Are the days of Passover and Pentecost represented also around the portal at Beth Alpha? We can only suggest that some elements in the panel, which have been argued over, may be relevant. On one side of the flanking candelabra is a stalk with five flowers branching off; its counterpart on the other side is a woody trunk from which issue six flowering (or perhaps fruit-laden) branches. These may represent the grain of Passover and the fruit tree of Pentecost. This suggested interpretation should be weighed against another: "Less familiar objects are the flowering rod of Aaron on the right of the Ark, and the barren rod on the left."[51] Or, one branch has been considered as the rod of Aaron, with the other standing for the Israelite tribes.[52] Goodenough suggests that they stand for the "Tree of Life."[53] Each of these ideas has merit, although it is difficult to see in the flowering branch a "barren rod." However, the identification suggested here, that the branches are associated with the festivals, has the dual advantage of fitting these elements into the pattern established by their companion sacred objects of a motif of Days of Judgment, and with the appropriate notion that the mosaic is "more in keeping with rabbinical exegesis than with the pentateuchal narrative . . . that the aggadic-theological thinking of the rabbis of the synagogue lies embedded herein."[54]

The grave doors of Kefar Yasif and Ovalin can be interpreted as manifestations of the ancient celestial portal, with their internal iconographical consistency of carved designs. And these doors, in turn, help to explain the sky-borne aspirations expressed in the Beth Alpha mosaic. The pedimented portal in the synagogue mosaic is not, of course, in any sense a sepulchral doorway; rather, both doors are derived from the basic motif of the door as an embodiment of the celestial sphere, and as the entrance to the dwelling place of the Divine. When the portal is seen within this context, it becomes clear that no purpose is served by attempting to pin down the precise identification of each portal in Judaic art as Torah shrine, or Ark, or Temple, for each of these is a specific application of the all-embracing cosmic theme.[55] For Marianos and Hanina the portal of the mosaic was probably simply a "shrine," a more or less realistic picture of the sacred closet for the scrolls of the synagogue. They knew it to be holy, and they may have had a vague awareness that it was in some way connected with the realm of the most high, but artists are seldom theologians. Specific reference to the sacred portal as part of the Torah shrine is clearly stated in the paintings of the catacombs in Rome (Photo 27) and on the gold glass vessels, where the doors are opened to reveal the scrolls neatly stacked on shelves. On the other hand, the Roman gold glass that depicts the portal, with its building behind, surrounded by an arcade, and flanked by two free-standing columns, must be taken as a picture of the Temple of Jerusalem (Photo 28). But most of the representations of the sacred portal lack this specific denotation.

It is beyond our subject to enter into the vexing question of the theological significance of the Ark of the Temple, whether it represents the seat or footstool of Yahweh or the container of the Tablets of the Law or the lots.[56] What is important for the pictorial appearance is that each of these attributions suggests the celestial role of the container and its doors. The Ark as the divine seat would be consistent with the ancient Oriental pictorial documentation of the throne of the god as a temple or altar-shrine. One scholar suggests that the Jewish artists picked up the motif of the pedimented shrine from Roman iconography as standing for the Mercy Seat, because the Jews no longer knew the original form of the Seat.[57] Beyond the Old Testament account, there is no indication of the appearance of the Ark in the later history of the Temple. The original Ark of the Temple probably dropped out of sight and was destroyed during the reign of Manasseh.[58]

In the Municipal Museum at Haifa is preserved a Jewish portal that demonstrates the multi-valence symbolism of the door in Jewish iconography (Photo 46). The door is a single stone slab carved to represent double, paneled doorleaves. Rising from the median strip is the *menorah*. The door jambs are carved with birds perched on amphorae. The lintel carries antefixes of scallop shell design with the second *menorah* in the middle. We would hasten to identify this ensemble as a Torah shrine, except that it is a tomb door. It is, of course, first of all the celestial portal; but it is here used as the entrance to the land of the dead.

Once again, the standard iconography of Judaic art is employed on the portal. The vessels on the door jambs are regularly associated with the *menorah*. They may contain the oil for the lamps, as has been suggested, and so signify the promise of immortality. The Hellenized Phoenician paintings in the Palestinian catacombs of the second century B.C. at Marisa (Mareshah) show the immediate precursors of the amphorae in a funerary setting.[59] The rather roughly drawn birds on the Haifa portal (that came from Kefar Tamra, near Shefar'am) are not easy to identify. The one on the left jamb has a crest that indicates it is a peacock, while the one on the right, with its long legs and extended neck belongs to the same family as the birds that climb the pediment at Beth Alpha.[60] The peacock has long acted as a symbol of immortality and apotheosis. The mosaic in the synagogue of Hamman-Lif portrays peacocks in their accustomed position on either side of a cantharos with spouting water; peacocks and similar long-necked birds appear in early Christian art flanking the sacred portal. A sixth century A.D. metal bookcover from Syria, for example, shows the motif of peacocks standing on either side of the arch of the portal which enshrines a holy figure.[61] It is this pattern which is drawn, in more lively form, on the pediment of the Beth Alpha portal. The celestial habitat of the birds is also found in the Roman catacombs; in a Jewish tomb at Torlonia the peacock stands next to the star-studded arcade which imitates the canopy of heaven.

The line of shell antefixes is well-known as entablature decoration on Classical sarcophagi which follow the miniature temple format. The portal painted above the Torah shrine at Dura-Europos carries the same pattern (Photo 16). The *menorah* on the Haifa portal stands in place of the solar disk on the lintels of pagan shrines. The median strip that divides the panels of the stone slab, appears to be a garland and, hence, would be related to the wreath of victory (a common funerary motif) that symbolizes triumph over death.[62] The *menorah* crowning the garland would, then, be quite appropriate.

The sacred portal, used as a tomb door in the Haifa model, is also scratched upon the catacomb walls at Beth She'arim. There, lions rather than birds stand on the roofline. One of these wall-carvings places the *menorah* inside the portal, as on the Haifa door, thus sanctifying the candelabrum, placing it within its celestial home. These several forms of the sacred portal, descended from the palace-shrine of the gods, use the straight entablature, the arch, and the triangular pediment. As in the second millennium Semitic iconography, the doorleaves may be portrayed, or else just the doorposts, the columns to support the lintel. Copying Classical architectural patterns, the Jewish artists draw their portals with triangular pediments and with arches. In the pagan world, the gods are placed within the celestial portal, which forms an *aedicula* or *naiskos*. But the Jews substitute symbolic forms: the *menorah* in place of the god, and, as in the Torah niche at Dura-Europos, the lozenge in a square.[63] The sacred portal depicted on a ceramic lamp, decorated with antefixes and shell entablature, encloses the lozenge (Photo 47).[64]

The sarcophagi and ossuaries that were carried in through the sacred portals of the tomb continue the decorative use of the portal motif in its many variations. The Jews of the early Christian centuries buried their dead in different types of receptacles. Those of expensive material and more elaborate design reflect the higher social and economic level of the families. Sarcophagi are made of both imported marble and local stone. Found at Beth She'arim are fragments of fully ornamented marble sarcophagi whose strongly Hellenized figural relief work indicates that they belonged to a wealthy family which could afford imported art. Probably the social prestige alone of such a family accounts for this audacious intrusion of patently pagan sculpture in ground sanctified with the bones of sages.[65] Lead coffins with die-cast decoration were also current in the ancient world and were used by the Jews of the time.[66] The lead coffins are made of two sheets of lead, bent and soldered to form the sides.[67] Secondary burials (*i.e.* reburial of the bones after the body had decayed) were made in small stone and wood chests. Of wood coffins, nothing remains, but the presence of a few nails in the catacombs guarantees the use of these less expensive receptacles by poorer families. The Jerusalem Talmud mentions burying bones in cedar boxes.

It is a commonplace to refer to the coffin as the house of the dead. Even in neolithic times, as we have seen, the mortal remains were placed in a "house." But the house of the dead was not the same as the house of the living; the dead resided in the house that is the other world, in the regions above or below, where the infernal or celestial gods resided. The Jews of the Holy Land still kept this burial tradition in the last centuries of Roman rule. That is, the later Jewish burials were made in caskets that carried the symbols of the celestial palace-shrine, the sacred portal, and were themselves made in the form of a "house of the dead." The Jewish funerary equipment that reflects this tradition does so in the idiom of contemporary Classical burial vessels (Photo 48). The borrowing of Hellenized forms indicates the adoption of current burial styles that continue the tradition of ancient concepts. Burial in catacombs is probably of Oriental origin, for it was not an established tradition in the West. The Etruscans carved out burial "houses" in the soft tufa rock, but this form of burial is intrusive in Italy. We have already noted the early Italian use of the ceramic "hut-urn" for burial (Photo 37); it and the later Etruscan funerary house may both be evidence of Eastern importation. The Christian and Jewish catacombs of Rome also probably derive from the East, where the use of natural caves for burial gave rise to excavated chambers that developed into the long, underground corridors with halls and vaults.

The custom of translating the dead into the cosmic house

may also be seen in the Mediterranean on a sarcophagus from the Cretan site of Hagia Triada. This well-known example of Minoan painting depicts a funerary setting, part of which shows the deceased in front of his "house of the dead." Terra cotta sarcophagi from Clazomenae of the sixth century B.C. present a later, Greek version of the concept embodied in the earlier "hut urns." The Clazomenae vessels are made in the form of shrines with pillared façade and entablature painted around the opening. It has been proposed that these funerary palace-shrines were thought of as *aediculae* within which the deceased stood, and that the later Greek funerary stele portraying the dead enshrined in a portal was a sculptural continuation of the more primitive mode.[68] But the shrine motif was also directly continued in Graeco-Roman sarcophagi made as miniature temples, complete with colonnade and entablature.

The bone chests of Palestine, which date from the second century B.C. to the end of the second century A.D., are clearly within this iconographical setting, for they follow architectural models.[69] There is no other way to interpret one of the ossuaries found in a cemetery located outside the western wall of the Old City of Jerusalem on the Mount of Olives. This box is carved to show the regular courses of stone walls decorated with rosettes; cornice and pediment complete the "building."[70] The typical Jewish ossuary is not so realistically detailed, but is still obviously designed as a model building. Significantly, the architectural detail of the temple-shrine that persists, when all other architectural motifs are eliminated, is the representation of the celestial portal. The portal is placed in the center of the long side of the box, frequently defined with doorjambs, paneling, and flat or arcuated lintel. The geometrical rosettes of the tomb doors here flank the sacred portal to the other world (Photo 49).[71] An ossuary fragment from the cemetery mentioned above (Dominus Flevit) simply shows an arcuated niche between six-leaved rosettes. Two horn-like projections are drawn out from the haunch of the arch, the vestigial remains of *acroteria*.[72]

While the ancestry of the sacred portal can be traced far back into the dim recesses of Near Eastern prehistory, we must

look to the West for the more immediate parentage of the ossuary doors. Such sacred doors are well-illustrated on Classical
sarcophagi,[73] and the theme is splendidly represented on the
monument to the Haterii that carries the relief of an elegantly
decorated temple-tomb.[74] Goodenough, in his photographic
corpus of early Jewish artifacts, illustrates over a hundred stone
ossuaries that provide the limited range of decoration used by
the Jewish artists. The dominant motif is the geometrical rosette
in combination with arcades, sacred doors, "trees," garlands,
columns, and vases. The tree is substituted on the ossuaries for
the usual Jewish symbol, the *menorah*, which appears with such
infrequency that it cannot be considered as a regular part of
ossuary design. In Goodenough's catalog of ossuaries, the *menorah* is represented only once.[75] But its omission does not indicate that it was prohibited in funerary art, for it is found in
the catacombs and on the marble and lead caskets. We must
conclude, then, that the significances of *menorah* and tree are
so closely related, that the latter can be substituted for the for-
mer. The tree form degenerates on the ossuaries into a simple
columnar shape, but on some chests, the design is picked out
by a zigzag line that describes a form intermediate between
menorah, tree, and column.[76] Hence, we have here another
example of the assimilation of the three ancient, cosmic symbols,
and a further indication of the pictorial origin of the *menorah*.

The sacred doors of the ossuaries follow the pattern of variations with which we are already familiar: straight lintels with
antefixes, arcuated lintels, triangular pediments with *acroteria*,
and flanking, free-standing columns. The doorleaves are drawn
plain, or represented as paneled, or made with a lozenge pattern
in the same manner as the grid design on the Kefar Yasif stone
door. The ivy, with its heart-shaped leaf, that figures prominent-
ly on Classical sarcophagi, is also used.

Thus the range of motifs open to the artist is very restricted.
The cosmic valence of the designs is arranged in different ways,
but extraneous elements are not introduced, except for lozenges,
diamonds, zig-zags, and other minor ornamental elements easily
cut by the chisel. The stone sarcophagi, on the other hand offer

a broader range of designs, no doubt because of the number and proximity of pagan examples from which the Jewish artists could adopt and adapt.[77] At Beth She'arim, the carvers of sarcophagi went directly to Graeco-Roman models, sometimes setting down a seemingly random assortment of motifs without any attempt at integrating the design or following through with a unified pictorial program. But behind this apparent catch-as-catch-can carving of individual motifs on the stone walls of the chests, there is the familiar emphasis on heavenly elements and the sacred portal.

A sarcophagus from Beth She'arim shows the expanded architectural symbolism of the portal represented on the ossuaries (Photo 50). The shorthand technique of the ossuaries that represents the door between two columns, to signify that the chest is a celestial abode, developed from the container carved as a miniature building. A fourth century B.C. Etruscan urn, for example, has an arcuated portal between columns at one end; the long sides of the chest represent the flank of the building; and the lid is the architrave.[78] The Beth She'arim example has the long face of the chest carved with columns supporting a lintel. It is based on the columnar sarcophagi of the Classical world which place figures and mythological scenes in the spaces of the arcades.[79] These columnar sarcophagi are picked up in the Roman East by Christian artists and transmitted by them back to the West.[80] The theme of the portal as symbolic of the heavenly sphere is still vital in early Christianity where the sarcophagus as the palace-shrine then also portrays the heavenly city:

> It is the city of God, namely the Church . . . . If interpreted in this manner, the continuous series of city-gates may be considered as a symbol of the Church whose successive stages—prototypes, foundations, and spreading—are represented on the four sides.[81]

Both the Christian columnar sarcophagi of the fourth century A.D. and the Jewish examples come from the common source of East Graeco-Roman art.[82] There is no reason to see the Jewish examples as the intermediary between Classical and Christian.

One Beth She'arim sarcophagus shows the double-leaved portal flanked by columns,[83] while the more interesting example (Photo 50) from the same cemetery mentioned above has the long side of the chest carved as an arcade with six columns.[84] In three of the arcades are pictured small columns with vertical fluting. These are undoubtedly the same columns that appear between the rosettes on the ossuaries and must carry the same meaning; that is, they refer us back to the celestial pillar, to the astral significance of the *menorah*, and, hence, they properly belong in the arcade of heaven. In one of the arcades of this sarcophagus is a low stand supporting a deep, bowl-shaped form; rising from it are two spiraling columns that widen at the center and terminate in points. The reference here is to the incense altar of the Temple. A plaque from Dura-Europos pictures a horned altar from which rises a spiral of smoke made in a similar manner, confirming the identification of the sarcophagus design (Photo 51).[85] The placing of incense altars within arcades is not unusual. The lintel of a Nabataean temple has carved on it a series of arcuated lintels, terminating at either end in a six-pointed geometrical rosette, enclosing a series of altars with ascending smoke.* The third motif carved on the sarcophagus is of a man resting on a tall spear with a leaping animal before him. Several explanations as to his identity have been offered, based on similar representations on pagan sarcophagi: the hunter and his dog, Meleager and the Caledonian boar, Artemis and her hind, or Dionysus and his lion. The theme of a hunter in combat, which is used on Christian sarcophagi,[86] does not seem to fit the passive, almost contemplative scene of the Beth She'arim example. Much closer to that spirit is the Meleager, on the sarcophagus called by his name, who stands under an arcade, resting on his spear, his dog seated by him.[87] For want of more comparative Judaic material, we can only suggest that Meleager is portrayed, without knowing why the Jewish artist has used this theme, except as a borrowing from the Classical model.

---

* *Alt TB*, Taf. clxxxi, No. 452; *Sym*, VI, 291 and I, 153. Gressmann distinguishes between three of the altars which he says have iconic pillars on them —*masseben*—and two which are flaming.

The pagan motifs and models combined with the heavenly motif make this sarcophagus instructive for its eclecticism. The celestial palace-shrine of old is still alive in it, but now the Jewish artist has transformed it into the Roman format of a peripteral temple. The arcade design became popular all over the Hellenized East, as decoration for architecture and for the smallest of household goods; it encloses, and hence sanctifies, all manner of symbols and figures, the abstract and animal signs being most popular with the Jews.[88] A quick review of the decorated sarcophagi of Beth She'arim impresses one with the random selection of motifs taken from the pagan world. We find lions drinking from a bowl, hanging garlands with bearded mask, wreaths, bucrania, grapevine, and shells. It follows, of course, that these motifs have to do with the hoped-for heavenly resting place, for they are borrowed from pagan funerary monuments.

One further sarcophagus from Beth She'arim should be briefly noted. It is of stone, with a lid in imitation of Roman models; it represents a temple pediment with acroteria and the familiar classical moldings and beadings (Photo 52). The front panel shows a discontinuous assemblage of designs framed by a grapevine and an interlacing pattern under a triple fascia. The framed panel, which seems to be unfinished as is the remainder of the carving, shows flanking animals, a wreath enclosing the six-pointed geometrical star or rosette, and two portal-shrines crowned with scallop shells. Sanctified in one shrine is a lion. We have seen the lion in Judaic art usually flanking a holy symbol; here it may be the old solar beast in the door of heaven.[89] It is less likely that it stands, in this setting, for the heroism of the Jews,[90] or as the symbol of the Law.[91] The solar attribution of the lion on this sarcophagus is supported by the presence of an eagle in the other, identical niche. The eagle, also, as we have seen, has its ancient solar affinities.

The eagle in the portal-shrine comes from the art world outside that of the Jews. We have seen something of its ancient character; there remains to review the role it held in the pagan world contemporaneous with Judaic art. In a well-argued study of Roman funerary art, the Belgian scholar Cumont summarizes the symbolic content of the eagle in display position as follows. The eagle appears in East Roman (particularly in Syrian) art on funerary monuments with its old connection with the solar power. But it takes on additional meaning in the Roman world as

19. Drawing of dipinto of eagle in niche from Dura-Europos (see Photograph 53).

the messenger of the sun, the vehicle that conveys the souls of the dead to the sky, "to the star that has created them." Thus, the eagle carries the wreath of victory (signifying triumph over death), and, with the deifying of the Caesars, the eagle carries the emperor himself, or a divine trinity:[92]

> The Oriental belief, adopted by the Romans, that the sacred eagle carried the dead prince to the world of the gods, is translated in the Empire into a number of figural monuments: bas-reliefs, carved stones, medallions with the legend *Consecratio*, testifying to its diffusion. There is seen sometimes the complete figure of Caesar made divine, sometimes only his bust, placed on an eagle, the wings wide open, which lift them up into the air.[93]

The East-Roman monuments that Cumont catalogs show the eagle in the pediment, our old architectural concept of the solar lintel, and the eagle in display position within a pedimented shrine, just as it appears on small clay lamps and on the Beth She'arim sarcophagus.[94] The association of eagle and God in the Semitic world is found in the fourth century B.C. on a coin that shows a male figure seated on a winged, wheeled throne with a bird in his hand. The coin is inscribed to Yahu (i.e. YHWH: the Hebrew characters of *Y, H, V*).[95] Whether it is the same eagle that stands on a horned altar within a pedimented shrine at Dura-Europos (Photo 53, Fig. 19) cannot be determined, but certainly an eagle on an altar must have to do with a form of divinity, and must also be the pagan prototype for the Jewish symbol.[96]

Finally, we can return to the world of Marianos and Ḥanina at Beth Alpha, and to the culminating panel in the mosaic. The flowered curtains which stood before the Holy-of-Holies in the Temple are drawn back to reveal the symbols of the celestial residence of the Divine. Lions, birds, *menorah,* ritual utensils, and trees are gathered together, assembled about the pedimented sacred portal; the basic meaning of the portal as the palace-shrine of the heavenly Dweller is never lost. As the architectural concretion of God's house, it holds His Tablets, His Torah. It is the Temple because it also holds God's seat and footstool. And, as the heavenly precinct, its doors close upon the realm of the pious dead who are gathered under His throne.

· VI ·

The Altar and the Heavenly Palace

In the discussion of the Oriental palace-shrine, we found that the deity's palace on earth could be represented in and depicted by the altar dedicated to him. The heavenly mountain was architecturally interpreted as the ziggurat; then, in turn, the altar was formed in the shape of a miniature ziggurat. The emblem of the palace-shrine, the sacred portal, persists in the representation of the altars, as is indicated by the appearance of the doorposts, either standing on the altar or flanking it. The altar can well be thought of as the *cathedra,* the seat of the deity, for it is not only the place of his presence but is also symbolic of his residence. Ancient Semitic representations on sealings document the assimilation of the divine throne with the altar.[1] Here, then, is another dimension of the sacred portal as being associated with the altar. In a moment we shall look at some of the later illustrations of this connection between the sacred portal and the altar.

If the heavenly portal and the altar, the house and the seat of the divine, are assimilated in ancient Near Eastern iconography, does the altar play a distinctive part in Judaic iconography along with the portal motif? The altar is, of course, important in the Old Testament narrative; its shape, size, material, and manner of construction are carefully outlined.[2] In Judaism, the altar was unique to the Temple of Jerusalem once the Temple was established, and it could well have become the symbol for the Temple after the building was destroyed. And yet, the horned altar of the Temple does not become part of the iconographical repertory of the Jewish artist. We have the frequent representation of the altar of the Akedah, to be sure, and an altar can be identified on the columnar sarcophagus from Beth She'arim. There are two other, possible appearances of altars on Jewish

20. Horned altar (?) graffito on Jewish ossuary. (after: *Sym*, III, fig. 224)

ossuaries (Fig. 20),[3] but the scant number of such representations only emphasizes the lack of a continuing tradition. By contrast, the altar is omnipresent in contemporary pagan art of the East. Perhaps, Goodenough suspects, it is because the altar was a basic pagan symbol that it was shunned by Jewish artists.

> The menorah became popular, the altar did not, probably because the altar was common to so many religions, while the menorah could become the unique sign of Judaism—also because the menorah could be, and was, used in home and synagogue.[4]

Such, indeed, may be the reasons that account for the absence of the horned altar, but, as Professor Goodenough's encyclopedia of Jewish symbols so well documents, the Jews were not at all loath to accept pagan symbols. We may suggest a different resolution to this curious, apparent disappearance of the altar from Jewish iconography. Perhaps the altar is not absent, but has been assimilated with the sacred portal, and the portal motif also stands for the Temple altar when it appears in Judaic art. While there is no direct Jewish evidence for this subterranean appearance of the altar in Judaic art, there are some strong indications that point in that direction, indications common to Jewish and non-Jewish iconography. If the portal and altar are combined into one visual motif in the surrounding pagan world, then there is a reasonable basis for arguing that this aspect of the portal was carried over into Jewish symbolism also. We must ask, then, how strong was this tradition of portal-as-altar in the ancient world, and did this iconographical tradition persist through the early Christian centuries?

The ceramic incense burners from the Palestinian littoral, that were discussed before, were made in the form of miniature shrines (Photo 36). The Megiddo pottery shrine dates from approximately the same period as that of the Solomonic Temple.[5] Because this ceramic burner is roughly contemporaneous with the Temple, it is interesting to find that the Megiddo shrine is supported at its corners by human-headed animals who are strongly reminiscent of the Solomonic cherubim described as part of the Temple furnishings (I Kings 6:23-28).[*] The Temple cherubim act as supports for the Ark.[6] The Ark itself, it has been argued, was originally conceived of as the *cathedra*, the throne of YHWH the invisible; that is, the Ark represented His palace-shrine.[7] One of the chief sources for this identification of the Ark as YHWH's throne is found in the similarity between the Biblical description of the cherubim supporting the Ark and the common representation in Oriental art of deities seated on thrones that are composed of the two fantastic beasts which are the prototypes of the Biblical creatures.[8] The cherubim of the pagan world have a solar affiliation, for they have attributes of the solar lion which symbolizes that august power. It has even been suggested that the Biblical cherubim, like their counterparts, the lions of the sun god, may stand for the invisible God of the Jews.[9]

A sequence of Persian coins offers an instructive example of the process by which a structure which holds an altar is grad-

---

[*] Heads decorating small altars or *thymaterions* persisted in the East in Hellenistic times, *viz.*, a green glaze altar from Dura-Europos: M. I. Rostovtzeff, *Excavations at Dura-Europos, Preliminary Report of Seventh and Eighth Seasons* (New Haven, 1939), pp. 381-382, Pl. xl, 3.

ually transformed into an altar but with the retention of the original portal even after its function as a means of entrance to a building has disappeared (Fig. 22). This series of coins, with the enigmatic structure that it portrays on the reverse sides, is

21. The tower at Naqsh i-Rustam.

of significance in our present context because it again illustrates, now in Persian art, the iconographical persistence of the portal motif in the last centuries of the pre-Christian Era. But before examining these numismatic illustrations, we must digress briefly to review a troublesome problem in Persian architecture; the pertinence of this "Persian problem" will be speedily apparent, for it brings us back not only to the relationship of sacred portal and altar, but also to the funerary aspect of the portal.

The structures in question are two masonry towers found on Iranian soil at two sites that figure large in the history of the Achaemenian empire: Pasargadae and Naqsh-i-Rustam (Fig. 21). The towers bear modern names, the "Prison" and the "Ka'aba of Zoroaster," which in no way reflect the ancient designations of the building. The towers have a square plan, are set

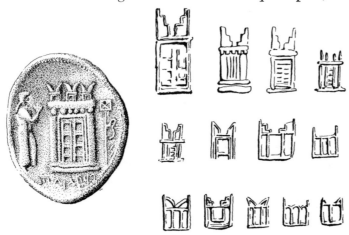

22. Persian coins with tower motif. a. tetradrachma of Bagates I. b. tower on coin of Autophradates I. c.-l. towers from coinage between *ca.* 150-100 B.C. m.-n. towers from hemidrachma and Obol of Autophradates II.

on a stepped base, and are capped by a heavy, dentilated cornice. The door is set high in the wall, approached by a masonry stairway; an interior staircase leads up to the roof. A later tower of the same type, located in Iran at Nurabad, seems to have had a stepped roofline. The tower of Pasargadae probably dates to the time of Cyrus, *circa* 549–529 B.C.; that of Naqsh-i-Rustam probably belongs to the reign of Darius, 521–495 B.C. The Nurabad tower was built sometime in the last three centuries B.C. The eminent Iranian archaeologist, Ernst Herzfeld, considered these buildings to be the royal tombs of the Achaemenians.[10] A number of the most qualified scholars on the several aspects of ancient Persian culture (among whom are Sarre, Sprengling, Wachtsmuth, Ghirshman, Erdmann, Zaehner, and Duchesne-Guillemin) have argued from a variety of evidence that the towers are fire altars or fire temples, and have no funerary connections whatsoever.[11] It is these towers which are obviously illustrated on the Persian coin sequence (Fig. 22), and they have been labeled tower-shaped fire temples.[12] Perhaps because of

Herodotus' statement that the Persians had neither temple nor altar, similarly shaped structures portrayed on Persian sealings found at Persepolis have been cautiously described as "altar-shaped" or "altar (?)."[13] André Godard who, after decades spent in the service of that area of study, is one of the most qualified scholars to speak on Iranian art and archaeology, has taken an intermediate position: the tower "was probably at first the temporary tomb of Achaemenid royalty, which at a later period, perhaps, became the official temple in which the royal standards were kept." But the similar structures on the coins he admits as possibly fire temples.[14] The opinion of Henri Frankfort, late of the Oriental Institute in Chicago and the Warburg Institute of London, is categorical: there were no Iranian temples.[15]

Herzfeld refused to accept as of substantive importance an inscription on the Ka'aba of Zoroaster that infers a fire ritual was performed in the tower. The composer of the inscription, he held, lived too many centuries after the construction of the tower to know or remember its original function. But Herzfeld did not comment on the numismatic depictions of the towers, which seem to represent the all-too-familiar scene of a royal figure sacrificing at an altar (the tower) over which floats the acknowledging sky-god (Ahura-Mazda?). Herzfeld argued that Persian temples, whose remains he identified, do not in the least resemble the towers. Rather, the towers are modeled after Vannic (in the region of Lake Van in the Caucasus) and Assyrian architecture, domestic or military.[16] But, in opposition, it has been pointed out that the great free-standing Tomb of Cyrus at Pasargadae and the tombs of Achaemenids cut into the living rock of the mountains at Naqsh-i-Rustam show the proper form of Persian sepulture, and these monuments are in no way related to the tower structure. The free-standing tomb of Cyrus, a huge masonry "sarcophagus" with a domed top, mounted on a high pedestal, would represent the earlier form of burial; the rock-cut tombs were used in later generations after the capital of the Achaemenids had been moved from Pasargadae to Persepolis. It would be highly unlikely that a third and radically different type of burial chamber would have been used, contemporaneously with the other two, for the same family.

Arguing against the fire altar attribution, Herzfeld insisted
that if we would know what Persian altars looked like, we need
but glance at the flaming altar depicted on the rock wall above
the tomb at Naqsh-i-Rustam: a table-size model composed of
stepped base, rectangular die, and broad table top. Or, the
official fire altars of the state are to be found in the twin monolithic altars on a raised platform at the same location.[17] Surely
it is reasonable to ask, as Herzfeld did, why the towers should be
designated as vessels for the sacred flame when there is unmistakable evidence for true Persian altars.

The defenders of the fire temple theory, to pursue the problem a bit further, demonstrate that the architectural features
of the towers militate against their being built as tombs. A tomb
does not require a permanent masonry stairway leading to the
door; but an altar, frequently used, does. The tower door is too
small, the interior too cramped to accommodate a royal sarcophagus for which there are no proper quarters inside. The narrow,
winding staircase of the interior would hardly hold the solemn
cortege of a royal burial; but on the other hand, the flat roof, its
elevation, and the modest interior space would well serve the
needs of the priests who made their offerings under the open
sky.

Without going into more detailed argumentation, it can be
seen that the Persian towers have aspects that make them
neither temples nor tombs and equally strong characteristics of
both. However, the prehistoric shrines and funerary equipment
that we have examined suggest that the designations of altar
and tomb are not necessarily mutually exclusive.

The major portion of the evidence that we have examined
comes from people who speak Semitic languages, and it is probably representative of a distinct cultural continuum as opposed
to that of Indo-Iranian language peoples. It is true that Indo-
Iranian and Semitic cult practices may have basic and funda-
mental differences, but quite the contrary holds true when
Achaemenian and Assyrian art and architecture are compared.
In spite of important, lingering native Iranian elements, Persian
material culture is strongly dependent upon that of the nations
to the west. The design on the Persian coin sequence that dis-

[131]

plays the tower is uniquely Iranian, but the format and the individual elements of the composition are Assyrian stock-in-trade. The coins depict a royal figure standing before a structure made up of, chiefly, a double-leaved doorway, with a ban-

23. Crenellated portal. From Neo-Assyrian cylinder sealing. (after: *Corpus*, no. 676.)

ner or insignia to one side, and a winged deity hovering overhead (Fig. 22). This format has a clear Assyrian authority.[18] The structure depicted on the earliest coins of the series is carefully delineated: the building is tower-shaped, stands on a stepped socle, has corner pilasters that frame a large door, and is capped by a dentilated cornice which supports three, small, horned altars (Fig. 22a).[19] The design is an accurate copy of the actual tower, except for the convention of the oversize door. Whether the three small altars displayed on the roof of the towers on the coins once stood on the roof of the towers at Pasargadae and Naqsh-i-Rustam, cannot be proved now; however, there is no reason to doubt the existence of such altars, for in all other respects the artist of the coins is faithful to the original.

The contrast in size between the door of the building on the coins and that of the actual tower need not trouble us now: it results from the pictorial shorthand we have seen in operation in the ancient East, a device that uses the portal to take the place of and stand for the building. Crenellated portals similar to those depicted on the coins appear early in Mesopotamia and continue on into Neo-Assyrian times and beyond (Fig. 23).[20] The later coins in the sequence that depict the tower lack the clear, detailed rendering of the earlier; by the second half of the second century B.C. the elements of the design become increasingly schematic and even border on the careless. The tower is converted into a doorway only, crowned with hornlike merlons (Fig. 22b-e). What had been precisely defined as paneled door-leaves are now simply indicated by a few vertical marks (Fig. 22g-1). Still, however, the general format remains the same, so that there is no question but what the same structure is intended throughout. The coinage of Autophradates II (*circa* 150–100 B.C.) for example, shows a tower that is a bare rectangle with one or two interior vertical lines denoting the door, and two horns on the cornice line (Fig. 22m-n). This particular numismatic sequence documents the continuing devaluation of craftsmanship in the course of those restless years in the Near East when Hellenism vainly strove to tide the surge of Iranian nationalism, but it also demonstrates the several steps in the transformation of the tower into an altar only. That is, the slow transformation shows how the original concept of a building with altars on its roof changes into an altar; only the persistent inclusion of the portal indicates beyond doubt its architectural genesis. Eventually, the tower motif is abandoned in Parthian coinage. The successors of the Parthian in Iran, the Sasanians, re-establish the altar on their coins, but now it is a flaming altar completely different in design and not related to the earlier, tower motif.

The coin sequence would appear to indicate that the tower was a sacred shrine, complete with royal standards, to which the ruling dynasty came in worship or commemoration. The monument was under the protection of the wing-borne deity to whom offering was made on the rooftop altars. Its restricted interior space guarantees that it was no temple but a place sacred to the royal family and the god of the state. We have noted that, since neolithic times, burial receptacles have assumed the shape of miniature shrines. Perhaps the towers also had a funerary role, even if they were not permanent burial places as Herzfeld insisted. It can be suggested that the wooden prototypes of the towers (the architectural features of these structures indicate that they are based on wooden buildings) were commemorative shrines that held the dead, either inside or exposed on the roof. By the time of Cyrus the permanent burial of royal dead was made elsewhere, in structures similar

 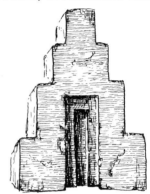

24. Assyrian battlemented altar from relief. (after: Barnett, *Assyrian Palace Reliefs*, no. 134)

25. Stone merlon with carved portal from balustrade at Persepolis.

to the monolithic tomb of Cyrus at Pasargadae; but the tower may have served, then, as a temporary repository for the body, as Godard suggests. The tower may have been used over and over again to house the newly deceased until the body was ritually prepared for the final, elaborate state funeral, and perhaps until the permanent tomb had been constructed. Thus, the tower would require a fixed means of entrance, rooftop altars for the fitting commemorative ceremonies, and the shrine-like setting. We may have some insight into the nature of the ceremony that took place on the roof. Above the lintel of the carved façade that opens into the burial chamber in the rock wall at Naqsh-i-Rustam (that is, on the *roof* of the building indicated by the rock carving) stands the king before a table altar. This scene may well picture dynastic commemorative ceremonies that took place on the tower monuments—monuments to the past rulers of Achaemenid Persia.*

One further point increases the possibility of this hypothesis. The cornice line of the Persian tower, as shown on the coins,

* The scene of the Achaemenian king before a crenellated altar over which the winged god floats is repeated on Persian cylinder sealings, *viz.*, R. S. Young, "Progress at Gordion, 1951-52," *University Museum Bulletin*, XVII (1953), 14, Fig. 10.

has stepped battlements which are directly in the tradition of Assyrian altars (Fig. 24).[21] Battlemented altars were still in use in Hellenized Phoenicia.[22] But the same type of format is used, for example, by the Nabataeans who line the cornice of their rock-cut tombs with merlons.[23]

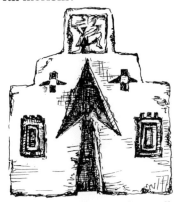

26. Stone merlon with carved crenellated portals from temple area at Surkh Kotal.

What we hope to emphasize in this protracted examination of the Persian tower is that the appearance of a door opening on an altar is the result of the same type of architectural synecdoche used in old Oriental sealings, shrines, funerary urns, and the like. Even the flaming altar represented on the Persian rock-carved tomb façades has inscribed on its die an opening made of inset rectangles which has been recognized, quite correctly, by Erdmann as a "door of epiphany." This type of portal motif appears elsewhere in Persian architecture as a symbolic element. The great terrace of Persepolis, which recent opinion holds to be a sacred rather than a secular complex of buildings,[24] had crenelations decorating the parapets and probably the roofline of the buildings. Each merlon has inscribed in it the rectangle denoting a doorway (Fig. 25). This decorative motif continued in use in post-Achaemenid times on temple buildings such as, for example, the one at Surkh Kotal in Bactria (Afghanistan) which dates from the last quarter of the first century B.C. to the first half of the first century A.D. (Fig. 26).[25] The center of these merlons carries an arrow-shaped slot (a symbol once associated with the god, Marduk); on either side of the arrow is a triple-framed rectangular opening crowned with three, small squares.

Here we have, in a sacred architectural environment, a sturdy survivor of the old ziggurat-altar with its sacred portal.[26] Moving westward, we find the same design at Syrian Palmyra[27] on an altar that has the triple-framed portal topped by three merlons,

27. *Left.* Altar with double-doors on coin of Agrippa.
(after: Reifenberg, *Ancient Jewish Coins*, no. 104)

28. *Center.* Altar with double-doors on coin of Tiberius. (after:
Sjöqvist, "Excavations at Morgantina, 1961," fig. 26a)

29. *Right.* Altar with portal opening on coin of Volusianus. (after:
Kadmon, *Corpus Nummorum Palaestinensium* II, no. 230)

dedicated to the god, Aglibôl Shalma.* A coin of Agrippa II, dated 86 A.D., with a portrait of Domitian on the obverse, shows an altar with a double-paneled door crowned by merlons (Fig. 27).[28] On a Tiberian coin, paneling and door-pulls are clearly marked on the double doors of the altar (Fig. 28).[29] A coin of Gallienus (150–255/256 A.D.) has a hemispherical object (possibly a baetyl between horns) on top of an altar with a center-opening inscribed with horizontal lines. These lines have been described as steps leading up to the altar, but because they are placed inside the altar, not before it, they must stand for the door paneling.[30] A mid-third century A.D. coin of the Emperor Volusianus, found at Caesarea Maritima, has only a framed rectangular opening in the altar (Fig. 29).[31] A stone altar from Alexandria continues the tradition of the portal. The die of the altar is a portal with double-hung doorleaves; one doorleaf stands ajar (Fig. 30). The top of the altar has an architectural cornice complete with dentils and horns that have assumed the role of oversize acroteria.[32]

---

* Aglibol, a moon deity, is one of the Palmyrean trinity composed of Bel (supreme god, the equivalent of Zeus), Yarhibol (sun), and Aglibol.

What does this accumulated evidence (of which only some scattered examples are cited here) for the use of the portal in altars indicate? Primarily, it is confirmation of a continuous Eastern tradition that carried over into the Roman world, of

30. Roman altar with carved doors ajar. (after: Smith, "The Iconography of the Sacrifice of Isaac," fig. 4)

transforming a building—tomb or shrine—into an altar. The process of transformation is the same as that which combined the design of burial chest, shrine, and altar. The portal persists as the identifying feature. The Persian coins clearly demonstrate how stepped battlements, or merlons, of the East are later substituted for the horns of the altar and assume the shape of oversize acroteria. Thus it is that the Alexandrian altar is crowned with corner decorations that are somewhat ambiguous: they serve as acroteria on the pictured façade, but their size indicates their origin in the horns of the altar.

In the Hellenized East there is found another example of the altar conceived in the shape of a shrine. A coin from Emessa has depicted on it an altar mounted on a stepped base with a double row of arcades on the die. On the table of the altar is a cone-shaped object standing on a rectangular base.[33] Such cones mounted on horned altars are known from their appearance on coins of the Emperor Macrinus (168–218 A.D.) (Photo 54) from Byblos, assuring us that the structure on the Emessa coin is indeed an altar. An object related to the depicted altar on the coins was found in Beirut; carved from a single block of stone is the cone-shaped *betyl* within an arcade mounted on four pillars. Carved on the face of the *betyl* in its *aedicula* is a relief of Helios in the wheel of the zodiac.[34] From Parthian Hatra comes a similar type of altar with four figures carved in-the-round, each standing in his own *aedicula*, or miniature temple.[35] An equally Hellenized version of the sacred door of appearance on an altar comes from the Nabataean site of Khirbet-et-Tannur, excavated by Professor Nelson Glueck of Hebrew Union College. This altar is made up of a socle holding corner piers that support a lintel with the usual oversize horns formed as palmette *acroteria*. The top of the altar has a central cup-depression for incense.[36] Within the openings framed by the piers are two winged goddesses, *tyches,* holding branches and victory wreaths (Photo 55). On the front is carved the partially draped figure of Zeus-Baal (Photo 56). There would appear to be, then, little question but that these various representations depict the altar as a model shrine with the deity manifest in the door of his heavenly palace. The same theme appears, in more schematic form, on a gypsum altar from Dura-Europos. Drawn on one side is an arcuated portal within which are displayed cult symbols, one of which is the Semeion, identified by Ingholt as the emblem of the god Heavens.[37]

Hence, the architectural iconography that, in both the East and the West, forms the basis for the later Judaic symbols had assimilated the sacred portal and the altar of the god. With this background we can with some assurance interpret a seemingly casual design scratched on a Jewish stone ossuary: a cross-hatched panel with three vertical projections on top that terminate in small points (Fig. 20). It has been suggested that these projections are flames on an altar,[38] but the comparable material discussed above, particularly that found on the Persian coins, shows them to be the horns of an altar-shrine. While the cross-hatching may only be a decorative fill, used to define the design, it should be remembered that the doors of shrines are similarly crosshatched to indicate the doorleaves and, thereby, confirm Professor Goodenough's rather enigmatic note that "the cross-

31. Portal design on lintel from synagogue at Chorazin.

hatching seems to me interesting." On one of the walls of the synagogue at Dura-Europos, in the scene which has been identified as depicting the contest between Elijah and the prophets of Baal on Mt. Carmel, is portrayed an altar that holds the sacrificial bullock (I Kings 18:17-40). The die of the yellow altar contains a black rectangular opening within which stands a man. The figure portrayed in the altar may be the man concealed inside as the Midrash relates.[39] But regardless of the story involved, the iconography is that of an altar with a portal.

Another indication of the altar combined with the portal in Judaic art is found on small clay lamps. One such lamp has on it a small portal of the type familiar in Judaic art: two squat columns support very large *acroteria* made in the shape of horns. These "horns" are about the same size as the columns that support them. Between the "horns" is the shell motif; enshrined in the portal is the lozenge (Photo 47).[40] The Jewish artists used the horns and palmette *acroteria* interchangeably. The niche carved on the stone lintel from Chorazin is of the same style as that on the lamp, but the acroteria follow the classical design (Fig. 31).[41] The identical motif, with the horns transformed into floral *acroteria*, is picked up by the Christian artist. A Coptic, carved, wooden lintel enshrines the cross rather than the lozenge; on either side of the portal are wreathed rosettes, precisely the combination of motifs that appears on the Jewish ossuaries (Fig. 32).[42] A Christian glass chalice portrays the portal-shrine; the curtains of the portal are tied back to reveal—not the deity, not the Jewish Ark or Temple—the sanctified symbol of the god-

32. Portal on wooden Coptic lintel. (after: Dalton, *Byzantine Art and Archaeology,* 60, 33)

head (Photo 57). It is interesting to note on the clay lamp just cited (Photo 47) that the nozzles for the wicks, eight in number (which may indicate that this is a Chanukah light), are arranged across the top of the arcuated portal; is this design accidental or planned? A dim echo of the flaming altar? The horned altar with a portal persists in later Biblical iconography, to be found in the traditional scene of the sacrifice of Isaac as interpreted by Christian miniaturists.*

To return, finally, to the portal depicted in the Beth Alpha mosaic, we find that the oversize, horn-like *acroteria* closely resemble those of the altar-shrines under discussion, suggesting that the altar motif may well form a significant part of the iconographical background for the synagogue "shrine." Mrs. Wischnitzer-Bernstein has questioned the meaning of these

---

* *Viz.,* the altar depicted in the Etchmiadzin Gospels. (Illustrated in A. M. Smith, "The Iconography of the Sacrifice of Isaac," *AJA,* XXVI [1922], Fig. 4.) The Gospels are dated in the tenth century A.D., but Dalton has suggested that the illustrations go back to a sixth century source. Later opinion holds the illustrations to be contemporary with the text, i.e., 989 A.D. (D. T. Rice, *Byzantine Art,* 2nd ed. [Harmondsworth, 1954], 133).

[140]

horns at Beth Alpha, and has decided that they cannot be *acroteria* at all. However, she still sees them as architectural accessories of the Ark, as rain spouts, the chain of drops suspended from them representing rain: "The ark is the repository of God's blessing and of the heavenly gift, rain, a pledge of survival."[43] The fertility motif implicit in rain is most ancient; in ancient Oriental iconography a god-of-the-flowing-vase pours out the waters of abundance. And so Raphael Patai finds this concept of fertility imbedded in the symbolism of the Temple, for "it is from the Temple that waters pour forth bringing fertility to the world. . . ."[44]

But, keeping in mind the association of altar and shrine, we may suggest a different source for the horns of the mosaic portal. We have mentioned that the several devices in this mosaic panel have an integral relationship in that they may stand for the important Jewish holidays. On the most holy of these days, that of Atonement, the High Priest sprinkled the blood of the sacrifice on the horns of the altar.[45] If an artist were to represent such a motif, how would he draw it: perhaps as droplets running from the horns. The inappropriate size of the "horns" argues against their being waterspouts; but, as we have seen, the size is quite in keeping with that of horns on altars. The Atonement theme implicit in the blood-sprinkled horns would, once again, establish the internal consistency of the thematic material of the Beth Alpha mosaic, from the Patriarchal sacrifice at the entrance to the sacrifice of Atonement, from the altar of Abraham to the altar of the Temple. Birds, we may mention, have long been associated with altars, and perhaps that is why they are not out of place on what we may name the "altar-shrine" of Beth Alpha.

· VII ·

Sources of Style for
Marianos and Hanina

W E DO NOT possess sure information on the means by
which pictorial consistency was maintained in the ancient world
over long distances and through the centuries. We assume that
standard motifs and designs obtained a common currency by
being handed down from master to apprentice and by being
copied back and forth. Marianos and Ḥanina were probably
journeymen artists who, as we have seen, utilized the standard
designs of the day. While they may never have traveled far from
the Galilee, they still had ample opportunity to see firsthand a
variety of Roman and Oriental art from which they could draw.
Certainly they were not restricted to the mosaics of other synagogues; Roman temples, baths, and other public buildings, as
well as Christian church decoration were available to them.

It is possible that Marianos and his son drew the several
elements of their Beth Alpha design from a copybook handed
down from master to pupil. However, pattern books, as such,
have not been found. Trial pieces, models, and thumb-nail
sketches have been recovered, and these provide some information on the habits of early artists. Certainly many designs were
memorized, but complex patterns formed of several elements
which are dependent for their effect upon precision of ordering
and detail must have been recorded. But no matter from what
sources the Beth Alpha artists borrowed, their mosaic is unique
among synagogue mosaics in its particular three part composition. Until other, prior, examples are found, we must attribute to
the genius of this team the unusual knitting together of a novel
iconographical whole.

[143]

Because of the general similarity of designs, it is beyond question that Marianos was familiar with mosaics in neighboring synagogues and churches. He could easily have been influenced by local Jewish copies of this typical Roman design or he could have made his own copies of Roman zodiac mosaics. However, the drawing style of the Beth Alpha mosaic suggests that Marianos may have borrowed more directly from another art form, that of the weaver and rug maker. The over-all impression that one has of the drawing style of the Beth Alpha mosaic, as indeed of many other mosaics, is that of a large carpet. It is a commonplace to note that ancient mosaic floors and carpets are quite similar, that they share designs and individual motifs, that one could be used as a substitute for the other. But it is important to reaffirm this relationship, for it provides some insight into both the means by which the iconography of Beth Alpha was transmitted and the formation of the stylistic characteristics of its mosaic.

Patterns taken from rugs and wall-hangings and then translated into mosaics can be found as early as, for example, the clay cone mosaics that sheath the massive half-columns at the fourth millennium B.C. site of Warka in Mesopotamia. The glazed brick walls of Assyria and Persia, as well as their figural stone relief work, reflect carpet and tapestry designs. Mesopotamian and Iranian stuccowork of the early centuries on either side of the birth of Christ, and the extensive stucco modeling of the later Sasanians, demonstrate the continuance of the technique of transferring patterns from one medium to another. A detailed knowledge of the exact relationship of the later mosaic patterns to the patterns of carpets is lacking and, perhaps, may never be gained, because so few ancient textiles are preserved.[1] But some isolated textile fragments preserved by unusually fortuitous circumstances confirm the ease with which designs in one medium were worked out in another medium. For example, the design of birds framed in a network pattern, which became the stock-in-trade of mosaicists, is well-preserved in a textile fragment now in the Cooper Union Museum (Photo 17).

In antiquity, Oriental and Egyptian woven and embroidered materials were world-famous for their richness and complexity. They were noted for their startling representations of human as well as plant forms and animal designs.[2] Ezekiel (27:24) particularly mentions the esteem in which Assyrian and Median fabrics were held. The Romans, who well knew how to take advantage of the cultural achievements of the foreigner, imported huge stocks of the famous Babylonian materials.[3]

The richest source today for the study of ancient fabrics is Egypt where climatic conditions favor the preservation of fragile stuffs. The Coptic textiles from Christian Egypt concern us here because of their date—the first six centuries of the Christian Era—and their proximity to the ancient East. They certainly carry many patterns that are common to mosaics.* A dramatic illustration of rug format and its connection with mosaic designs is found in a Coptic rug fragment from Antinoë that dates to the early fifth century A.D. (Photo 58). The fragment shows a part of the rich assortment of rug designs from which mosaicists could have copied: squares, meanders in perspective, interlocking rectilinear shapes, knots, frets, insets, all-over motifs, to name a few.[4] Whether this particular bit of fabric copies mosaic designs, or the opposite, is a moot question. The point is that Coptic fabric, such as this, is sure proof that rugs and mosaics of this period shared a common repertoire of designs, and, hence, that designs could be, and must have been freely exchanged between the two art forms. As models to be used for the copying of designs, textiles recommend themselves far more than do mosaics. Cloth stuff is easily transportable, no matter how large the piece; it can be stored, used, moved about and re-used in any surroundings. Textiles can diffuse their patterns as far as the merchant caravan can travel. Durable, relatively inexpensive, and capable of being produced in the household, they reach the eye of everyone, not the least that of the artist. Mosaics, of course, are completely inflexible, permanent installations, and surely there can have been no comparison between the quantities of mosaics and

* Mosaic floors with animals in net-work patterns, commonly found in early churches, seem clearly to imitate textile originals; the device, for example, is well-known in Coptic fabrics.

of textiles in antiquity. In every way textiles appeal as the best means for transmitting complex patterns and designs.

The ancient Jew, like his non-Jewish neighbor, was actively engaged in weaving and used carpets and tapestries for decoration.[5] There is some assurance that textile furnishings, in addition to the draperies and curtains of the Torah shrine, were brought into the synagogue also.[6] In talmudic times, at least, weaving was not simply a household craft, but an established profession.* The Jews of Alexandria from the second century B.C. through the fifth century A.D. were known for their choice textiles (*Judaica vela*) on which were depicted fabulous beasts (that is, they contained figural representations as well as abstract designs).[7]

The earlier synagogues of the Galilee, those dating to the third and fourth centuries A.D., have undecorated stone floors; mosaic flooring represents a later development in synagogue architecture. For a number of reasons—the talmudic reference to mats being brought into the synagogue, the Jewish occupation of carpet-making, the common use of textiles in Oriental buildings—we should expect that the bare stone floors of the synagogue, and even the later historiated floors, were covered with small rugs. Further, the sudden shift from plain stone to elaborately decorated mosaics may not have been as sudden as it appears to be at first, but, rather, may indicate that the congregations were already fully accustomed to having decoration on the floors of the prayer halls prior to their decision to allow colorful pictorial decoration as a permanent part of the building. The prior use of rugs and mats would considerably help in explaining why the change from stone to pagan mosaic floors should have been accepted by pious elders when these mosaics were clearly outside the Law. If the Jewish community had been thoroughly familiar with pagan designs in their everyday fabrics that were brought into the synagogue, the transition to mosaics would not have been so much a foreign intrusion as a minor modification of an accepted form: retention of old patterns and

* R. Eleaza b. Perata referred to himself as a master of weavers, Babylonian Talmud 'Abodah Zarah 17b.

designs in the synagogue with but a change in materials, from fabric to stone tesserae.

Striking evidence of this translation of floor decoration from one material into another is to be found in the mosaic floor of a prayer hall on the Greek island of Aegina. The synagogue there, built by the archisynagogus, Theodorus, in the first part of the fourth century A.D., carries a mosaic floor that, in design, is only a carpet.[8] It is made up of all-over abstract rug patterns. One of its repeated motifs, that of interlaced loops, is found on the Antinoë rug fragment mentioned above, while a four-petaled form in the center of the mosaic is found in an unusually well-preserved saddle blanket of the fifth century B.C., probably of Persian manufacture, excavated in a Siberian tomb.[9] These two examples are not given in an attempt to establish, or even suggest some sort of direct copying of patterns between Persian, Coptic, and Greek artists, although certain relationships do exist as part of a complex history of cross influences, but rather to indicate the interchange of designs between textiles and mosaics. It is not pertinent here to enter into a discussion of such cross-cultural ties, but it may be mentioned that while Persian art work was carried into the Siberian hinterlands, the Persians knew and used Greek patterns and designs, and also employed Greek artists from Asia Minor. The Copts, on the other hand, knew Greek art intimately, for it had been firmly established in Egypt during the long Ptolemaic rule of the Hellenistic period.

It is interesting to speculate whether the introduction of mosaics into synagogues in ancient Palestine marks the change in the Jewish attitude toward the use of figural representation in the prayer hall. What separates the earlier, plain stone floors from the mosaic ones is probably not simply a difference in aesthetics, but a radical change in concept, the marked, though not complete, collapse of Jewish abhorrence of image-making. Sculpture appears always to have been too closely associated with the pagan idol to have become part of the Jewish aesthetic. It is true that the relief work of the catacombs and ossuaries is, technically, sculpture, as are also the animal and floral reliefs on architectural moldings and cornices of the synagogues. But relief carving, like painting and mosaic, does not have the physical presence, the concrete reality of the free-standing figure carved in the round. The plastic image has a potency because, unlike the illusionistic image of painting and mosaic, it is a distinct entity, palpable to the touch, measurable, occupying space; the Jews, quite rightly, feared the pagan influence of its magic. Only a few carved lions found amongst the architectural remains of the synagogue ruins testify to the existence of Jewish sculpture, but sculpture rendered completely harmless by reason of its setting in the synagogue.

The material to be gleaned from the rabbinical writings and the third century paintings of the Dura-Europos synagogue illustrates Jewish acceptance of representational art; such tolerance is mandatory before mosaics can be made part of the holy buildings. Without the textile originals we cannot know for sure, but it is reasonable to suppose that the first use of mosaics in Palestine documents that point at which the Palestinian Jew, long accustomed to images in rugs and mats, could accept the translation of such designs from temporary into permanent decoration. Certainly more conviction on the part of the congregation in the appropriateness of figural decoration in the synagogue was required in order to have images laid in mosaic, and hence to become an integral part of the building, than was needed to bring in rugs that could be removed, taken away. Once again, textiles form an easy means of transition, this time from a religious attitude that mistrusted all manner of images to one that admitted and encouraged figural images in the most holy of Jewish buildings after the destruction of the Temple of Jerusalem.

That rug patterns are used at Beth Alpha is abundantly clear. The floor of the central hall, as defined by the north and south walls and the two rows of basalt pillars, is designed as one large rectangular "rug," complete with a border pattern and insets. Even though the floor continues beyond the central nave, between the pillars into the aisles, the mosaic is disposed as if it were a rectangular rug and does not extend around the floor, as is quite usual in mosaics that cover the entire floor in one continuous design regardless of the irregular shape of the space and the intervening architectural elements. As the drawing of the floor plan shows (Photo 1), several small mosaic rugs are strewn over the aisle floors. Each of these decorative mosaics has its own individual, self-contained design. Thus, what at first glance seems quite strange to our Western aesthetic sensibilities —the lack of a comprehensive design with a sense of balance and symmetry that covers the entire mosaic floor with a unified plan —is perfectly well explained if we visualize these different and contrasting patterns as fossil rugs. The lack of unity in the mosaics does not reflect a naive love of variety or lack of aesthetic control by folk artists, but rather it speaks of a continuation of the rug tradition.

Keeping in mind this carpet orientation, we can then perhaps understand a troubling feature of the Beth Alpha synagogue: why did the congregation first expend a goodly sum to have an elaborate mosaic laid, and, then, sometime later, have no feeling about covering up portions of this expensive floor with stone furnishings? But covering parts of rugs with furniture is not surprising, and such may have been the attitude of the congregation toward the mosaic. Very probably, the mosaic itself was partly covered with small rugs thrown over it.

The fact that a stone *bema* was constructed on top of that portion of the mosaic that contains, as we have seen (Photo 3), some of the most significant symbols of Jewish iconography, may help us to understand the sixth century Palestinian Jew's attitude toward religious symbols also. Does this casual covering of the mosaic reflect in some measure a degree of casualness toward the images? Does the fact that, in the first place, the sacred images are depicted on the floor, where they could and would be stepped on, lessen their potency as living, meaningful symbols in the Jewish mind? Eastern Christianity was sufficiently concerned at one time over the blasphemous implications of having the faithful walk on holy symbols and portraits made in mosaic to have forbidden by law the placing of such holy images on floors where they would be desecrated. However, the Beth Alpha mosaic may not indicate a diminution in the meaningfulness of Biblical scenes and sacred symbols at all; rather, it may be taken as a demonstration of how cautious one must be in drawing any conclusions based upon the assumption that the equation between the religious symbol and the degree of sanctity it holds is necessarily unchangeable. So rigid an attitude toward symbols is not justified historically. The sacredness of a symbol is dependent upon its location, position and, most important, its utilization. There is no question but that the Jewish sages were aware of these distinctions, that they are not merely extrapolations from the art evidence. The reasoning is finely drawn in the Babylonian Talmud:

> Behold in the Synagogue of Shaph-weyathib in Nehardea a statue was set up; yet Samuel's father and Levi entered it and prayed there without worrying about the possibility of suspicion! It is different when there are many people together. ('Abodah Zarah 43b).

That is, the efficacy of an idol is dependent upon the circumstances under which one contacts it. Another passage notes that "what is treated as a deity is prohibited, what is not treated as a deity is permitted (44b)." Or, in another place, the law states that Jews may use the garden or bathhouse of pagans even if an idol is present *providing* no advantage comes to the idol from the visit; that is, provided payment is not given, nor recognition made of the use to which the idol is put (51b). For the present purpose, the close and analogical reasoning set forth in the Talmud is not as significant as the fact that the rabbis' extensive deliberations make clear the relative position which idols held. Were the potency of a symbol considered to be always the same, the prohibitions would have been absolute and the matter beyond discussion.

The mosaic of Beth Alpha occupies, as does so much of religious art, an ambivalent position. On the one hand it portrays material drawn from the profound depths of Jewish belief; on the other hand, the portrayal is cast into an ornamental, decorative framework where it may be obscured, covered, and walked upon. The decorative aspect does not necessarily diminish the significance of the things represented, and the ambivalence may be partly explained by the Jewish attitude toward images. In so far as images and the worship of images are forbidden, the Jew may have dismissed from his mind the idea that the mosaic representation had to do with images. For it is also true that the basic concern was one of image-making, that is, the three-dimensional sculptural form, the physical idol. It is stated in 'Abodah Zarah 43a that:

> A man may not make . . . . a candelabrum after the design of its [the Temple's] candelabrum. He may, however, make one with five, six or eight branches, but with seven he may not make it even though it be of other metals.

Yet, despite the prohibition, stone models that follow the design of the Temple candelabrum were in use.[10] Although the law was violated in fact, it may not have been violated in spirit as long as the representation was not held sacred; the *menorah* is a significant symbol, laden with content in the Jewish mind, but it is not a holy object to be held in piety because it is an image of something else. Judaism does not have cult objects to which prayers are addressed or upon which devotional services are oriented. The figure of Abraham in the Beth Alpha mosaic is not, in this sense, comparable to the Christian saint portrayed in mosaic. Prayers are not made to or directed at the Old Testament figure in the manner in which Catholic devotions may address a saint or martyr. Jewish commemorative inscriptions ask that the benefactor or deceased be remembered, not by patriarch or prophet, but by Jewry. It is within a framework such as this, then, that the mosaic can be assessed as a decorative religious element within the prayer hall.

Although no Jewish carpets or rugs of this period have been found as yet, it is reasonable to suppose that decorative fabrics, carrying significant Jewish symbols and illustrating Jewish history, were used in the synagogue, and that it was this textile tradition that found continuation in the work of many Jewish mosaicists. The format and technique of the mosaic from the synagogue of Na'aran (located a few miles northwest of Jericho), which closely resembles that of Beth Alpha, adds strength to this assumption. Its floor is also elaborately decorated with the zodiac wheel and sun chariot at the hub, and with various Hellenic interlocking border patterns. One section, containing inscriptions and a candelabrum, seems to be an exact copy of woven and sewn work.[11] The small, border fretwork and the scatter pattern in the field resemble nothing as much as modern cross-stitching. The zodiac and seasons motif is not a Jewish conception, as has been pointed out, but was taken without serious alteration from the Hellenic world where it may have been used in fabrics also.

This problem of establishing the Jewish models from which complex Jewish compositions evolved became acute in modern scholarship with the astounding discovery of the synagogue of Dura-Europos whose walls are covered with narrative scenes loosely based on Biblical history.[12] Suddenly, and quite without warning, large-scale, narrative Judaic art was found to be flourishing in the first half of the third century A.D. in a caravan outpost of the East. The murals still stand without parallel or predecessor in the sphere of Judaic art, but they certainly could not have been unique. Chiefly because of these murals we now know that the Jews of the late Roman period had a well-developed pictorial tradition, used complicated iconographical schemes, and had established a mode of narration keyed to the vital episodes and heroes of Jewish religious history. The sources of this pictorial tradition have been sought, without success, in hypothetical illuminated Jewish manuscripts. The Classical world had illuminated manuscripts, to be sure, but no Jewish ones have been recovered.

Ancient illustration of Jewish Biblical manuscripts is quite possible, although the only evidence that can be introduced is negative. Even the addition of gold to heighten the letters in the Bible was subject to question.[13] Extra-Biblical literature, haggadic lore (that is, the legends and stories of the Jews that have their roots in the Bible),[14] may have been the vehicle that carried and developed Jewish pictorial illustrations, as some commentators suggest. No such example, however, of an illustrated haggadic manuscript from these early centuries has yet been found. The fragmentary manuscripts that have been recovered in the Dead Sea caves carry no illustrations. Even apocryphal versions of stories from Genesis, such as the so-called "Seventh Scroll," or "Lamech Scroll," written in Aramaic, are unadorned.[15] Perhaps more prosperous and cosmopolitan communities than those of the Dead Sea region may have had more elaborate, illuminated rolls. The possibility remains that Jewish manuscripts now lost along with other fragile materials, such as fabrics, were the media through which the Jewish symbolic and narrative compositions and formulae of presentation fossilized in the mosaics, were developed and established.

Hence, the Beth Alpha mosaic may indicate that there is a lost chapter in the story of ancient Judaic art, that of the textile, the *judaica vela*. Marianos may have borrowed his entire composition from textile designs that had already absorbed Classical motifs and designs. Classical figural elements would have been taken over also, and become part of the Jewish textile worker's stock-in-trade. Hellenic narratives—stories taken from classical myth and legend—would have been adopted by the weaver, and disguised with haggadic content. Possible traces of this process can be found in the Sacrifice scene at Beth Alpha. This suggested textile tradition is not, of course, an assured fact, but it offers, like that of the manuscripts, another possible source for style and iconography.

The drawing style in the Beth Alpha mosaic is fairly simple: contours are drawn with a single or double row of tesserae, and the shapes they enclose are filled in with flat colors. Thus the patterns take on a linear aspect which is strongly reminiscent of the craft of the textile worker. The lines of tesserae appear to echo stitching or the thread lines made on a simple loom, particularly in such details as the curly hair and beard, the flames of the altar, and the heads of the beasts. The artists made no attempt to give the figures a feeling of mass, to modulate the colors so as to define plastic, three-dimensional form. Rather they worked by a rule of arbitrary simplification that never violates the planar surface of the floor with counterfeit depth or bulk. The direct simplification and abstraction of anatomy, and the resultant stilted, puppet-like action of the figures are obvious. Effects of light and shadow are converted into formalized, decorative patterns. The mimetic, imitative aspect of art is expunged in favor of a rigid adherence to conventional signs and signals. By contrast, we need but glance at the pavement mosaics of the synagogue at Hamman-Lif. Here, the full force of Alexandrian illusionistic art is still alive and vigorous: the figures turn with natural ease; shading is delicately picked out in the colored cubes; and the tesserae are set so as to follow and emphasize the contours of the bodies (Photos 59, 60).

At first, the eye sees in the Beth Alpha mosaic all the traits of folk art; it has a charming simplicity and stylistic ingenuosity that frequently is the mark of the untrained artist who is removed from his contemporary art scene.* Yet a description of Marianos and Ḥanina as talented folk artists is singularly incomplete, not only because it fails to consider the twentieth century demonstration that such characteristics as described here can be the property of the most sophisticated artist, but also because it attributes much that is simply and basically Oriental in its conception to lack of training. It is easy for eyes trained in the West to be deceived, partly because of the Western orientation in art, and partly because the Beth Alpha panels come so close to their Classical counterparts that they can be taken as inept copies. There is some truth here, for the panels do have a Classical heritage, but, in order to grasp the Oriental aspects of the mosaic which make it into something other than folk art, the Classical and Oriental stylistic elements need to be distinguished from each other. Of the three panels, the scene of the Akedah offers the richest material for analysis because it contains, in addition to the symbolic elements, a narrative, pictorial setting.

The "reading" of the Akedah scene across the picture plane, in this case from left to right, from the servants on one side,

---

* "The mosaic shows the main stylistic features of the Late Antique and Byzantine Period, though restricted to the sphere of folk-art: rigid frontality, absence of naturalistic space—instead, symbolic indication of landscape by means of scattered tree branches; a linear style with stress on outlines; ornamentalization of details such as hair, eyes, etc. Although the mosaic masters obviously did their best to render the Biblical story as literally as possible, the result is far from being naturalistic." (P. P. Kahane, "Classical and Local Elements in the Art of the Ancient Land of Israel," *Atti del settimo congresso internazionale di archeologia classica,* III 1958 [Rome, 1961], 24-25.)

through the central figures, to the altar at the other extreme, is well within the Oriental tradition of pictorial presentation. The composition follows the processional mode of organizing figures in a scene—figures next to each other in a long line that disregards arrangement in depth. The figures also adhere to the general inclination to avoid overlapping of elements which, perceived in depth, would be behind and partially concealed by elements in front of them. The result is a standard convention in Near Eastern art which must be interpreted by the Western eye as indicating by means of the processional device composition in depth. In the ancient Oriental aesthetic, overlapping, and hence the partial concealment which destroys the complete unity of a form, means a loss of visual and tactile clarity and is best avoided. The evocative power of a significant form is reduced if the form is partially concealed.

The figure of Isaac seems to float awkwardly just beyond the finger tips of his father. How are we to interpret this pose? Does Abraham hold the youth close to him, or does he hold him at arm's length in preparation for the impending blow, or does he place him on the altar? However, such questions imply an art style which attempts to interpret a dramatic action in a single scene. The mosaic does not depict a scene from a story, but rather offers a presentation of an event whose importance, as we have seen, lies in its symbolic, and not its narrative, character. Marianos, well within the Oriental sphere of artistic thinking, presents the essential elements of the symbolic presentation. The physiological reality of the individual figures and the psychological reality of the relationship between these figures are irrelevant factors. Isaac floats at the tip of Abraham's outstretched hand because that position makes perfectly clear his symbolic (which is far more important than his physical) position. He must not overlap, and hence obscure, either the altar or his father; they are both too important in the iconography to bear partial concealment. The artist has clearly established the symbolic relationship between the three critical elements— father, son, and altar—with splendid clarity of design: the body of the youth swings precipitously between the flames of sacrifice and the obedient father. Even the fingers of Abraham cannot be concealed, as they would be if the artist had shown the hand in the act of grasping. While Marianos placed the youth just beyond the fingers of Abraham so as to maintain the integrity of the hand, Assyrian relief-carvers, for example, solved the same problem in a slightly different manner: the libation bowl held in the raised hand of the Assyrian king is treated as if it were transparent so that the king's fingers, that should be concealed behind the bowl, are carved in fine detail.

To place the youth at the foot of the altar, or beside his father on the ground, as occurs in Westernized versions of the Sacrifice scene, enhances the realistic narrative, but it also reduces the visual impact and clarity of the symbol of the Akedah. A youth standing beside his father, before an altar, does not imply the absolute obligation of the Akedah. There can be no question, however, of the meaning of Marianos' presentation; here is an unequivocal presentation of the fixed relationship between Abraham (Israel) and God.

In the East, scale is also a matter of symbolic convention. The size of a figure does not denote its relative position in the composition (near or far), but rather its relative importance. This symbolic use of size is, of course, another symptom of an art style where the concept to be communicated transcends the need for optical reality. Hence, Abraham towers over the servants. We must be careful to guard against attributing disproportions to ineptness or to a child's view of the world when we deal with ancient Oriental art. In this respect, the frontal orientation of the figures, a common feature of children's art, should not be wrongly interpreted as a naive characteristic. Frontality is one of the basic traits of late Oriental art, to become a decisive, stylistic element in Byzantine art. Its introduction in the East is symptomatic of the Oriental resurgence as the classicism of the Hellenistic world began to lose its political and cultural control of the East.[16] Equally Near Eastern is the emphasis on decorative treatment of natural form. The patterning and decorative simplification which guide the hand of Marianos are part of his Oriental inheritance.

These stylistic traits of the panel merely serve as illustrations for the Oriental rationale that has formulated the mosaic as a whole. Marianos and Ḥanina were not folk artists, but rather late Oriental artists. Their work should be seen as representing the closing phase of a great Eastern tradition. This Oriental tradition had but recently (in terms of its long history that stretches over three thousand years) swallowed the foreign elements of Mediterranean Classicism, and although they were badly digested, these elements were assimilated in the aesthetic culture of Marianos' time. It is the uncomfortable mixing of Oriental and Classical in this late Oriental mosaic that is chiefly responsible for any dismissal of the work as naive folk art: Marianos' Akedah clearly shows Classical elements transmuted by the Oriental hand.

The usual, Oriental manner of composing this type of scene would place all the figures on a common ground line, but here the figures stand at successively higher levels on the picture plane as the eye moves from right to left; that is, the scene, for all its Oriental processional qualities, shows traces of having been influenced by compositions that are organized in depth on a diagonal, receding plane. Abraham occupies the immediate foreground; the servant with the goad is stepped back several paces; the other servant with the animal is moved off toward the background. This slight evidence of illusionistic depth composition is confirmed by the positions of the heads: as the figures "recede" in space, the heads approach the top border of the panel. The beast tied to the bush first appears to be arbitrarily inserted into a cramped space; however, his pose is explainable as the result of the compromise between the Oriental conceptual mode and Western illusionism. The spacing of the figures permits a theoretical reconstruction of the scene, a recasting into a spatially formulated prototype with the composition organized in depth (Fig. 33). There is a strong Graeco-Roman tradition in painting mosaics upon which to base such a diagonal composition. While the subject is far different from that of the Akedah, the portrayal in a mosaic from a Roman villa at Corinth shows the compositional prototype: the receding plane, the scattered bits of vegetation, and the modeling of the bodies which, in the Beth Alpha donkey, is transformed into decorative color patterns.

This echo of Classical spatial composition in the Akedah scene is reinforced by other, significant traces of Western illu-

33. Hypothetical reconstruction of the Sacrifice of Isaac at Beth Alpha employing Western depth perspective.

sionism. The seemingly shapeless fall of Abraham's robe is, on the contrary, planned to form a meaningful silhouette. The patriarch's pose is a late Classical convention: the torso is frontally presented with the left leg in profile flexed at the knee, the right leg is seen full front, the head turned back in opposition to the movement of the left leg, and the arms carry out the action of the figure across the body. In the Classical world this standard format was used to represent figures in action; the convention persisted up into the late Medieval and early Renaissance periods. Giotto, for example, shows his mastery of the dramatic possibilities of the stance when he employs it for the figure of Christ of the *noli me tangere* in the Arena Chapel. It is this same action stance that is depicted in the Akedah, where, however, it is compromised by Oriental conventions, such as the turning of the feet and the flatness of the body. A small gem that depicts in miniature the Akedah, also shows Abraham in this pose with his head turned back to look at the divine hand and the ram.[17] Here, the Classical affiliation is clear in the disposition of the feet, the sculptural profile, and the swing of the draped robe.

The far more Hellenized versions of Abraham that appear in Coptic textiles show the same action pose with the dramatic aspect of the scene heightened by a greater sense of urgency: Abraham's knee is acutely flexed, as if he were striding off in one direction while he abruptly turns back in the opposite direction to grasp the hair of Isaac.[18] The partial nudity of Abraham in these Coptic representations is a sure index as to how directly the format has been taken from pagan Hellenistic sources. The convention of the action pose for Abraham is still used in the Etchmiadzin Gospels of the late tenth century A.D.[19] In contrast, an earlier representation on a fourth or fifth century A.D. tapestry fragment from Egypt reveals all the Classical traits noted, but, as at Beth Alpha, the format has come under strong Orientalizing influence, as is indicated by the looser silhouette.[20]

The strange, airborne pose of Isaac also has a solid foundation in the Classical world, where flying figures of gods are presented in this stance. Once again we must see in this pose, not the ingenuous fixing of the figure into an arbitrary attitude, but rather the adaptation of a Classical pose to the Oriental mode of frontal presentation. The two rather anomalous lobes attached to the boy's neck are the decorative interpretations of his flying cloak. Coptic examples of the scene place the wind-tossed cloak above Abraham. A winged figure of Hellenized proportions from Ḥadda (Afghanistan) is precisely in the pose of Isaac,[21] while Orientalized precedence for the frontally presented figure with flying cloak and arms thrown across the body can be found in the Parthian representations of that other youthful hero, Mithra.[22] In the Mithra relief from Dura-Europos (Photo 20) the hero wears the Iranian costume, short tunic and pleated trousers tucked into soft, low boots, the cape tied over his shoulders flying out to one side; one leg sharply flexed, the other extended and, because the figure is shown full front, the action of the arms across the body. This is the exact format that is followed by the Beth Alpha artists in their depiction of Isaac: an old Hellenistic-Syrian conventionalized mode of representation with Iranian overtones. The impression of violent movement, reinforced by the fluttering cape, betrays Western influence, for the temporal aspect that such movement implies is foreign to the static timelessness of late Eastern religious compositions. The three vertical lines of dark tesserae on Isaac's short tunic are all that remain of the folds of the garment.[23]

The degree of inventiveness in the Beth Alpha composition can be measured to some extent by looking back over other, more clearly classicizing, representations of the scene. As is to be expected, when the Akedah is found on Roman soil, as in the catacomb paintings, Classical format is dominant. The painting in the fourth century A.D. catacomb of the Cemetery Jordanorum shows an imperious, bearded Abraham leading Isaac to the altar by his hand.[24] Isaac, unmindful of the burden of faggots he lightly carries on his shoulder, trustfully looks to his father. On the other side of Abraham, the goat anxiously peers at the patriarch who dominates the stage with raised arm, brandishing a particularly wicked blade, before the blazing altar. The Roman artist has dwelt upon the dramatic moment, building upon the tense interaction of the actors caught up in this spiritual crisis. The Graeco-Roman standards of art are obvious in the plastic figures that are organically operative in lively and expressive attitudes, and in the use of cast shadows and foreshortening.

In the late Hellenistic versions of this drama found in the Coptic textiles, the theme takes on a decorative, dance-like aspect (Photo 17). The weavers most frequently play upon the dynamic contrast of poses, portraying Abraham striding off in one direction as he reaches back across his body to grasp the hair of the kneeling Isaac who turns in the opposite direction.[25] The violent posing of the figures and the swift gesturing, it has been suggested, is a typical Coptic effect.[26] But the emphasis on musculature and the nude figure, on the three-quarter view pose and turning stance, and the inclusion of a beardless Abraham are typical characteristics of late Hellenistic art. Hence, the original format for the Sacrifice scenes may be sought in the Classical sphere.

Probably Greek pictorial representations of the hero slaying his adversary or engaged in sacrifice formed the stylistic basis for the Jewish and Christian Akedah. There are many examples from which to choose, but a fourth century B.C. painting may be offered as a paradigm. The painting shows Achilles slaughtering Trojan captives before the wooden catafalque of his beloved Patroclus.[27] Achilles stands in the flexed knee pose, nude save for his windblown cape, sword drawn across his body, while with his left hand he grasps the hair of the captive. Even the slight detail of having the left foot of Achilles stand on the leg of the prisoner is faithfully copied in the Coptic scenes of the Akedah. The pose of the kneeling Trojan about to be dispatched is interchangeable with that of the equally desperate Isaac.[28] The poses are stereotyped in Coptic work of the fourth and fifth centuries A.D., and in the sixth and seventh centuries A.D. a few traces still remain of the Classical prototype: the position of the knife, the stepping pose, the grasping of the hair, and the position of the bound and kneeling Isaac. In the later examples, the Judeo-Christian content finally overwhelms the Classical influences: Isaac sits upon the altar, the sacrificial beast is placed in the forefront, and the patriarch who turns raptly to the divine hand is completely clothed, as Eastern tradition would require.[29]

The partial renunciation in Coptic design of Classical format and style may be due to local inspiration and native taste, or to the strong pressure of Near Eastern art on the Christian artists of Egypt. Such an influence would not be unexpected, for it would simply have followed the road that Christianity took as it moved out from the Holy Land. Indeed, the land route by which Orientalizing influences came down into Egypt may be traced in Nabatea, which lies along the way. There are marked similarities between the art of Nabatea and that of Coptic Egypt which would bear fruitful exploration.[30]

The Dura representation of the sacrifice (Photo 16), on the other hand, adheres closely to the principles of Classical pictorial illusionism, in spite of its Oriental aspects. The scene is composed in depth; the eye of the observer is forced to move up and back into the composition. The stylistic gulf that separates the third century artist of Dura from the sixth century mosaicists of Beth Alpha is not merely one of time. Marianos and Ḥanina retain Classical elements (indeed, they had no choice), but the restive Oriental mode of depiction, that was becoming insistent in the third century, predominates in the sixth. The static, symbolic, presentational verism of the East has replaced the dynamic, dramatic, representational realism that courses through the Akedah scene in the Christian catacombs of Rome, in Coptic art, in the Jewish Durene murals, and in Jewish gold glass. Classical pictography is completely assimilated in the Beth Alpha mosaic, but it is still discernible if only in conventionalized features. The process of assimilation produces, for the Western eye, such seemingly awkward results as the disjointed bodies, dangling poses and puppet-like stances, and flat composition. To label this evidence of the collision of Eastern and Western art as simply folk art is to miss the genesis of a style.* In a metaphorical sense, we may speak of the Akedah panel of Beth Alpha as symptomatic of artistic schizophrenia: the opposing aesthetic propositions of East and West are caught up in one style, but constantly threaten to destroy the integrated whole. The Classical, axial turning of the human figure is forced into the pattern of Oriental, frontal orientation; composition in depth is wedded to planar organization; optical realism and tactile verism merge. But, whereas schizophrenia can be destructive in the human personality, in the art of Beth Alpha the unstable combination of opposing elements brings into being a sense of drama and immediacy, a focusing of attention on symbolic content made manifest with a directness and simplicity that characterizes religious art at its best.

Marianos and Ḥanina clearly stand closer to the Oriental art tradition than do many of their fellow Jewish artists who follow the realistic illusionism of the West. The old call, "Orient or Rome?" still sounds in the Beth Alpha mosaic. Late Classical format, Western themes, and pan-Hellenic symbols are accommodated by the Oriental personality of the artists. The work

* Coptic art has recently been discussed as a symptom of the antinaturalism and abstraction of "maladjustment to nature": J. Shapley, "A New Reading of Old Egyptian Textiles," *Journal of Aesthetics and Art Criticism* XX (1962), 383. The suggestion is interesting, but it ignores the historical position of antinaturalism in the East and, particularly, the resurgence of orientalisms in the early centuries of the Christian Era as the Classical style waned.

that results from this bringing together of two distinct traditions is not, however, a loose amalgam; rather, it is a new stylistic entity that is neither "Orient" nor "Rome." The mosaic offers a fresh artistic expression in which the technical subtleness of the West is tempered by Oriental directness of expression, in which Western variety and humanism are modified by the conceptual patterning of the Orient. Naturalism and formalism are wedded to produce a tense, dramatic style. To view the mosaic as either decadent Oriental or debased Classical is to miss the point.

The Mediterranean and Oriental worlds were never, of course, hermetically sealed off one from the other. The sudden military and political intrusion of Alexander the Great and his inheritors into the Oriental scene in the late fourth century B.C. was one climax in the play of cultural cross-currents that ebbed and flowed for millennia in this small corner of the world. For that reason we are able to trace the thematic material of Beth Alpha back through the art of both regions; there is a continuity of motifs that did not stop at the Asiatic shores of the Mediterranean. We cannot demand that visual motifs retain a single denotation as they move from one culture to the next over long periods of time. We can only ask whether a motif serves as an archetype for a consistent complex of related conceptions. The portal does; it is a basic image in the ancient visual arts, laden with the powerful concept of the home of the divine and the promise it holds out to man. It is small wonder that the Jewish artist adopted it to serve as one of his primary symbols.

· ABBREVIATIONS ·

AAAO   H. Frankfort, *Art and Architecture of the Ancient Orient* (Harmondsworth, 1954).
AJA   *American Journal of Archaeology.*
Anc Rec AB   D. D. Luckenbill, *Ancient Records of Assyria and Babylonia* II (Chicago, 1927).
Anc Rec E   J. H. Breasted, *Ancient Records of Egypt* III (Chicago, 1906).
Anc Syn   E. L. Sukenik, *Ancient Synagogues in Palestine and Greece* (Oxford, 1934).
ANET   J. B. Pritchard, ed., *Ancient Near Eastern Texts* (Princeton, 1955).
Alt TB   H. Gressmann, *Altorientalische Texte und Bilder zum alten Testament* II (Berlin, 1927).
BA   *Biblical Archaeologist.*
Beth Alpha   E. L. Sukenik, *The Ancient Synagogue of Beth Alpha* (London, 1932).
Bull Rab   Bulletin, *Louis M. Rabinowitz Fund for the Exploration of Ancient Synagogues* (Jerusalem), I-III (1949, 1951, 1960).
Corpus   E. Porada, *Corpus of Ancient Near Eastern Seals in North American Collections* I (Washington, 1948).
Cyl S   H. Frankfort, *Cylinder Seals* (London, 1939).
DE Syn   C. H. Kraeling, *The Excavations at Dura-Europos, Final Report* VIII, part 1: *The Synagogue* (New Haven, 1956).
Frey CII   J.-B. Frey, *Corpus Inscriptionum Iudaicarum*, II (Rome, 1952).
Gly Mes   P. Amiet, *La Glyptique mesopotamienne archaïque* (Paris, 1961).
Gotteshaus   W. Andrae, *Das Gotteshaus und die Urformen des Bauens im alten Orient* (Berlin, 1930).
HUCA   *Hebrew Union College Annual.*
IEJ   *Israel Exploration Journal.*
JNES   *Journal of Near Eastern Studies.*
JPOS   *Journal of the Palestine Oriental Society.*
Manuel   G. Contenau, *Manuel d'archéologie orientale*, I-IV (Paris, 1927-1947).
PEQ   *Palestine Exploration Quarterly.*
QDAP   *Quarterly of the Department of Antiquities of Palestine.*
RB   *Revue biblique.*
REJ   *Revue des études juives.*
Sym   E. R. Goodenough, *Jewish Symbols in the Graeco-Roman Period* I-VIII (New York, 1953-1958).

· NOTES ·

Chapter II

1. Concerning the eponymous artists appointed by Moses, Bezalel, and Oholiab (Exodus 31:1-4): F. Landsberger, "Jewish Artists Before the Period of Emancipation," *HUCA*, XVI (1941), 325-326. For a summary of the general question of most ancient Judaic art: W. F. Albright, "Was the Age of Solomon Without Monumental Art?" *Eretz-Israel*, V (1958), 1-9.
2. N. Avigad, Report on the Congress of the Israel Exploration Society, *IEJ* 8 (1958), 277-278. In the Appia catacomb in Rome there is reference to a painter named Eudoxius; H. J. Leon, *The Jews of Ancient Rome* (Philadelphia, 1960), p. 233.
3. See Frey, *CII*, Nos. 757, 762, 763, 781, 803 and 804 for donors and Nos. 806 and 809 for quantities.
4. For 'Alma: Frey, *CII*, No. 973; R. Hestrin, "A New Aramaic Inscription from 'Alma," *Bull Rab* III, 65-67.
5. Hestrin, *loc. cit.*; Frey, *CII*, No. 984; *Anc Syn*, p. 71.
6. Frey, *CII*, par. 1166; *Anc Syn*, p. 77. In general, the basic source is the excavation report: *Beth Alpha*.
7. N. Tsori, "Notes and News: Beth Shean," *IEJ*, XIII (1963), 148-149. At the time of this writing, the mosaic is unpublished. I owe the information to the kindness of Dr. Asher Hiram, Jerusalem, who writes me that the Beth Shan (Beit-Shean) mosaic lacks the "primitive" aspect of the Beth Alpha, and that it does not contain the scene of the Sacrifice.
8. *Beth Alpha*, pp. 52-53.
9. E. L. Sukenik, "Notes: A New Discovery at Beth Alpha," *Bull Rab*, II, 26; B. S. J. Isserlin, "Some Recent Archaeological News from Israel," *PEQ* (1952), p. 46.
10. Frey, *CII*, Par. 1165; *Anc Syn*, p. 77; C. Watzinger, *Denkmäler Palästinas*, II (Leipzig, 1935), 114. For Justin I, A. A. Vasiliev, *Justin the First* (Cambridge, 1950).
11. As Suggested by M. Avi-Yonah, "Mosaic Pavements in Palestine," *QDAP*, II (1933), 10.
12. *Sym* I, 243.

13. Frey, *CII*, Par. 895. Also, on an ossuary appears the name Hanania bar Menahem: B. Bagatti and J. T. Milik, "Nuovi scavi al 'Dominus Flevit,'" *Liber Annus, Studii Biblici Franciscani*, IV (1954), 273.

14. See: D. Kaufmann, "La Synagogue de Hamman-Lif," *REJN* XIII, (1886), 52; J. B. Frey, "La Question des images chez les Juifs à la lumière des récentes découvertes," *Biblica*, XV (1934), 285-286.

15. J. Gutmann, Review of *Israel Mosaics, The Reconstructionist*, XXVII (1961), 26.

16. Bibliography gathered in A. Parrot, *Archéologie mesopotamienne: les étapes* I (Paris, 1946), 391-392.

17a. Viz. descriptions recorded in II Sam. V:11, II Chron. ii.

17b. I Kings 7:21; II Chron. 3:17. See below for sources and iconography of the two columns.

18. V. Müller, "Types of Mesopotamian Houses," *Journal of the American Oriental Society* LX (1940), 158 ff.

19. Y. Yadin, "Excavations at Hazor, 1958, Preliminary Communiqué," *IEJ*, IX (1959), 81-83.

20. A. Rowe, *The Four Canaanite Temples of Beth Shan*, I (Philadelphia, 1940), Pls. vi and viii.

21. As one would suspect, there is much speculation concerning the architecture and decoration of the Temple, ranging from enthusiastic flights of exotic fancy to analytical reconstructions based on extant comparative material. For the latter interpretations:
General:
   Watzinger, *op. cit.*, I (1933), 89 ff.
   G. E. Wright, "The Steven's Reconstruction of the Solomonic Temple," *BA*, XVIII (1955), 41-44.
   W. F. Albright, *Archaeology and the Religion of Israel* (Baltimore, 1942), pp. 143 ff.
   L.-H. Vincent and A.-M. Steve, *Jérusalem de l'Ancien Testament* (Paris, 1956), chap. xiv.
   A. Parrot, *The Temple of Jerusalem* (New York, 1955).
   P. L. Garber, "Reconstructing Solomon's Temple," *BA*, XIV (1951), 1-24.
   L. Waterman, "The Damaged 'Blueprints' of the Temple of Solomon," *JNES*, II (1943), 284-294.
   G. Contenau, *Manual* III, 1779.
   L.-H. Vincent, "La Description du temple de Solomon," *RB*, XVIII (1907), 515-542.
Dating:
   M. B. Rowton, "The Date of the Founding of Solomon's Temple," *Bulletin of the American Schools of Oriental Research*, CXIX (1950), 20-22.
Furnishings:
   F. Landsberger, *A History of Jewish Art* (Cincinnati, 1946), pp. 100-106.

J. L. Myres, "King Solomon's Temple and Other Buildings and Works of Art," *PEQ* (1948), pp. 14-41.

Orientation:

J. Morgenstern, "The Book of the Covenant," *HUCA*, V (1928), 45 ff.

K. Kenyon, *Archaeology in the Holy Land* (London, 1960), p. 245.

Reconstructed Model:

P. L. Garber, "A Reconstruction of Solomon's Temple," *Archaeology,* V (1952), 165 ff.

22. C. W. McEwan, "The Syrian Expedition of the Oriental Institute of the University of Chicago," *AJA*, XLI (1937), Fig. 4.

23. For "synagogue," "synod," and Jewish corporations, see M. Radin, *The Jews Among the Greeks and Romans* (Philadelphia, 1915), p. 362.

24. For the earliest inscriptional evidence: F. V. Filson, "Temple, Synagogue, and Church," *BA*, VII (1944), 77-88.

25. Cf. S. Zeitlin, "The Origin of the Synagogue," *Proceedings of the American Academy for Jewish Research* II (1931), 73 ff.

26. Hastings *et al.*, *Dictionary of the Bible*, "Synagogue," IV; *Encyclopaedia Biblica* (1903), cols. 483 ff; *Jüdische Lexicon* Iv/2 (1930), 790 ff; Helen Rosenau, "The Synagogue and the Diaspora," *PEQ* (1937), pp. 196-202.

27. Zeitlin, *loc. cit.;* Louis Finkelstein, "The Origin of the Synagogue," *Proceedings of the American Academy for Jewish Research*, I (1928-30), 49-59.

28. Cf. K. Galling, "Erwägungen zur antiken Synagoge," *Zeitschrift des deutschen Palästina-Vereins* LXXII (1956), 165-68.

29. J. Morgenstein, "The Origin of the Synagogue," *Studi orientalistici in onore di Giorgio Levi della Vida*, II (Rome, 1956), 192-201.

30. Cf. Syrian churches in H. C. Butler, "Architecture, Southern Syria," *Princeton University Archaeological Expeditions to Syria*, Div. II (Leyden, 1919).

31. The study of synagogue architecture is relatively recent. The first major survey of early synagogues, which is still valid in its major outlines, is that of H. Kohl and C. Watzinger, *Antike Synagogen in Galiläa* (Leipzig, 1916). Shorter, but important early studies are: S. Krauss, "Die galiläischen Synagogenruinen," *Gesellschaften für Palästinaforschung*, 3rd publ. (Berlin, 1911); Watzinger, *Denkmäler, op. cit.*, II 107-116; R. Krautheimer, *Mittelalterliche Synagogen* (Berlin, 1927); and a short notice of the (then) recent investigations, C. Watzinger, "Die antiken Synagogen Goliläas, neu Ausgrabungen und Forschungen," *Der Morgen* VI (1930), 356-367. The first, and still only fairly comprehensive survey in English is that of E. L. Sukenik, *Anc Syn*, which covers the finds up to 1930. Professor Sukenik established plans for a comprehensive survey of ancient synagogues after World War II; three bulletins have been issued so far, *Bull Rab* (1949, 1951, 1960). Goodenough, *Sym.* I, chap. 5, provides a convenient review. Notices of recent synagogue archaeology are reported in: Sh. Yeivin, *Archae-*

ological Activities in Israel, 1948-1955 (Jerusalem, 1955); Sh. Yeivin, *A Decade of Archaeology in Israel, 1948-1958* (Istanbul, 1960); M. Avi-Yonah, "Ten Years of Archaeology in Israel," *IEJ*, VIII (1958), 52-65.

The first major re-examination and synthetic study of synagogues in the Holy Land since the pioneering work of Kohl and Watzinger is by Dr. Asher Hiram, "Die Entwicklung der antiken Synagogen und altchristlichen Kirchenbauten im heiligen Lande," *Wiener Jahrbuch für Kunstgeschichte*, XIX (1963).

32. GENERAL: *Anc Syn*, pp. 37 ff; *Sym*, II, pp. 78 ff.

AEGINA: B. D. Mazur, *Studies on Jewry in Greece*, I (Athens, 1935); A. Reifenberg, *Ancient Hebrew Arts* (New York, 1950), p. 112; Notice, *RB*, XLV (1936), 462; Notice, *Archäologischer Anzeiger*, XLVII (1932), 164-165.

DELOS: A building first identified as a synagogue, was later rejected, but Goodenough, *Sym*, II, 71-75, prefers to leave the question open. If this building is a synagogue, it is the earliest such structure yet found, dating to the first centuries B.C. or A.D. A. Plassart, "La Synagogue juive de Délos," *RB*, XI (1914), 523-534; A. Plassart, "La Synagogue juive de Délos," *Mélanges Holleaux* (Paris, 1913), pp. 201-215; J. Juster, *Les Juifs dans l'empire romain*, I (Paris, 1914), 498 ff.; L. A. Mayer and A. Reifenberg, "The Synagogue of Eshtemo'a," *JPOS*, XIX (1941), 231, n. 2. Notice, RB, XLV (1936), 461-462. L.-H. Vincent, "Une ville gréco-romaine à Beit Djebrin," *RB*, XXXI (1922), 275.

ELCHE: E. Albertini, "Fouilles d'Elche," *Bulletin Hispanique*, IX (1907), 109–127.

ELEPHANTINE: Papyri from this Jewish settlement in Egypt mention a Jewish *temple*, not a synagogue. The building is described in the papyri, but no remains have been found of the structure: H. Idris Bell, *Cults and Creeds in Graeco-Roman Egypt* (Liverpool, 1953), 28 ff.; E. G. Kraeling, *The Brooklyn Museum Aramaic Papyri* (New Haven, 1953), 72-85, 100 ff.

MILETUS: Possible synagogue remains: A. von Gerkan, "Eine synagogue in Milet," *Zeitschrift für Neuetestamentliche Wissenschaft*, XXII (1921), 177-181; Notice, *RB*, XXXI (1922), 472-473.

OSTIA: Notice, *Bollettino d'arte* (1961), p. 316; Notice, *AJA*, LXVI (1962), p. 396; M. F. Squarciapino, "Die Synagoge von Ostia Antica," *Raggi, Zeitschrift für Kunstgeschichte und Archäologie*, IV (1962), 1-8; V (1963), 13-17.

PRIENE: Th. Wiegand and H. Schrader, *Priene, Ergebnisse der Ausgrabungen 1895-1898.* (Berlin, 1904), p. 480, Fig. 583.

ROME: No remains of the several synagogues of the large Jewish community have been found, but unsuccessful attempts have been made to locate those mentioned in the Jewish inscriptions: Leon, *op. cit.*, chap. 7.

SARDIS: G.M.A. Hanfmann, "The Fifth Campaign at Sardis," *Supplement, Annual Report of the Fogg Art Museum for 1962*; D. G. Mitten,

"The Synagogue at Sardis," *AJA*, LXVII (1963), 215; Notice, *AJA*, LXVII (1963), 188.

STOBI: A Marmorstein, "The Synagogue of Claudius Tiberius Polycharmus in Stobi," *Jewish Quarterly Review* XXVII (1936-37), 373-384.

HAMMAN-LIF: See n. 14 above; E. Renan, "La Mosaïque de Hamman-Lif," *Revue Archéologique*, III (1884) 273-275; F. M. Biebel, "The Mosaics of Hamman Lif," *Art Bulletin* XVIII (1936), 541-551.

33. The *Diplostoon* of Alexandria was destroyed, according to the Yerushalmi Talmud, during the reign of Trajan (116 A.D.). See *Anc Syn* p. 46, for talmudic sources; Watzinger, *Denkmäler, op. cit.*, p. 108; *Sym*, II, 86, for interpretation of building.

34. The material on the synagogue, excavated under the direction of Professor Clark Hopkins, is extensive. The final excavation report, with comprehensive bibliography, is now available: *DE Syn*. Also *Sym*, IX, X, XI.

35. 'Abodah Zarah (Strange Worship: Idolatry) is the tractate dealing with the prohibition of images. The most recent summary of the legal aspects of the injunction is by B. Cohen, "Art in Jewish Law," *Judaism*, III (1954), 165-176.

36. Yerushalmi Talmud, 'Abodah Zarah, 42d.

37. Cf. Landsberger, *op. cit.*, p. 150; E. E. Urbach, "The Rabbinical Laws of Idolatry in the Second and Third Centuries in the Light of Archaeological and Historical Facts," *IEJ*, IX (1959), 149-165.

38. S. Saphrai, "Beth She'arim in Talmudic Literature," *Eretz-Israel* V (1958), 206-212 (in Hebrew; English summary, p. 95).

39. For the dispersion of the Jewish communities: Juster, *op. cit.*, I, 179-212.

40. C. Roth, "An Ordinance Against Images in Jerusalem, A.D.66," *Harvard Theological Review*, XLIX (1956), 169-177.

41. *DE Syn*, pp. 343-346; M. Avi-Yonah, "Syrian Gods at Ptolemais-Accho," *IEJ*, IX (1959), 12. For economic and social determinatives, J. Gutmann, "The 'Second Commandment' and the Image in Judaism," *HUCA*, XXXII (1961), 161-174.

42. M. Burrows, *What Mean These Stones?* (New York, 1957), p. 232.

43. For the relationship between the Jewish "sky god," Yaho of Elephantine, and Ba'al Shamim, "Lord of the Skies," see A. Vincent, *La Religion des Judéo-Araméens d'Éléphantine* (Paris, 1937), pp. 120-127, 136-142.

44. 'Abodah Zarah 45b, 48a; for Asherah and the Old Testament, P. Torge, *Aschera und Astarte* (Leipzig, 1902).

45. 'Abodah Zarah 19b; citations in Urbach, *op. cit.*, pp. 158, 161.

46. M. I. Rostovtzeff, *Dura-Europos and Its Art* (Oxford, 1938), pp. 94 ff.; Rostovtzeff, "Dura and the Problem of Parthian Art," *Yale Classical Studies*, V (1935), 273 ff.; C. Hopkins, *The Excavations at Dura-Europos, Preliminary Report*, VI (New Haven, 1936), 147 ff.

47. Frey, *CII*, Par 825; Hopkins, *op. cit.*, pp. 167-168; R. du Mesnil du Buisson, "Inventaire des inscriptions palmyréniennes de Doura-Europos," *Revue des études sémitiques* II (1935; supplement to *REJ*, 1936), xxxii.

48. The final report on the Christian chapel at Dura-Europos has not appeared as yet. See: *The Excavations at Dura-Europos, Preliminary Report*, V (New Haven, 1934); A. von Gerkan, "Die frühchristliche Kirchenanlage von Dura," *Römische Quartalschrift*, XLII (1934), 214-232.

49. N. Avigad, "Excavations at Beth She'arim, 1958, Preliminary Report," IEJ, IX (1959), Pl. 24A; Avigad, "Excavations at Beth She'arim," *Eretz-Israel* (1959), Pl. xiv. 1.

50. Chéhab, *op. cit.*, p. 55, No. 35.

51. F. Cumont, "Un Fragment de sarcophage judéo-païen," *Revue Archéologique*, IV (1916), 1-16.

52. E. L. Sukenik, "The Present State of Ancient Synagogue Studies," *Bull Rab*, I (1949), Pl. iv; M. Avi-Yonah, "A New Fragment of the Ashdod Chancel Screen," *Bull Rab*, III (1960), 69, Pl. liv. 4.
    For the synagogue of El-Hammeh (Hammath-by-Gadara): *Anc Syn*, 81 ff.; Frey, *CII*, pars. 856-860 (with bibliography); M. Avi-Yonah, "Mosaic Pavements in Palestine," *QDAP*, II, IV (1933, 1935), 25, 188; E. L. Sukenik, "The Ancient Synagogue of El-Hammeh," *Journal of the Palestine Oriental Society*, XV (1935), 101-180.

53. G. M. Fitzgerald, *A Sixth Century Monastery at Beth-Shan* (Philadelphia, 1939), p. 10, Pl. iii, Fig. 5. Another of the same design from a Byzantine monastery in the vicinity of Massu'ot Itzhaq: Sh. Yeivin, *Archaeological Activities in Israel, 1948-1955, op. cit.*, Pl. xi, 5.

54. M.-J. Lagrange, "La Mosaïque de Chellal en Palestine," *RB*, XXVI (1917), 569-572; A. D. Trendall, *The Chellal Mosaic* (Canberra, 1942).

55. A. Soper, "The 'Dome of Heaven' in Asia," *Art Bulletin*, XXIX (1947), 225-248.

56. C. G. Jung, *Symbols of Transformation* (New York, 1958), p. xxv.

Chapter III

1. O. M. Dalton, "The Tessellated Pavement of Umm Jerar," *Burlington Magazine* 34 (1919), 9.

2. R. P. Hinks, *Catalogue of the Greek, Etruscan and Roman Paintings and Mosaics in the British Museum* (London, 1933), pp. 70-71, bibl.; Figs. 77, 132; Figs. 134, 156, for bird and fish motifs in individual frames.

3. Excellent color reproductions may be found in the lavish UNESCO World Art Series: *Israel Ancient Mosaics* (Paris: 1960), Pls. xxvi, xxvii. The bird in a cage motif also appears in contemporaneous Christian mosaics; *viz.* A. D. Trendall, *The Shellal Mosaic* (Canberra, 1942), Pl. ii, Figs. 4, 5.

4. E.g., the tomb at Khirbet Semmaka on Mt. Carmel: *Sym* III, Fig. 43.

5. *DE Syn*, p. 57.

6. *Pirke Rabbi Eliezer*, chap. 31.

7. L. Ginzberg, *The Legends of the Jews*, I (Philadelphia, 1913), 276-285.

8. *The Fathers ['Abot] According to Rabbi Nathan*, chap. i, trans. J.

Goldin, Yale Judaica Series, X. This is an amplification of the Pirke 'Abot (Chapters of the Fathers), a tractate of the mishnah, which contains, mainly, the rabbinical maxims on moral conduct. The text dates to the third-fourth centuries A.D., or slightly later. Cf. Babylonian Talmud, tractate Rosh hashanah, 26a.

9. See * in text *supra* on Midrash.

10. Midrash Rabbah I, chap. lvi.

11. For the various related interpretations of the Akedah in Christian iconography, K. Wessel, "Dei grosse Berliner Pyxis," *Rivista di archeologia cristiana*, XXXVI (1960), 288.

12. A compilation of types of presentations of this scene in A. M. Smith, "The Iconography of the Sacrifice of Isaac," *AJA*, XXVI (1922), 159-173. A check-list of Christian monuments portraying the Sacrifice and a survey of its meaning within the Christian context up through the Middle Ages is presented by I. S. van Woerden, "The Iconography of the Sacrifice of Abraham," *Vigiliae Christianae*, XV (1961), 214-255. The later iconography, with special reference to the pictorial device of an angel bringing the sacrificial ram is studied by M. Schapiro, "The Angel with the Ram in Abraham's Sacrifice: A Parallel in Western and Islamic Art," *Ars Islamica*, X (1943), 134-147.

13. A. Badawy, "L'Art copte, les influences hellénistiques et romaines," *Bulletin de l'institut d'Égypte*, XXXIV (1953), part ii, 49, Fig. 62.

14. On the "City-Gate" sarcophagus in S. Ambrogio, Milan: M. Lawrence, "City-Gate Sarcophagi," *Art Bulletin*, X (1927-28), 28, Fig. 4.

15. O. M. Dalton, *Byzantine Art and Archaeology* (Oxford, 1911), p. 191, Fig. 115.

16. A. C. Weibel, *Two Thousand Years of Textiles* (New York, 1952), pp. 82-83, Pl. 22, dated to *circa* 6th-7th centuries A.D.

17. In the Rheinisches Landesmuseum Trier; exhibited recently (1963) in the Jewish Museum, New York.

18. *Alt TB*, II, Taf. cxxxii, p. 332.

19. *Viz.*, W. S. Smith, *The Art and Architecture of Ancient Egypt* (Harmondsworth, 1958), Pl. 116A.

20. For a detailed extrapolation of astronomical material from rabbinical sources, W. M. Feldman, *Rabbinical Mathematics and Astronomy* (London, 1931).

21. E. Weidner, "Der Tierkreis und die Wege am Himmel," *Archiv für Orientforschung*, VII (1931), 173-175; W. F. Albright and P. E. Dumont, "A Parallel between Indic and Babylonian Sacrificial Ritual," *Journal of the American Oriental Society*, LIV (1934), 124-125.

22. B. L. van der Waerden, "History of the Zodiac," *Archiv für Orientforschung* XVI (1952-53), 217-218, 225; for a summary of astronomical and astrological knowledge in the ancient world: O. Neugebauer, "The History of Ancient Astronomy, Problems and Methods," *JNES*, IV (1945), 1-38.

23. Babylonian Talmud, tractate 'Abodah Zarah iii.

24. Babylonian Talmud, tractate Shabboth 156:a-b.

25. See the description of the zodiac and seasons in John of Gaza: G. M. A. Hanfmann, "The Seasons in John of Gaza's Tabuli Mundi," *Latomus*, III (1939), 111 ff.

26. The synagogue at Yafia (Iaphia, Yafa), located 3 kilometers southwest of Nazareth: M. Avi-Yonah, "Places of Worship in the Roman and Byzantine Periods," *Antiquity and Survival*, II (1957), 264, Fig. 1; E.L. Sukenik, "The Ancient Synagogue at Yafa near Nazareth, Preliminary Report," *Bull Rab*, II (1951), 6-24; Sh. Yeivin, *A Decade of Archaeology in Israel, 1948-58* (Istanbul, 1960), p. 43; S. Krauss, "Nouvelles découvertes archéologiques de synagogues en Palestine," *REJ*, LXXXIX (1930), 411-412; L.-H. Vincent, "Vestiges d'une synagogue antique à Yafa de Galilée," *RB*, XXX (1921), 434-438; H. Lietzmann, "Notizen," *Zeitschrift für die neutestamentliche Wissenschaft*, XX (1921), 254; B. S. J. Isserlin, "Some Recent Archaeological News from Israel," *PEQ*, (1952), 46; *Sym*, III, Figs. 992-994.

27. The mosaic at 'Ain Douq, accidentally discovered in 1918, had been badly mutilated by iconoclasts. The synagogue is located approximately 6½ kilometers from modern Jericho, northeast of Jerusalem: L.-H. Vincent, "Le Sanctuaire juif d' 'Aïn Douq," *RB*, XXVIII (1919), 532-563; L.-H. Vincent, "La Synagogue de Noarah," *RB*, XXX (1921), 442-443, 579-601; L.-H. Vincent, "Un Sanctuaire dans la région de Jericho," RB, LXVIII (1961), 163-173; M. Avi-Yonah, "Mosaic Pavements in Palestine," *QDAP*, II, 20-22; Frey, *CII*, Par. 1197-1207; S. Krauss, "Nouvelles découvertes archéologiques de synagogues en Palestine," *REJ*, LXXXIX (1930), 395 ff; C. Watzinger, "Die antiken Synagogen Galiläas, neue Ausgrabungen und Forschungen," *Der Morgen*, VI (1930), 362-363.

28. 'Isfiya synagogue: M. Avi-Yonah, "A Sixth Century Synagogue at 'Isfiya," *QDAP*, III, 118-131; M. Avi-Yonah, "Mosaic Pavements in Palestine," *QDAP*, II, 70; "Archaeological News," *AJA*, XXXVIII (1934), 303-304.

29. Anon. "Excavations in Palestine and Trans-Jordan, 1938-39: esh Sheikh Ibreiq," *QDAP*, IX, 213.

30. Dr. Asher Hiram graciously supplied me with a photograph of the drawing of the floor found in 1962. B. Lifshitz, "Die Entdeckung einer alten Synagoge bei Tiberias," *Zeitschrift des Deutschen Palästina-Vereins*, LXXVIII (1962), 180-184.

31. *Sym*, III, Figs. 513, 541; *Anc Syn*, p. 26.

32. *Viz.*, the Roman mosaic from Bingen, Rhineland: K. Lehmann, "The Dome of Heaven," *Art Bulletin* XXVII (1945), Fig. 14.

33. Examples collected in M. J. Vermaseren, *Corpus Inscriptionum et Monumentorium Religionis Mithriacae* (Hague, 1956).

34. H. P. L'Orange, *Studies on the Iconography of Cosmic Kingship in the Ancient World* (Oslo, 1953), p. 33, Figs. 14, 67.

35. F. Cumont, *Recherches sur le symbolisme funéraire des romains* (Paris, 1942), p. 174, Pl. xiv.

36. F. Cumont, "Un Fragment de sarcophage judéo-païen," *Revue archéologique*, 5th Ser. IV (1916), 1-16.

37. G. M. A. Richter, *Catalogue of Greek and Roman Antiquities in the Dumbarton Oaks Collection* (Cambridge, 1956), pp. 19-22, Pl. viii.

38. H. W. Beyer and H. Lietzmann, *Jüdische Denkmäler* I. *Die Jüdische Katakombe der Villa Torlonia in Rom* (Berlin, 1930), Taf. 4.

39. A. Soper, "The 'Dome of Heaven' in Asia," *Art Bulletin*, XXIX (1947), 225-248.

40. K. Weitzmann, *Ancient Book Illumination* (Cambridge, 1959), p. 6.

41. P. S. Ronzevalle, "Venus lugens et Adonis byblius," *Mélanges de l'université Saint-Joseph* 15 (1930), 12, Pl. xxxiv. Father Ronzevalle argues that the cart contains the betyle of a male god rather than the symbol of Astarte.

42. N. Glueck, "The Nabataean Temple of Khirbet et-Tânnur," *Bulletin of the American School of Oriental Research* 67 (1937), 6 ff.

43. G. M. Fitzgerald, *A Sixth Century Monastery at Beth-Shan* (Philadelphia, 1939); color plate in P. Hitti, *History of Syria* (New York 1951), opp. p. 360.

44. R. Patai, *Man and Temple in Ancient Jewish Myth and Ritual* (London, 1947), pp. 76-77.

45. *Viz.*, in mosaic (*opus sectile*) on the wall of the basilica of Junius Bassus, Rome: Lübke-Pernice, *Die Kunst der Römer* (Vienna, 1958), Fig. 399; in a sixth century A.D. Byzantine silk now in Aix-la-Chapelle: E. Flemming, *Encyclopaedia of Textiles* (London, 1958), Pl. 24.

46. O. Wulff and W. F. Volbach, *Spätantike und koptische Stoffe ausägyptischen Grabfunden* (Berlin, 1926), p. 17, Pl. 46; O. M. Dalton, *Byzantine Art and Archaeology* (Oxford, 1911), p. 61.

47. E. E. Herzfeld, "Der Thron des Khosrô: I. Typus des Sonnen—und Mondwagens in der sasanidischen Kunst," *Jahrbuch der preuszischen Kunstsammlungen*, XLI (1920), 105 ff.

48. E. E. Urbach, "The Rabbinical Laws of Idolatry in the Second and Third Centuries in the Light of Archaeological and Historical Facts," *IEJ*, IX (1959), 235; I. Sonne, "The Zodiac Theme in Ancient Synagogues and in Hebrew Printed Books," *Studies in Bibliography and Booklore*, I (1953), 11.

49. *Sym*, VIII, 2, 214 ff.

50. Mishnah Yoma, V:1.

51. *Sym*, I, 253.

52. Sonne, *op. cit.*, pp. 8-12.

53. E. L. Sukenik, "Designs of the Torah Shrines in Ancient Synagogues in Palestine," *Palestine Exploration Fund, Quarterly Statement* (1931), pp. 22-25; K. Galling, "Erwägungen zur antiken Synagoge," *Zeitschrift des deutschen Palästina-Vereins* LXXII (1956), 163-178; E. G. Budde, *Aramarium und* χιβωίσς. *Ein Beitrag zur Geschichte des antiken Mobiliars* (Würzberg, 1940).

54. Gold glass: F. Cabrol and H. Leclercq, *Dictionnaire d'archéologie chrétienne et de liturgie*, V, pt. 2 (1923), "fonds de coupes," Par. 1826 ff.

Chapter IV

1. E.g., Eusebius, *Ecclesiastical History*, Book X, 4.
2. M. Holleaux, "Fouilles au temple d'Apollon Ptoos," *Bulletin de corre-spondance héllenique*, XII (1888), 395.
3. C. F. Lehmann-Haupt, "Materialien zur älteren Geschichte Armeniens und Mesopotamiens," *Abhandlung der königlichen Gesellschaft der Wissenschaften zu Göttingen*, neue Folge, IX (1907), 89; *Cyl S*, p. 297.
4. H. Frankfort, *Kingship and the Gods* (Chicago, 1948), pp. 307-309.
5. B. Goldman, "An Oriental Solar Motif and Its Western Extension," *JNES*, XX (1961), 239-247.
6. For identification of the "saw" as the attribute of the sun god: Th. Dombart, "Das babylonische Sonnentor und die 'Säge des Šǎmaš'", *Journal of the Society of Oriental Research*, XII (1928), 4-24.
7. G. Komoróczy, "Cinq cylindres-sceaux de la mésopotamie archaïque," *Bulletin du musée national hongrois des beaux-arts*, XIX (1961), 10-14.
8. *Corpus*, Nos. 178-183; *Cyl S*, Pl. xviii, g; L. Legrain, *Culture of the Babylonians and Assyrians* (Philadelphia, 1925), Nos. 187-192; L. Legrain, *Seal Cylinders, Ur Excavations*, X (Philadelphia, 1951), Nos. 238-241; O. Weber, *Altorientalische Siegelbilder* (Leipzig, 1920), Nos. 375-382.
9. A. Ungnad, "Ausgangstore," *Die Religion der Babylonier und Assyrier* (Jena, 1921), p. 58; C. D. Gray, *The Šǎmaš Religious Texts* (Chicago, 1901), p. 13.
10. F. Martin, *Textes religieux assyriens et babyloniens* (Paris, 1903), K2906, K2401.
11. *Cyl S*, Pl. xix, a; Weber, *op cit.*, Nos. 375, 376; G. Contenau, *Every-day Life in Babylon and Assyria* (London, 1954), p. 249. For the inter-pretation of a unique seal showing the morning sun posed "as a runner ready to start" from between two mountain gods: Comte du Mesnil du Buisson, "Le Lever du soleil dans le cylindre hittite du Louvre," *Syria*, XXXVI (1959), 145-147.
12. *Corpus*, No. 188.
13. *Alt TB*, No. 319.
14. E. D. Van Buren, *Symbols of the Gods in Mesopotamian Art, Analecta Orientalia* XXIII (Rome, 1945), sign H₁.
15. H. H. von der Osten, *Ancient Oriental Seals in the Collection of Mr. Edward T. Newell* (Chicago, 1934), Nos. 54, 55.
16. *Cyl S*, Text Fig. 11.
17. On Babylonian cities as the earthly reflection of heavenly patterns: E. Burrows, "Some Cosmological Patterns in Babylonian Religion," S. H. Hooke, ed., *The Labyrinth* (London, 1935), pp. 60-62.
18. M. Lambert and R. Tournay, "Le cylindre A de Gudea," *RB*, LV (1948), 408 ff; T. H. Gaster, "Myth and Story," *Numen*, I (1954), 190-191.
19. I Kings 3:5 and 9:2; Exod. 25:9, 40; Exod. 31:1-4.

20. H. L. Ginsberg, trans., I. Mendelsohn, ed., *Religions of the Ancient Near East* (New York, 1955), pp. 236 ff.

21. *Anc Rec AB*, p. 247.

22. Doors and Gates in Mesopotamia: *Gotteshaus*, pp. 36-38; Lambert and Tournay, *op. cit.*, p. 421; E. D. Van Buren, "The Guardians of the Gate in the Akkadian Period," *Orientalia*, New Ser., XVI (1947), 324.

23. For a full discussion of the Classical and Christian theophanies at the gate: E. B. Smith, *Architectural Symbolism of Imperial Rome and the Middle Ages* (Princeton, 1956), chap. I.

24. Frankfort, *op. cit.*, pp. 305-306.

25. E. Porada, "A Lyre Player from Tarsus," S. S. Weinberg, ed., *The Aegean and the Near East* (New York, 1956), Pl. xviii, g; P. Amiet, "Le Temple ailé," *Revue d'assyriologie et d'archéologei orientale*, LIV (1960), Fig. 9; W. H. Ward, *The Seal Cylinders of Western Asia* (Washington, 1919), No. 930.

26. Van Buren, *Symbols, op. cit.*, sign C4; *Corpus*, Nos. 222, 233; Legrain, *Culture, op. cit.*, Nos. 161-163; *Cyl S*, p. 1, xxii, g, i; Legrain, *Seal Cylinders, op cit.*, Nos. 227-231.

27. Van Buren, "The Guardians of the Gate," *op. cit.*, p. 326.

28. E. Heinrich and W. Andrae, *Fara* (Berlin, 1931), Taf. 72g; L. Legrain, *Ur Excavations*, III (Philadelphia, 1936), Pl. 18.

29. *Manuel*, IV, Fig. 1107.

30. *Gly Mes*, p. 117.

31. S. H. Hooke, *Babylonian and Assyrian Religion* (Oxford, 1962), pp. 41-42; Text: *ANET*, 333.

32. *Gly Mes*, Pl. 111, No. 1474.

33. *Corpus*, No. 202.

34. For the problem of three-dimensional rendering in ancient art: H. A. Groenewegen-Frankfort, *Arrest and Movement* (Chicago, 1951).

35. For the reign, *circa* 1130-1100 B.C.: R. Labat, "Elam and Western Persia," *Cambridge Ancient History* (1964), rev. fas. II, 32.

36. E. Porada, *Alt-Iran* (Baden-Baden, 1952), pp. 53-54; J.-E. Gautier, "Le 'Sit Samši in Šušinak," *Délégation en Perse, Mémoires*, XII (Paris, 1911), 144, inscription.

37. L.-H. Vincent, "La Notion biblique du Haut-Lieu," *RB*, LV (1948), 253 ff.

38. Vincent, *op. cit.*, p. 254.

39. Gautier, *op. cit.*, 122, Fig. 133.

40. *Cyl S*, Pl. xviii, k.

41. H. Lenzen, *Die Entwicklung der Zikurrat* (Leipzig, 1941), p. 60.

42. *Gly Mes*, No. 271.

43. *Gly Mes*, Nos. 37, 577, 578.

44. For the dwelling place of the god on the ziggurat: Lenzen, *op. cit.*, p. 60; H. Gressmann, *The Tower of Babel* (New York, 1928).

45. W. Amdrae, *Das Gotteshaus und die Urformen des Bauens im alten Orient* (Berlin, 1930), 17-18, Fig. 10.

46. Van Buren, "The Guardians of the Gate," *op. cit.*, p. 312.

47. *Iliad* V (Rieu translation).
48. Frankfort, *op. cit.*, p. 305; A. Salonen, *Die Türen des alten Mesopotamien. Annales Acadamiae Scientiarum Fennicae*, Ser. B., CXXIV (1961), 29.
49. Frankfort, *op. cit.*, pp. 305-306.
50. Salonen, *op. cit.*, p. 20; T. Jacobsen, "Parerga Sumerologica," *JNES*, II (1943), 118.
51. Kinnier Wilson, trans., D. W. Thomas, ed., *Documents from Old Testament Times* (London, 1958), p. 10.
52. *AAAO*, Pl. 119; *Corpus*, Nos. 771, 793.
53. *Manuel*, III, Figs, 760, 795; *Corpus*, Nos. 640, 641, 726.
54. B. Pering, "Die geflügelte Scheibe in Assyrien," *Archiv für Orientforschung* VIII (1933), 291-292.
55. Weber, *op. cit.*, Abb. 646a.
56. E. F. Schmidt, *Persepolis* II, *Oriental Institute Publications*, 69 (Chicago, 1957), Pl. 6.
57. J. Duchesne-Guillemin, *La Religion de l'Iran* (Paris, 1962), pp. 163, 207.
58. Andrae, *op. cit.*, 16-17.
59. H. Güterbock, "The Composition of Hittite Prayers to the Sun," *Journal of the American Oriental Society*, LXXVIII (1958), 240, ll. 29-30.
60. C.F.A. Schaeffer, *Ugaritica*, III (Paris, 1958), 3-14, Figs, 2, 4, 13, 14, etc.
61. E. Akurgal, "Early Period and Golden Age of Ionia," *AJA*, LXVI (1962), 377.
62. J. Friedrich, "Das Siegel des hethitischen Königs Hattušili III," *Artibus Asiae*, VI (1937), 188, Abb. 6. For Hittite *aediculum*: A. H. Sayce, "The Hieroglyphic Inscription on the Seal of Subbiluliuma," *Archiv für Orientforschung* VII (1931), 184-185. For hieroglyphic reading of the *aediculum*: E. O. Forrer, "Die sogenannte Hethitische Bilderschrift," *American Journal of Semitic Languages and Literature*, XLVIII (1932), 138-140.
63. B. Trell, "The Naophoroi of Greek Imperial Coins," *AJA* LXVI (1962), 200.
64. H. Z. Koşay, *Alacahöyük* (Ankara, n.d.); O. R. Gurney, *The Hittites* (Harmondsworth, 1952), Pl. 15; K. Bittel, *Die Felsbilder von Yazilikaya* (Bamberg, 1934), E. Akurgal, *Kunst der Hethiter* (Munich, 1961), Pls. xix, 78.
65. G. Loud, "The Hittites at Megiddo?" *Mélanges Syriens*, II (Paris, 1939), 557-558.
66. Akurgal, *op. cit.*, Pl. xxi, an excellent photograph that clearly shows its architectural character; O. Meyer, *Reich und Kultur der Chetiter* (Berlin, 1914), Taf. xiii; *Manuel* I, 199; *Alt TB*, 150-151.
67. S. Lloyd, *Early Anatolia* (Harmondsworth, 1956), p. 146; K. Bittel, "Beitrag zu Eflân-Pinar," *Bibliotheca Orientalis*, X (1953), 2-5, Taf. i-iii.
68. "The Egyptian Temple," *Biblical Archaeologist Reader* (New York, 1961), p. 152.

69. *Anc Rec E*, p. 101; H. H. Nelson, *Medinet Habu Reports. Oriental Institute Reports*, X (Chicago, 1931), 21-27.

70. A. Gardiner, *Egyptian Grammar* (Oxford, 1950), sign-list: N1; K. Kees, *Der Götterglaube im alten Ägypten*² (Berlin, 1956), 223.

71. N. M. Davies, *Picture Writing in Ancient Egypt* (London, 1958), Pl. xvii, 5.

72. H. Bonnet, *Reallexikon der ägyptischen Religionsgeschichte* (Berlin, 1952,) *Schu*.

73. Von der Osten, *op. cit.*, No. 534.

74. *Alt TB*, 101, Taf. cxliv, No. 354.

75. *Alt TB*, Taf. ccix, No. 520; *Manuel*, II, 1470, Fig. 891.

76. *Anc Rec E*, p. 229.

77. R. Dussaud, *L'Art phénicien du II*ᵉ *millénaire* (Paris, 1949), p. 107, Fig. 69.

78. *AAAO*, Fig. 96.

79. G. A. Eisen, *Ancient Oriental Cylinder and Other Seals, Oriental Institute Publications*, XLVII (Chicago, 1940), 129, Pl. xvi; Amiet, *op. cit.*, Fig. 9.

80. Ward, *op. cit.*, No. 939.

81. *Alt TB*, Taf. cxvii, No. 277.

82. A. B. Cook, *Zeus*, II (Cambridge, 1925), 45; 47 ff., for the Milky Way as the celestial road leading to the god's house.

83. *Metamorphoses*, II, 1-18.

84. M. J. Vermaseren, *Mithras, the Secret God* (London, 1963), p. 157.

85. G. Contenau, *La Civilization d'Assur et de Babylone* (Paris, 1937), Fig. 20.

86. *Viz.*, *AAAO*, Pl. 146.

87. *Anc Rec AB*, p. 62.

88. *Anc Rec E*, pp. 179, 229.

89. Of the extensive literature on the "sacred tree," the following present the major aspects: E. Dhorme, "L'Arbre de verité et l'arbre de vie," *RB*, XVI (1907), 271-274; N. Perrot, "Les Représentations de l'arbre sacré sur les monuments de Mesopotamie," *Babyloniaca*, XVII (1937); U. Holmberg, "Der Baum des Lebens," *Annales Academiae Scientiarum Fennicae*, Ser. B, XVI (1923), 1-157; H. Kühn, "Die Lebensbaum und Beterschnallen der Völkerwanderungzeit," *IPEK*, XVIII (1949-53), 33-58; J. de Morgan, *Délégation en Perse, Memoirs*, XII (Paris, 1911), 156 ff; R. D. Barnett, *A Catalogue of the Nimrud Ivories* (London, 1957), 85-87; H. Schmökel, "Ziegen am Lebensbaum," *Archiv für Orientforschung*, XVIII (1958), 373-378; G. Lechler, "The Tree of Life in Indo-European and Islamic Cultures," *Ars Islamica*, IV (1937), 369-416; *Sym*, VII, chap. 3.

90. Gressmann, *op. cit.*, 58 ff.

91. F. J. Hollis, "The Sun-Cult and the Temple at Jerusalem," in S. H. Hooke, ed., *Myth and Ritual* (Oxford, 1933), p. 110.

92. W. F. Albright, *Archaeology and the Religion of Israel* (Baltimore, 1953), pp. 167-168.

93. Tractate 'Erubin V, 22c (Jerusalem Talmud).

94. *Jewish War*, Excursus vi (Williamson translation).

95. *Anc Rec E*, 179, 229.

96. I Kings vii:15-22; II Chronicles iii:15-17. Resumé of the various ex-planations of the origin and significance of the pillars of the Solomonic Temple: R. B. Y. Scott, "The Pillars Jachin and Boaz," *Journal of Biblical Literature* LVIII (1939), 143-149.

97. Cf. J. Obermann, "The Divine Name *YHWH* in the Light of Recent Discoveries," *Journal of Biblical Literature*, LXVIII (1949), 317-318.

98. Van Buren, "The Guardians of the Gate," *op. cit.*, p. 326.

99. *Ibid.*, p. 316.

100. W. F. Albright, "Two Cressets from Marisa and the Pillars of Jachin and Boaz," *Bulletin of the American School of Oriental Research*, LXXXV (1942), 18-27.

101. Y. Yadin, "Excavations at Hazor, 1958, Preliminary Communique," *IEJ*, IX (1959), 81-83.

102. Lenzen, *op. cit.*, 59-60; W. Andrae, *Das Gotteshaus und die Urformen des Bauens im alten Orient* (Berlin, 1930), Taf. IV. The clay altars were found at Level G at Assur, dated to *circa* 2700 B.C.

103. K. Galling, *Der Altar in den Kulturen des alten Orients* (Berlin, 1925), p. 20; *Corpus*, No. 220; *Cyl S*, Pls. xxii, j and xxiv, f.

104. *Cyl S*, Pl. xx, k.

105. M. A. Beek, *Atlas of Mesopotamia* (London, 1962), Figs. 256, 257, 258.

106. H. G. May, "Material Remains of the Megiddo Cult," *Oriental Institute Publications*, XXVI (Chicago), Pl. 13.

107. A. Jirku, *Die Welt der Bibel* (Stuttgart, 1957), Taf. 32; *Manuel*, III, 1396, Fig. 857; M. Lods, "Autel ou réchaud? à propos du 'brûle-parfums' de Taanak," *Revue de l'histoire des religions*, CIX (1934), 129-147; concerning its date in ninth-eighth centuries B.C., R. de Vaux, "Les Chérubins et l'arche d'alliance," *Mélanges de l'Université Saint-Joseph*, XXXVII (1960-1961), 117-118.

108. A. Moortgat, "Tell Chūēra," *Archiv für Orientforschung*, XX (1963), Abb. 38-40.

109. A. Evans, *Palace of Minos*, II, (London, 1928), part 1, Fig. 70 bis.

110. Concerning the sacrificial aspects of incense burning: A. H. Godbey, "Incense and Poison Ordeals in the Ancient Orient," *American Journal of Semitic Languages and Literatures*, XLVI (1930), 217-238.

111. J. H. Iliffe, "A Model Shrine of Phoenician Style," *QDAP*, XI (1944), 91-92, Pl. xxi.

112. British Museum No. 27526; also an Egyptian shrine model of Roman times, R. D. Barnett, *A Catalogue of the Nimrud Ivories* (London, 1957), Fig. 59.

113. Jirku, *op. cit.*, Taf. 87.

114. *Alt TB*, p. 152, Taf. ccx, No. 523; Harden, *op. cit.*, pp. 197, 304, Pl. 23; general discussion of the shrine type, J. Birmingham, "The Chronology of Some Early and Middle Iron Age Cypriote Sites," *AJA*, LXVII (1963), 18.

115. Evans, *op. cit.*, pp. 128-129, Figs. 63-64.

116. *Viz.*, a protogeometric (850-800 B.C.) shrine from Crete: R. W. Hutchinson, *Prehistoric Crete* (Harmondsworth, 1962), Fig. 68.

117. Principal discussions of the so-called hut urns: F. Behn, *Hausurnen* (Berlin, 1924); W. R. Bryan, *Italic Hut Urns and Hut Urn Cemeteries, Papers and Monographs of the American Academy in Rome*, IV (Rome, 1925); J. Sundwall, *Die italischen Hüttenurner; Acta Academiae Aboensis Humaniora*, IV, No. 5 (Finland, 1925); Evans, *op. cit.*, 130 ff.; H. Müller-Karpe, *Vom Anfang Roms; Mitteilungen des deutschen archaeologischen Instituts, roemische Abteilung*, Fünftes Ergänzungsheft (1959), 87 ff.

118. Müller-Karpe, *op. cit.*, pp. 88, 92, says that house models equal cult room models.

119. J. Perrot, "Une tombe à ossuaires du ive millénaire à Azor, près de Tel-Aviv," *'Atiqot*, III (1961), pp. 1 ff. For derivative European examples: Behn, *op. cit.*, p. 58, Taf. 25; Perrot, *op. cit.*, Fig. 20.

120. *Viz.*, Jemdet Nasr seal: *Art of the Ancient Near East in Boston; Boston Museum of Fine Arts*, Fig 3; *Corpus*, Nos. 24, 25.

121. Perrot, *op. cit.*, p. 12, n. 51, Fig. 21 (No. 1).

122. P. Bar-Adon, "Expedition C—The Cave of the Treasure," *IEJ*, XII (1962), 220 ff., Pl. 40; A. Moortgat, *Alt-Vorderasiatische Malerei* (Berlin, 1959), Pl. 4.

123. H. Payne, *Perachora, The Sanctuaries of Hera Akraia and Limenia* (Oxford, 1940), Pl. 96.

Chapter V

1. S. N. Kramer, "Death and Nether World According to the Sumerian Literary Texts," *Iraq*, XXII (1960), 63.

2. Texts: *ANET*, 52 ff, 106 ff.

3. The "geography" of the land of the dead is reviewed in: M.-J. Lagrange, "Études sur les religions sémitiques," *RB*, XI (1902), 234-238.

4. F. Cumont, *Oriental Religions in Roman Paganism* (New York, 1956), pp. 126-127.

5. I. Lévi, "Les Morts et l'avènement de l'ère messianique," *REJ*, LXIX (1919), 122-128. For a collection of rabbinic literature that deals with death and afterlife: C. G. Montefiore and H. Loewe, *A Rabbinic Anthology* (London, 1938), chap. xxxi.

6. J. Goldin, *The Fathers According to Rabbi Nathan*, Yale Judaica Series, X (New Haven, 1955), chap. XII.

7. *Ibid.*, chap. XIX.

8. Babylonian Talmud, Berakoth, 15b, 18b.

9. Translation of catacomb epitaph in H. J. Leon, *The Jews of Ancient Rome* (Philadelphia, 1960), pp. 248-249.

10. *Sym* I, pp. 66, 84.

11. J. Pinkerfeld, "Two Fragments of a Marble Door from Jaffa," *'Atiqot*, I (1955), 92.

12. E.g., a chambered tomb in the Cedron Valley: M.-R. Savignac, "Nouveaux ossuaires juif avec graffites," *RB*, XXXIV (1925), 253-266.
13. F.-M. Abel, "Deux tombeaux à meule à Abou Ghoch," *RB*, XXXIV (1925), 275-279. New Testament references in Matthew 27:60; Mark 15:46.
14. N. Avigad, "Excavation at Beth She'arim, 1954," *IEJ*, V (1955), 219.
15. M. Avi-Yonah, *Oriental Art in Roman Palestine, Studi Semitici,* V (Rome, 1961), 36.
16. L. Y. Rahmani, "Jewish Rock-Cut Tombs in Jerusalem," *'Atiqot*, III (1961), Pl. xv, Nos. 6, 7.
17. *DE Syn*, p. 108, Pl. lvii.
18. *Sym* III, Figs. 45, 48.
19. W. M. Calder, ed., *Monumenta Asiae Minoris Antiqua*, I (Manchester, 1928), Nos. 130, 298, 385, 401, etc.
20. L. Heuzey, "Monuments de la Palestine," *Comptes Rendus, Académie des inscriptions et belles-lettres* (1905), pp. 344-347; R. Dussaud, *Les Monuments palestiniens et judaïques* (Paris, 1912), pp. 88-89, Fig. 118. Collection: Louvre, AO 3989; 0.78 x 0.62m.
21. Collection: Israel Department of Antiquities.
22. B. Goldman, "The Asiatic Ancestry of the Greek Gorgon," *Berytus*, XIV (1961), 1-23; J. B. W. Perkins and R. G. Goodchild, "The Christian Antiquities of Tripolitania," *Archaeologia*, XCV (1953), Pls. xv, e and xix, d; B. Bagatti, "Edifici cristiani nella regione del Nebo," *Rivista di archeologia cristiana*, XIII (1936), Fig. 5; *Alt TB*, Taf. clxxxi.
23. *Sym* III, Figs. 109-222.
24. Avigad, *op. cit.*, Pl. 31A.
25. *Viz.*, the lintel from Yafa: L.-H. Vincent, "Vestiges d'une synagogue antique à Yafa de Galilée," *RB*, XXX (1921), 434-438; E. L. Sukenik, "The Ancient Synagogue at Yafa Near Nazareth," *Bull Rab*, II, Pl. ii.
26. For the symbolism of the shell in antiquity: A. A. Barb, "Diva Matrix," *Journal of the Warburg and Courtauld Institutes*, XVI (1953) 205 ff.; *Sym*, VIII, part 2, 105; A. Hiram, *Die Entwicklung der antiken Synagogen und altchristlichen Kirchenbauten im Heiligen Lande* in *Wiener Jahrbuch für Kunstgeschichte*, XIX (1963), 53; M. Bratschkova, "Die Muschel in der antiken Kunst," *Bulletin de l'institut archéologique bulgare*, XII (1938), 1-131; K. Galling, "Erwägungen zur antiken Synagoge," *Zeitschrift des deutschen Palästina-Vereins*, LXXII (1956), 173.
27. M. Hours-Miedan, "Les Représentations figurées sur les stèles de Carthage," *Cahiers de Byrsa*, I (1950), Pl. IIc.
28. J. Ferron, "Inscriptions juives de Carthage," *ibid.*, pp. 175-206.
29. *Sym*, I, 152; III, Nos. 388-389.
30. For explanation of the solid base on the *menorah* rather than the base made of three legs: M. Kon, "The Menorah of the Arch of Titus," *PEQ* (1950), pp. 25-30; W. Wirgin, "On the Shape of the Foot of the Menorah," *IEJ*, XI (1961), 151-153.
31. Heuzey, *op. cit.*, p. 345.
32. For five-branch candelabra: *Sym*, III, Figs. 439, 942, 1012, etc. The

problem of the prohibition against, but the repeated representation of the *menorah*: E. R. Goodenough, "The Menorah Among Jews of the Roman World," *HUCA*, XXIII (1950-51), part 2, 450.

33. *Sym*, III, Fig. 65; Istanbul relief, *Sym*, III, Fig. 97. For the iconography of the *menorah* placed on the head of a man: M. Smith, "The Image of God," *Bulletin of the John Rylands Library*, XL (1957-58), 473-512.

34. Avigad, *op. cit.*, Fig. 12.

35. H. Ingholt, H. Seyrig, and J. Starcky, *Recueil des tessères de Palmyre* (Paris, 1955), Pl. 13, Nos. 88, 512. There is some question as to the use to which these clay lozenges were put; Seyrig suggests that they were used to collect food rations on holidays, H. Seyrig, "La Religion palmyrénienne d'après un livre récent," *Syria*, XVI (1935), 394 ff.

36. H. Ingholt, *Parthian Sculptures from Hatra, Connecticut Academy of Arts and Sciences*, XII (1954), Pl. iv, 2, 3.

37. P. Hommel, "Giebel und Himmel," *Istanbuler Mitteilungen*, VII (1957), 15 ff.

38. G. W. Elderkin, "Architectural Detail in Antique Sepulchral Art," *AJA*, XXXIX (1935), 524.

39. A. Strong, *Apotheosis and After Life* (London, 1915), pp. 176-177, Pl. xxiii (relief found at Preturo, near the Sabine Amiternum).

40. G. Scholem, "The Curious History of the Six-Pointed Star," *Commentary*, VIII (1949), 243-251; E. L. Ehrlich, *Symbolik der Religionen*; "Der Davidstern," *Kultsymbolik im alten Testament und im nachbiblischen Judentum* (Stuttgart, 1959). For early examples: J. B. Pritchard, *The Water System of Gibeon* (Philadelphia, 1961), p. 20, Nos. 305, 358, 259.

41. Ingholt, *op. cit.*, p. 27.

42. For Biblical and rabbinic references: Ehrlich, *op. cit.*, "Die Menōrā."

43. Josephus, *Jewish Wars*, Excursus vi.

44. H. Lietzmann and H. W. Beyer, *Jüdische Denkmäler*, I, in *Die jüdische Katakombe der Villa Torlonia in Rom* (Berlin, 1930), pp. 16 ff; *Sym*, VIII, part 2, 218.

45. *De Vita Mosis*, II, 102.

46. For the relationship between *menorah* and "sacred tree": Smith, *op. cit.*, pp. 473-512; Z. Ameisenowa, "The Tree of Life in Jewish Iconography," *Journal of the Warburg Institute*, II (1938-39), 326-345; H. Strauss, "The History of the Seven-branched Candlestick of the Hasmonean Kings," *Journal of the Warburg and Courtauld Institutes*, XXII (1959), 6-16. Biblical description, Exod. 26:31-37.

47. M. Dothan, "Some Aspects of Religious Life in Palestine during the Hyksos Rule," *Antiquity and Survival*, II (1957), 129, Figs. 2-4, 20.

48. W. Wirgin, "The Menorah as Symbol of Judaism," *IEJ*, XII (1962), 141.

49. G. F. Hill, *Catalogue of the Greek Coins of Palestine in the British Museum* (London, 1914), p. 219, Pl. xxiii, No. 11.

50. A. Reifenberg, *Ancient Jewish Coins*, 3rd ed. (Jerusalem, 1963), p. 17;

M. Avi-Yonah, "Ten Years of Archaeology in Israel," *IEJ*, VIII (1958), 58; on a clay lamp of the late first, early second centuries A.D., S. Applebaum, "A Lamp and Other Remains of the Jewish Community of Cyrene," *IEJ*, VII (1957), 154-157.

51. J. Leveen, *The Hebrew Bible in Art* (London, 1944), p. 63.
52. R. Wischnitzer, "The Beth Alpha Mosaic: A New Interpretation," *Jewish Social Studies*, XVII (1955), 135.
53. *Sym*, I, 253.
54. J. Gutmann, Review of *UNESCO, Israel Mosaics*, in *The Reconstructionist*, XXVII (1961), 26-27.
55. The various arguments on the identification of the pedimented portal are reviewed in C. Wendel, *Der Thoraschrein im Altertum* (Halle, 1950), pp. 29-30. Also see H. Rosenau, "Some Aspects of the Pictorial Influence of the Jewish Temple," *Palestine Exploration Fund, Quarterly Statement* (1936), pp. 157-162, where an attempt is made to distinguish between different types of buildings.
56. See: E. Nielsen, "Some Reflections on the History of the Ark," *Vetus Testamentum, Supplement,* VII (1960), 61-74, for the matter of the Ark as divine throne and as cupboard for the Covenant; M. Haran, "The Ark and the Cherubim: Their Symbolic Significance in Biblical Ritual," *IEJ*, IX (1959), 30-38, 89-94, for the Ark as throne and footstool; P. R. de Vaux, "Les Chérubins et l'arche d'alliance," *Mélanges de l'université Saint-Joseph,* XXXVII (1960-61), 91-124, for the cherubim forming YHWH's seat, and the Ark as his footstool; W. R. Arnold, *Ephod and Ark* (Cambridge, 1917), identifies the Ark as containing the Lots.
57. Rosenau, *op. cit.*, p. 158.
58. M. Haran, "The Disappearance of the Ark," *IEJ*, XIII (1963), 46 ff.
59. For the catacombs of Marisa: J. P. Peters and H. Thiersch, *Painted Tombs in the Necropolis of Marisa* (London, 1905).
60. *Sym*, VIII, chap. 9, catalogs the birds that appear in Jewish art.
61. Ch. Diehl, "Un Nouveau trésor d'argenterie syrienne," *Syria*, VII (1926), 122, Pl. xxxi.
62. F. Cumont, "L'Aigle funéraire des syriens et l'apothéose des empereurs," *Revue de l'histoire des religions*, LXII (1910), 142 ff. E. R. Goodenough, "The Crown of Victory," *Art Bulletin*, XXVIII (1946), 139-159.
63. *DE Syn*, Pl. xxiv.
64. *Sym*, III, Fig. 282.
65. E. R. Goodenough, "Pagan Symbols in Jewish Antiquity: The Vine, The Eagle, The Lion," *Commentary*, XXIII (1957), 77. For differences in styles of carving and in format as reflecting social status rather than different periods: Avi-Yonah, *Oriental Art in Roman Palestine, op. cit.*, p. 21.
66. L. Y. Rahmani, "Roman Tombs in Shmuel ha-Navi Street, Jerusalem," *IEJ*, X (1960), 140 ff; N. Avigad, "Excavations at Beth She'arim, 1958: Preliminary Report," *IEJ*, IX (1959), pp. 216 ff; M. Avi-Yonah, "Lead Coffins from Palestine," *QDAP*, IV (1935), 139 ff; M. Avi-Yonah, "Three Lead Coffins from Palestine," *Journal of Hellenic Studies*, L (1930), 300-

312; E. von Mercklin, "Untersuchungen zu den antiken Bleisarkopha-gen," *Berytus*, III (1936), 51-75.

67. M. Chéhab, "Sarcophages en plomb du musée national libanais," *Syria*, XVI (1935), 65.

68. G. W. Elderkin, "Architectural Detail in Antique Sepulchral Art," *AJA*, XXXIX (1935), 518.

69. Dating of ossuaries: L.-H. Vincent, "Sur la date des ossuaires juifs," *RB*, XLIII (1934), 564-567.

70. B. Bagatti and J. T. Milik, *Gli scavi de "Dominus flevit"* (Jerusalem, 1958), Pl. 19, fot. 42, 44.

71. For ossuaries and the door to Hades: F. Cabrol and Leclercq, *Dictionnaire d'archéologie chrétienne et de liturgie*, XIII (Paris 1937), Par. 22 ff.

72. Bagatti, Milik, *op. cit.*, Pl. 20, fot. 50.

73. F. Cumont, *Recherches sur le symbolisme funéraire des romains* (Paris, 1942), p. 307, Pl. xxx, 2, sarcophagus in the Vatican Museum.

74. C. Bailey, ed., *The Legacy of Rome*, 2nd ed. (Oxford, 1924), Fig. 48.

75. *Sym*, III, Fig. 198.

76. L.-H. Vincent, "Nouveaux ossuaries juifs," *RB*, II (1902), 103 (Fig. 1), ossuary from the Jewish cemetery on the Ladies of Sion property, south of the Mount of Olives.

77. Bibliography of Jewish funerary objects contained in P. P. Kahane, "Tombs at *Ḥuqoq*," *'Atiqot*, III (1961), 144-147.

78. R. Demangel, "Grilles de fenêtres en Égypte et triglyphes grecs," *Syria*, XVI (1935), Fig. 14.

79. C. Watzinger, *Griechische Holzsarkophage aus der Zeit Alexanders des Grossen* (Leipzig, 1915).

80. In general on Christian sarcophagi, J. Wilpert, *I sarcofagi cristiani antichi*, 5 vols. (Rome, 1929-36); for the history of Late Roman, Early Christian sarcophagi see C. R. Morey, *Sardis, V, The Sarcophagus of Claudia Antonia Sabina and the Asiatic Sarcophagi* (Princeton, 1924), part 1, 90-93, in which Morey argues that the format derives from the Roman *scenae frons*, i.e., is based on the architecture of the stage façade; for summary of different theories held see H. Stern, "Nouvelles recherches sur les images des conciles dans l'église de la nativité à Bethléem," *Cahiers archéologiques*, III (1948), 101.

81. A. Katzenellenbogen, "The Sarcophagus in S. Ambrogio and St. Ambrose," *Art Bulletin*, XXIX (1947), 253.

82. M. Lawrence, "City-Gate Sarcophagi," *Art Bulletin*, X (1927-28), 1-59; M. Lawrence, "Columnar Sarcophagi in the Latin West," *Art Bulletin*, XIV (1932), 103-185. Cf. G. Kleiner, "Hellenistische Sarkophage in Kleinasien," *Istanbuler Mitteilungen*, VII (1957), 1-10.

83. N. Avigad, "Excavations at Beth She'arim, 1955," *Eretz-Israel*, V (1958), 171-188 (Hebrew, English summary).

84. N. Avigad, "Excavations at Beth She'arim, 1958," *IEJ*, IX (1959), 211-212, Pl. 22b.

85. M. I. Rostovtzeff, "Dura and the Problem of Parthian Art," *Yale Classical Studies*, V (1935), Fig. 44.

[185]

86. A. Ferrua, "Il cimitero sopra la catacombe di Domitilla," *Rivista di archeologia cristiani*, XXXVI (1960), 194-195, Fig. 13.
87. Cumont, *Recherches, op. cit.*, p. 332, Pl. xxxv, 3. A funerary stele from Orchomenos also shows the famed hunter of the Calydonian boar, resting upon his spear with his dog at his feet, S. Reinach, *Répetoire de reliefs grecs et romains*, II (Paris, 1912), 373, No. 3.
88. Cf. collection of clay lamps in *Sym*, III, Figs. 259-286.
89. Lion in antiquity: *Sym*, VII, chap. 2; R. D. Barnett, *A Catalogue of the Nimrud Ivories* (London, 1957), pp. 71 ff.
90. S. Krauss, "Nouvelles découvertes archéologiques de synagogues en Palestine," *REJ*, LXXXIX (1930), 394.
91. *Sym*, VIII, part 2, 31.
92. E.g., the apotheosis on coins, L. Kadman, *Corpus Nummorum Palestinensium*, II, *The Coins of Caesarea Maritima* (Jerusalem, 1957), No. 112.
93. Cumont, "L'Aigle funéraire," *op. cit.*, p. 137.
94. *Ibid.*, p. 127, Fig. 10.
95. Hill, *op. cit.*, p. 181, Pl. xix, No. 29.
96. Rostovtzeff, *op. cit.*, Fig. 55.

Chapter VI

1. H. Danthine, "L'Imagerie des trones vides et des trones porteurs de symboles dans le proche orient ancien," *Mélanges syriens offerts à M. René Dussaud*, II (Paris, 1939), 857-866.
2. H. M. Wiener, *The Altars of the Old Testament* (Leipzig, 1927).
3. *Sym*, III, Nos. 214, 224.
4. *Sym*, I, 129.
5. The chronology for the Iron Age which is followed here is that of Sh. Yeivin, *A Decade of Archaeology in Israel, 1948-58* (Istanbul, 1960).
6. I Kings 8:6-7; II Chron. 5:7-8. For the name "cherub," its origin and the old Oriental representations, R. de Vaux, "Les Chérubins et l'arche d'alliance," *Mélanges de l'université Saint-Joseph*, XXXVII (1960-61), 97 (bibliography, n. 1); P. Dhorme and L.-H. Vincent, "Les Chérubins," *RB*, (1926), 328-358, 481-495; W. F. Albright, "What Were the Cherubim?" *BA*, I (1938), 1-3.
7. H. G. May, "The Ark—A Miniature Temple," *American Journal of Semitic Languages and Literatures*, LII (1936), 215-234; "Bulletin," *RB*, XVI (1907), 313.
8. On the identification of the cherubim and Ark: W. F. Albright, *Archaeology and the Religion of Israel* (Baltimore, 1953), p. 148, n. 65; R. D. Barnett, *A Catalogue of the Nimrud Ivories* (London, 1957), p. 86; M. Haran, "The Ark and the Cherubim: Their Symbolic Significance in Biblical Ritual," *IEJ*, IX (1959), 30-38, 89-94.
9. W. C. Graham and H. G. May, *Culture and Conscience* (Chicago, 1936), pp. 254-257.

10. E. E. Herzfeld, *Iran in the Ancient East* (Oxford, 1941), pp. 212-213, Pl. xli; E. E. Herzfeld, *Archaeological History of Iran* (Oxford, 1935), pp. 35-37.

11. F. Sarre, E. E. Herzfeld, *Iranische Felsreliefs* (Berlin, 1910), p. 4; M. Sprengling, "A New Pahlavi Inscription," *American Journal of Semitic Languages and Literatures*, LIII (1937), 140; F. Wachtsmuth, "Achaemenid Architecture," A. U. Pope, ed., *Survey of Persian Art*, I (New York, 1938), 311; R. Ghirshman, "La Tour de Nourabad," *Syria*, XXIV (1944-45), 175-193; K. Erdmann, *Das iranische Feuerheiligtum* (Leipzig, 1941), pp. 18 ff; R. C. Zaehner,*The Dawn and Twilight of Zoroastrianism* (London, 1961), Pls. 16, 17; J. Duchesne-Guillemin, *La Religion de l'Iran ancien* (Paris, 1962), p. 160.

12. H. H. von der Osten, *Die Welt der Perser* (Stuttgart, 1956), p. 108.

13. E. F. Schmidt, *Persepolis*, II (Chicago: Oriental Institute Publications, LXIX), 43 ff.

14. A. Godard, *L'Art de l'Iran* (Paris, 1962), pp. 115, 168.

15. H. Frankfort, *Art and Architecture of the Ancient Orient* (Harmondsworth, 1954), p. 224.

16. For the architectural equivalents, see now R. D. Barnett, "Persepolis," *Iraq*, XIX (1957), 74.

17. K. Erdmann, "Die Altäre von Naqsh i Rustem," *Mitteilungen der deutschen Orient-Gesellschaft zu Berlin*, LXXXI (1949), 6 ff.

18. E. E. Herzfeld, "Die Kunst des zweiten Jahrtausends in Vorderasien," *Archaeologische Mitteilungen aus Iran*, IX (1938), 55, No. 143.

19. The coin sequence can be conveniently followed in G. F. Hill, *Catalogue of the Greek Coins of Arabia, Mesopotamia and Persia* (London, 1922), Pls. xxviii-xxxii.

20. M. E. L. Mallowan, "Excavations at Brak and Chagar Bazar," *Iraq*, IX (1947), Fig. 19; *Corpus*, No. 676.

21. R. D. Barnett, *Assyrian Palace Reliefs* (London, n.d.), No. 134.

22. P. S. Ronzevalle, "Venus Lugens et Adonis Byblius," *Mélanges de l'université Saint-Joseph*, XV (1930), Pl. xxi, No. 8.

23. A. Kammerer, *Pétra et la nabatène* (Paris, 1929), Pls. 67, 71 (atlas).

24. K. Erdmann, "Persepolis: Daten und Deutungen," *Mitteilungen der deutschen Orient-Gesellschaft zu Berlin*, XCII (1960), 21-47; A. U. Pope, "Persepolis—Considered as a Ritual City," *Proceedings, Twenty-Second Congress of Orientalists*, II (Leiden, 1957), 58-66; A. U. Pope, "Persepolis as a Ritual City," *Archaeology*, X (1957), 123-130.

25. D. Schlumberger, *The Excavations at Surkh Kotal and the Problem of Hellenism in Bactria and India* (London, 1961), pp. 86-87.

26. D. Schlumberger, "Descendants non-méditerranéens de l'art grec," *Syria*, XXXVII (1960), Pl. vi, 1, 2; D. Schlumberger, "Le Temple de Surkh Kotal en Bactriane," *Journal Asiatique*, CCXL (1952), 433-453, Pl. viii, 1.

27. H. Ingholt, H. Seyrig, J. Starcky, *Recueil des tessères de Palmyre* (Paris, 1955), p. 21, No. 150.

28. A. Reifenberg, *Ancient Jewish Coins*, 3rd ed. (Jerusalem, 1963), Nos. 103, 104.
29. E. Sjöqvist, "Excavations at Morgantina (Serra Orlando) 1961: Preliminary Report VI," *AJA*, LXVI (1962), 140, Fig. 26a.
30. Hill, *op. cit.*, p. 15, Pl. iii, 5.
31. L. Kadman, *Corpus Nummorum Palaestinensium*, II, *The Coins of Caesarea Maritima* (Jerusalem, 1957), No. 230.
32. A. M. Smith, "The Iconography of the Sacrifice of Isaac," *AJA*, XXVI (1922), Fig. 4.
33. Ronzevalle, *op. cit.*, Pl. xxxii, 4d.
34. H. Seyrig, "Antiquités syriennes: une idole bétylique," *Syria*, XL (1963), 17-32, Pl. I.
35. D. Homès-Fredericq, *Hatra et ses sculptures parthes, étude stylistique et iconographique* (Istanbul, 1963), Pl. viii, 5.
36. G. E. Wright, "Herod's Nabataean Neighbor," *BA*, I (1938), 4, Fig. 3.
37. H. Ingholt, *Parthian Sculptures from Hatra* (New Haven, 1954), pp. 45-46, Fig. 7; Homès-Fredericq, *op. cit.*, pp. 41-42.
38. *Sym*, I, 129 and III, Figs. 224, 107.
39. *DE Syn*, 139-141, Pl. lxi, for the figure representing Hiel and the literary sources.
40. *Sym*, III, No. 282.
41. *Sym*, III, No. 497.
42. O. M. Dalton, *Byzantine Art and Archaeology* (Oxford, 1911), pp. 60, 33.
43. R. Wischnitzer, "The Beth Alpha Mosaic: A New Interpretation," *Jewish Social Studies*, XVII (1955), 137-139. Goodenough objects to Mrs. Wischnitzer-Bernstein's interpretation as an attempt to read medieval concepts into earlier symbols.
44. R. Patai, *Man and Temple in Ancient Jewish Myth and Ritual* (London, 1947), chaps. ii-iii *passim* (cf. p. 87 particularly).
45. Mishnah Yoma 5:4-5.

Chapter VII

1. M. Avi-Yonah, "Mosaic Pavements in Palestine," *QDAP*, II (1933), 85.
2. Silius Italicus, *Punica*, XIV, 656-660.
3. See B. Meissner, "Altorientalische Teppiche," *Orientalia*, n. s. XVI (1947), 166-168.
4. H. E. Winlock, "A Roman Tapestry and a Roman Rug," *Bulletin, Metropolitan Museum of Art*, XXVII (1932), 157-159.
5. Babylonian Talmud, Beẓah 30b.
6. Babylonian Talmud, Baba Bathra 8b.
7. J.-B. Frey, "La Question des images chez les juifs à la lumière des récentes découvertes," *Biblica*, XV (1934), 282.
8. For bibliography, *ibid.*, chap. I, n. 42.
9. In general, for the tombs, A. Mongait, *L'Archéologie en U.R.S.S.* (Moscow, 1959); S. I. Rudenko, *The Culture of the Population of the High Altai in the Scythian Period* (Moscow, 1953), in Russian.

10. E. R. Goodenough, "The Menorah Among Jews of the Roman World," *HUCA*, XXIII (1950-51), part 2, 449-492.

11. *Bull Rab*, I (1949), Pl. 3.

12. For the possible sources of the thematic material in the Dura syna-gogue murals: M. Avi-Yonah, *Studi Semitici*, No. 5, *Oriental Art in Roman Palestine* (Rome, 1961), p. 69; M. H. Ben-Shammai, "The Legends of the Destruction of the Temple among the Paintings of the Dura Synagogue," *Bulletin of the Jewish Palestine Exploration Society*, IX (1942), 93-97 (in Hebrew); H. Buchthal, *The Miniatures of the Paris Psalter* (London, 1938), pp. 18 ff; E. R. Goodenough, *By Light, Light* (New Haven, 1935); A. Grabar, "Images bibliques d'Apamée et fresques de la synagogue de Doura," *Cahiers archéologiques, fin de l'antiquité et moyen age*, V (1951), 9 ff; J. Leveen, *The Hebrew Bible in Art* (Lon-don, 1944); R. Wischnitzer, *The Messianic Theme in the Paintings of the Dura Synagogue* (Chicago, 1948); *DE Syn*.

13. Leveen, *op. cit.*, 4 ff.

14. Cf. L. Ginzberg, *The Legends of the Jews*, I (Philadelphia, 1913), ix.

15. N. Avigad and Y. Yadin, *A Genesis Apocryphon* (Jerusalem, 1956).

16. There is extensive material on the problem of frontality in ancient art; while the conclusion reached may not be acceptable, the basic division in opinion among scholars on the origin of the frontal pose is stated in E. Will, "Art parthe et art grec," *Etudes d'archéologie classique*, II (1959), 125-135.

17. *DE Syn*, Pl. xl, 4.

18. R. Forrer, *Die frühchristlichen Alterthümer aus dem Gräberfelde von Achmimpanopolis* (Strassburg, 1893), Pl. ix, 8; W. F. Volbach and E. Kuehnel, *Late Antique, Coptic and Islamic Textiles of Egypt* (New York, 1926), Pl. 22.

19. D. Talbot Rice, *The Beginnings of Christian Art* (London, 1957), p. 106.

20. E. Flemming, *Encyclopaedia of Textiles*, 2nd ed. (London, 1958), Pl. 1.

21. M. I. Rostovtzeff, "Dura and the Problem of Parthian Art," *Yale Clas-sical Studies*, V (1935), Fig. 58.

22. Viz., M. I. Rostovtzeff, ed., *Excavations at Dura-Europos, Preliminary Report Seventh and Eighth Seasons* (New Haven, 1939), Pl. xxiii.

23. For the Iranian costume: G. Widengren, "Some Remarks on Riding Costume and Articles of Dress among Iranian Peoples in Antiquity," *Studia Ethnographica Upsaliensia*, XI (1956), 228-276.

24. P. Styger, *Die römischen Katakomben* (Berlin, 1933), p. 193, Pl. 46.

25. Forrer, *op. cit.*, Pl. ix, 8.

26. A. Badawy, "L'Art copte, les influences hellénistiques et romaines," *Bulletin de l'institut d'Égypte*, XXXIV (1953), part 2, 49.

27. M. H. Swindler, *Ancient Painting* (New Haven, 1929), Fig. 447.

28. Volbach and Kuehnel, *op. cit.*, Pl. 22.

29. *Viz.*, Flemming, *op. cit.*, Pl. 8.

30. For a statement of the problem: E. Kitzinger, "Notes on Early Coptic Sculpture," *Archaeologia*, LXXXVII (1938), 181-215.

[189]

· BIBLIOGRAPHY ·

ANCIENT LITERARY SOURCES

Avigad, N. and Yadin, Y. *A Genesis Apocryphon.* Jerusalem, 1956.

Bacher, W. *Die Agada der Tannaiten.* 2 vols. Strassburg, 1890.

Bacher, W. *Die Agada der babylonischen Amoräer.* Frankfort-am-Main, 1913.

Breasted, J. H. *Ancient Records of Egypt.* 5 vols. Chicago, 1906-07.

Eusebius. *Ecclesiastical History.*

Ginzberg, L. *Legends of the Jews.* 5 vols. Philadelphia, 1913.

Goldin, J., trans. "The Fathers According to Rabbi Nathan," *Yale Judaica Series,* X. New Haven, 1955.

Gray, C. D. *The Šamaš Religious Texts.* Chicago, 1901.

Gressmann, H. *Altorientalische Texte und Bilder zum alten Testament.* 2 vols. Berlin, 1927.

Herodotus. *The Persian Wars.*

Homer. *Iliad.*

Josephus. *Jewish Wars.*

Kraeling, E. G. *The Brooklyn Museum Aramaic Papyri.* New Haven, 1953.

Loewe, H. and C. G. Montefiore. *A Rabbinic Anthology.* London, 1938.

Luckenbill, D. D. *Ancient Records of Assyria and Babylonia.* 2 vols. Chicago, 1926-27.

Martin, F. *Textes religieux assyriens et babyloniens.* Paris, 1903.

Mendelsohn, I., ed. *Religions of the Ancient Near East.* New York, 1955.

Montefiore, C. G. and H. Loewe. *A Rabbinic Anthology.* London, 1938.

Ovid. *Metamorphoses.*

Philo. *De Vita Mosis.*

Pirke Rabbi Eliezer.

Pritchard, J. B., ed. *Ancient Near Eastern Texts.* Princeton, 1955.

Silius Italicus. *Punica.*

Talmud, Babylonian.

Talmud, Jerusalem.

Thomas, D. W., ed. *Documents from Old Testament Times.* London, 1958.

Yadin, Y. and N. Avigad. *A Genesis Apocryphon.* Jerusalem, 1956.

[191]

DICTIONARIES, CATALOGS, LEXICONS

Amiet, P. *La Glyptique mesopotamienne archaïque.* Paris, 1961.

Avi-Yonah, M. "Mosaic Pavements in Palestine," *QDAP,* II (1933), 1-91.

Barnett, R. D. *A Catalogue of the Nimrud Ivories.* London, 1957.

Beek, M. A. *Atlas of Mesopotamia.* London, 1962.

Bonnet, H. *Reallexikon der Ägyptischen Religionsgeschichte.* Berlin, 1952.

Boston Museum of Fine Arts. *Art of the Ancient Near East in Boston.* Boston, 1962.

Cabrol, F. and H. Leclercq. *Dictionnaire d'archéologie chrétienne et de liturgie.* 15 vols. Paris, 1907-53.

Eisen, G. A. "Ancient Oriental Cylinder and Other Seals," *Oriental Institute Publications,* XLVII. Chicago, 1940.

Encyclopaedia Biblica.

Flemming, E. *Encyclopaedia of Textiles.* 2nd ed. London, 1958.

Frey, J.-B. *Corpus Inscriptionum Iudaicarum.* 2 vols. Rome, 1952.

Gardiner, A. *Egyptian Grammar.* Oxford, 1950.

Hastings *et al. Dictionary of the Bible.*

Hill, G. F. *Catalogue of the Greek Coins of Arabia, Mesopotamia and Persia.* London, 1922.

———. *Catalogue of the Greek Coins of Palestine in the British Museum.* London, 1914.

Hinks, R. P. *Catalogue of the Greek, Etruscan and Roman Paintings and Mosaics in the British Museum.* London, 1933.

Ingholt, H., H. Seyrig, J. Starcky. *Recueil des tessères de Palmyre.* Paris, 1955.

Jüdische Lexicon.

Kadman, L. *The Coins of Caesarea Maritima, Corpus Nummorum Palaestinensium,* II (1957). Jerusalem.

Leclercq, H., and F. Cabrol. *Dictionnaire d'archéologie chrétienne et de liturgie.* 15 vols. Paris, 1907-53.

du Mesnil du Buisson, R. "Inventaire des inscriptions palmyréniennes de Doura-Europos," *Revue des études sémitiques,* II (1935), 17-38.

von der Osten, H. H. *Ancient Oriental Seals in the Collection of Mr. Edward T. Newell.* Chicago, 1934.

Porada, E. *Corpus of Ancient Near Eastern Seals in North American Collections.* 2 vols. Washington, 1948.

Reifenberg, A. *Ancient Jewish Coins.* 3rd ed. Jerusalem, 1963.

Reinach, S. *Répertoire de reliefs grecs et romains.* 3 vols. Paris, 1909.

Richter, G. M. A. *Catalogue of Greek and Roman Antiquities in the Dumbarton Oaks Collection.* Cambridge, 1956.

Van Buren, E. D. *Symbols of the Gods in Mesopotamian Art, Analecta Orientalia,* XXIII. Rome, 1945.

Vermaseren, M. J. *Corpus Inscriptionum et Monumentorum Religionis Mithriacae.* Hague, 1956.

Volbach, W. F., and E. Kuehnel. *Late Antique, Coptic and Islamic Textiles of Egypt.* New York, 1926.

Volbach, W. F., and O. Wulff. *Spätantike und koptische Stoffe aus ägyptischen Grabfunden.* Berlin, 1926.

Ward, W. H. *The Seal Cylinders of Western Asia.* Washington, 1919.

Watzinger, C. *Griechische Holzsarkophage aus der Zeit Alexanders des Grossen.* Leipzig, 1915.

———. *Denkmäler Palästinas.* 2 vols. Leipzig, 1935.

———, and H. Kohl. *Antike Synagogen in Galiläe.* Leipzig, 1916.

Weber, O. *Altorientalische Siegelbilder.* Leipzig, 1920.

Wilpert, J. *I Sarcofagi cristiani antichi.* 5 vols. Rome, 1929-36.

Zunz, L. *Namen der Juden.* Leipzig, 1837.

GENERAL SOURCES

Akurgal, E. *Art of the Hittites.* New York, n.d.

Albright, W. F. *Archaeology and the Religion of Israel.* Baltimore, 1953.

———. *Archaeology of Palestine.* Harmondsworth, 1949.

Avi-Yonah, M. "Ten Years of Archaeology in Israel," *IEJ*, VIII (1958), 52-65.

———. "Oriental Art in Roman Palestine," *Studi Semitici*, V (1961). Rome.

Bailey, C., ed. *The Legacy of Rome.* 2nd ed. Oxford, 1924.

Barnett, R. D. *Assyrian Palace Reliefs.* London, n.d.

Beckwith, J. *Coptic Sculpture.* London, 1963.

Bell, H. I. *Cults and Creeds in Graeco-Roman Egypt.* Liverpool, 1953.

Bloch, R. *The Origins of Rome.* New York, 1960.

Burrows, M. *What Mean These Stones?* New York, 1957.

Contenau, G. *Manuel d'archéologie orientale.* 4 vols. Paris, 1927-47.

———. *La Civilization d'Assur et de Babylone.* Paris, 1937.

———. *Everyday Life in Babylon and Assyria.* London, 1954.

Cook, A. B. *Zeus.* 3 vols. Cambridge, 1914-40.

Cumont, F. *Recherches sur le symbolisme funéraire des romains.* Paris, 1942.

———. *Oriental Religions in Roman Paganism.* New York, 1956.

Dalton, O. M. *Byzantine Art and Archaeology.* Oxford, 1911.

Davies, N. M. *Picture Writing in Ancient Egypt.* London, 1958.

Duchesne-Guillemin, J. *La Religion de l'Iran ancien.* Paris, 1962.

Dussaud, R. *Les Monuments Palestiniens et judaïques.* Paris, 1912.

———. *L'Art phénicien du IIe millénaire.* Paris, 1949.

Ehrlich, E. L. "Symbolik der Religionen," *Kultsymbolik im alten Testament und im nachbiblischen Judentum.* Stuttgart, 1959.

Evans, A. *Palace of Minos.* 4 vols. London, 1921-35.

Feldman, W. M. *Rabbinical Mathematics and Astronomy.* London, 1931.

Frankfort, H. *Cylinder Seals.* London, 1939.

———. *Kingship and the Gods.* Chicago, 1948.

———. *Art and Architecture of the Ancient Orient.* Harmondsworth, 1954.

Godard, A. *L'Art de l'Iran*. Paris, 1962.

Goodenough, E. R. *By Light, Light*. New Haven, 1935.

———. *An Introduction to Philo Judaeus*. New Haven, 1940.

———. *Jewish Symbols in the Greco-Roman Period*. 11 vols. New York, 1953-64.

Gordon, P. *L'Image du monde dans l'antiquité*. Paris, 1949.

Graham, W. C., and H. G. May. *Culture and Conscience*. Chicago, 1936.

Gressmann, H. *The Tower of Babel*. New York, 1928.

Groenewegen-Frankfort, H. A. *Arrest and Movement*. Chicago, 1951.

Gurney, O. R. *The Hittites*. Harmondsworth, 1952.

Harden, D. *The Phoenicians*. London, 1962.

Herzfeld, E. E. *Archaeological History of Iran*. Oxford, 1935.

———. "Die Kunst des zweiten Jahrhtausends in Vorderasien," *Archaeologische Mitteilungen aus Iran*, IX (1938), 1-79.

———. *Iran in the Ancient East*. Oxford, 1941.

———, and F. Sarre. *Iranische Felsreliefs*. Berlin, 1910.

Hiram, A. *Die Entwicklung der antiken Synagogen und altchristlichen Kirchenbauten im heiligen Lande*, Wiener Jahrbuch für Kunstgeschichte, XIX (1963).

Hitti, P. *History of Syria*. New York, 1951.

Hooke, S. H. *Babylonian and Assyrian Religion*. Oxford, 1962.

Hutchinson, R. W. *Prehistoric Crete*. Harmondsworth, 1962.

Jirku, A. *Die Welt der Bibel*. Stuttgart, 1957.

Jung, C. G. *Symbols of Transformation*. New York, 1958.

Juster, J. *Les Juifs dans l'empire romain*. 2 vols. Paris, 1914.

Kammerer, A. *Pétra et la nabatène*. 2 vols. Paris, 1929.

Kanael, B. *Die Kunst der antiken Synagoge*. Munich-Frankfurt, 1961.

Kees, K. *Der Götterglaube im alten Ägypten*. 2nd ed. Berlin, 1956.

Kenyon, K. *Archaeology in the Holy Land*. London, 1960.

Kohl, H., and C. Watzinger. *Antike Synagogen in Galiläe*. Leipzig, 1916.

Krautheimer, R. *Mittelalterliche Synagogen*. Berlin, 1927.

Kuehnel, E., and W. F. Volbach. *Late Antique, Coptic and Islamic Textiles of Egypt*. New York, 1926.

Landsberger, F. *A History of Jewish Art*. Cincinnati, 1946.

Legrain, L. *Culture of the Babylonians and Assyrians*. Philadelphia, 1925.

Leon, H. J. *The Jews of Ancient Rome*. Philadelphia, 1960.

Leveen, J. *The Hebrew Bible in Art*. London, 1944.

Levy, G. R. *The Gates of Horn*. London, 1948.

Lloyd, S. *Early Anatolia*. Harmondsworth, 1956.

L'Orange, H. P. *Studies on the Iconography of Cosmic Kingship in the Ancient World*. Oslo, 1953.

Lübke-Pernice. *Die Kunst der Römer*. Vienna, 1958.

Mazur, B. D. *Studies on Jewry in Greece*. 2 vols. Athens, 1935.

Meyer, O. *Reich und Kultur der Chetiter*. Berlin, 1914.

Mongait, A. *L'Archéologie en U.R.S.S.* Moscow, 1959.

Moortgat, A. *Alt-vorderasiatische Malerei*. Berlin, 1959.

von der Osten, H. H. *Die Welt der Perser*. Stuttgart, 1956.

Parrot, A. *Archéologie mesopotamienne: les étapes*, I. Paris, 1946.

Patai, R. *Man and Temple in Ancient Jewish Myth and Ritual*. London, 1947.

Porada, E. *Alt-Iran*. Baden-Baden, 1962.

Radin, M. *The Jews Among the Greeks and Romans*. Philadelphia, 1919.

Reifenberg, A. *Ancient Hebrew Arts*. New York, 1950.

Rice, D. T. *Byzantine Art*. 2nd ed. Harmondsworth, 1954.

―――. *The Beginnings of Christian Art*. London, 1957.

Rostovtzeff, M. I. *Dura-Europos and Its Art*. Oxford, 1938.

Smith, E. B. *Architectural Symbolism of Imperial Rome and the Middle Ages*. Princeton, 1956.

Smith, W. S. *The Art and Architecture of Ancient Egypt*. Harmondsworth, 1958.

Steve, A.-M., and L.-H. Vincent. *Jérusalem de l'ancien Testament*. 2 vols. Paris, 1956.

Strong, Mrs. A. *Apotheosis and After Life*. London, 1915.

Styger, P. *Die römischen Katakomben*. Berlin, 1933.

Sukenik, E. L. *Ancient Synagogues in Palestine and Greece*. Oxford, 1934.

Swindler, M. H. *Ancient Painting*. New Haven, 1929.

UNESCO World Art Series: Israel Ancient Mosaics. Paris, 1960.

Ungnad, A. *Die Religion der Babylonier und Assyrier*. Jena, 1921.

Vasiliev, A. A. *Justin the First*. Cambridge, 1950.

Vermaseren, M. J. *Mithras, the Secret God*. London, 1963.

Weibel, A. C. *Two Thousand Years of Textiles*. New York, 1952.

Weitzmann, K. *Ancient Book Illumination*. Cambridge, 1959.

Yeivin, S. *A Decade of Archaeology in Israel, 1948-1958*. Istanbul, 1960.

―――. *Archaeological Activities in Israel, 1948-1955*. Jerusalem, 1955.

Zaehner, R. C. *The Dawn and Twilight of Zoroastrianism*. London, 1961.

SPECIAL STUDIES

Abel, F.-M. "Deux tombeaux à meule à Abou Ghoch," *RB*, XXXIV (1925), 275-279.

Akurgal, E. "The Early Period and the Golden Age of Ionia," *AJA*, LXVI (1962), 369-380.

Albright, W. F. "What Were the Cherubim?" *BA*, I (1938) ,1-3.

―――. "Two Cressets from Marisa and the Pillars of Jachin and Boaz," *Bulletin of the American School of Oriental Research*, LXXXV (1942), 18-27.

―――. "The High Place in Ancient Palestine," *Vetus Testamentum, Supplement*, IV (1957), 242-258.

―――. "Was the Age of Solomon Without Monumental Art?" *Eretz-Israel*, V (1958), 1-9.

―――, and P. E. Dumont. "A Parallel Between Indic and Babylonian Sacrificial Ritual," *Journal of the American Oriental Society*, LIV (1934), 107-128.

Ameisenowa, Z. "The Tree of Life in Jewish Iconography," *Journal of the Warburg Institute*, II (1938-39), 326-345.

Amiet, P. "Le Temple ailé," *Revue d'assyriologie et d'archéologie orientale*, LIV (1960), 1-10.

Andrae, W. *Die ionische Säule*. Berlin, 1933.

———. *Das Gotteshaus und die urformen des Bauens im alten Orient*. Berlin, 1930.

Anthes, R. "Mythology in Ancient Egypt," in S. N. Kramer, ed., *Mythologies of the Ancient World*. Garden City, 1961.

Applebaum, S. "A Lamp and Other Remains of the Jewish Community of Cyrene," *IEJ*, VII (1957), 154-162.

Arnold, W. R. *Ephod and Ark*. Cambridge, 1917.

Avigad, N. (Report on the Congress of the Israel Exploration Society.) *IEJ*, VIII (1958), 277-278.

Avi-Yonah, M. "Three Lead Coffins from Palestine," *Journal of Hellenic Studies*, L (1930), 300-312.

———. "Syrian Gods at Ptolemain-Accho," *IEJ*, IX (1959), 1-12.

———. "A New Fragment of the Ashdod Chancel Screen," *Bull Rab*, III (1960), 69.

Badawy, A. "L'Art copte, les influences héllenistiques et romaines," *Bulletin de l'institut d'Égypte*, XXXIV (1953), pt. 1, 151-205; pt. 2, 5-68.

Bagatti, B. "Edifici cristiani nella regione del Nebo," *Rivista di archeologia cristiana*, XIII (1936), 101-142.

Barb, A. A. "Diva Matrix," *Journal of the Warburg and Courtauld Institutes*, XVI (1953), 193-238.

Barnett, R. D. "Phoenicia and the Ivory Trade," *Archaeology*, IX (1956), 87-97.

———. "Persepolis," *Iraq*, XIX (1957), 55-77.

Behn, F. *Hausurnen*. Berlin, 1924.

Ben-Shammai, M. H. "The Legends of the Destruction of the Temple among the Paintings of the Dura Synagogue," *Bulletin of the Jewish Palestine Exploration Society*, IX (1942), 93-97. In Hebrew.

Birmingham, J. "The Chronology of Some Early and Middle Iron Age Cypriote Sites," *AJA*, LXVII (1963), 15-42.

Bratschkova, M. "Die Muschel in der antiken Kunst," *Bulletin de l'institut archéologique bulgare*, XII (1938), 1-131.

Bryan, W. R. *Italic Hut Urns and Hut Urn Cemeteries. Papers and Monographs of the American Academy in Rome*, IV. Rome, 1925.

Buchthal, H. *The Miniatures of the Paris Psalter*. London, 1938.

Budde, E. G. *Aramarium und* χιβωίδς. *Ein Beitrag zur Geschichte des antiken Mobiliars*. Würzberg, 1940.

Burrows, E. "Some Cosmological Patterns in Babylonian Religion," in S. H. Hooke, ed., *The Labyrinth*. London, 1935.

Busink, Th. A. "La Zikurrat de Dûr-Šarrukîn," *Compte rendu de la troisième rencontre assyriologique internationale*. Leiden, 1954.

Calder, W. M., ed. *Monumenta Asiae Minoris Antiqua*, I. Manchester, 1928.

Chéhab, M. "Sarcophages en plomb du musée national libanais," *Syria*, XVI (1935), 51-72.

Cohen, B. "Art in Jewish Law," *Judaism*, III (1954), 165-176.

Cumont, F. "L'Aigle funéraire des syriens et l'apothéose des empereurs," *Revue de l'histoire des religions*, LXII (1910), 119-164.

———. "Un Fragment de sarcophage judéo-païen," *Revue archéologique*, IV (1916), 1-16.

Danthine, H. "L'Imagerie des trones vides et des trones porteurs de symboles dans le proche orient ancien," *Mélanges syriens offerts à M. René Dussaud*, II (Paris, 1939), 857-866.

Demangel, R. "Grilles de fenêtres en Égypte et triglyphes grecs," *Syria*, XVI (1935), 358-374.

Dhorme, E. "L'Arbre de verité et l'arbre de vie," *RB*, XVI (1907), 271-274.

———, and L.-H. Vincent. "Les Chérubins," *RB*, XXXV (1926), 328-358, 481-495.

Diehl, Ch. "Un Nouveau trésor d'argenterie syrienne," *Syria*, VII (1926), 105-122.

Dombart, Th. "Das babylonische Sonnentor und die 'Säge des Šamaš'," *Journal of the Society of Oriental Research*, XII (1928), 4-24.

———. "Der zweitürmige Tempel-Pylon altaegyptischer Baukunst und seine religiose Symbolik," *Egyptian Religion*, I (1933).

Dothan, M. "Some Aspects of Religious Life in Palestine during the Hyksos Rule," *Antiquity and Survival*, II (1957), 121-130.

Dunand, M. "Notes sur quelques objets provenant de Saïda," *Syria*, VII (1926), 123-127.

Elderkin, G. W. "Architectural Detail in Antique Sepulchral Art," *AJA*, XXXIX (1935), 518-525.

Erdmann, K. *Das Iranische Feuerheiligtum*. Leipzig, 1941.

———. "Die Altäre von Naqsh i Rustem," *Mitteilungen der deutschen Orient-Gesellschaft zu Berlin*, LXXXI (1949), 6-15.

Ferron, J. "Inscriptions juives de Carthage," *Cahiers de Byrsa*, I (1950), 175-206.

Filson, F. V. "Temple, Synagogue, and Church," *BA*, VII (1944), 77-88.

Finkelstein, L. "The Origin of the Synagogue," *Proceedings of the American Academy for Jewish Research*, I (1928-30), 49-59.

Forrer, E. O. "Die sogenannte hethitische Bilderschrift," *American Journal of Semitic Languages and Literature*, XLVIII (1932), 137-169.

Frey, J.-B. "La Question des images chez les juifs à la lumière des récentes découvertes," *Biblica*, XV (1934), 265-300.

Friedrich, J. "Das Siegel des hethitischen Königs Hattušili III," *Artibus Asiae*, VI (1937), 177-190.

Galling, K. *Der Altar in den Kulturen des alten Orients*. Berlin, 1925.

———. "Erwägungen zur antiken Synagoge," *Zeitschrift des deutschen Palästina-Vereins*, LXXII (1956), 163-178.

Garber, P. L. "A Reconstruction of Solomon's Temple," *Archaeology*, V (1952), 165-172.

———. "Reconstructing Solomon's Temple," *BA*, XIV (1951), 1-24.

Gaster, T. H. "Myth and Story," *Numen*, I (1954), 184-212.

Gautier, J.-E. "Le 'Sit Samši' in Šušinak," *Délégation en Perse, Mémoires*, XII (Paris, 1911), 143-152.

Glasson, T. F. *Greek Influence in Jewish Eschatology*. London, 1961.

Godbey, A. H. "Incense and Poison Ordeals in the Ancient Orient," *American Journal of Semitic Languages and Literatures*, XLVI (1930), 217-238.

Goldman, B. "The Asiatic Ancestry of the Greek Gorgon," *Berytus*, XIV (1961), 1-23.

———. "An Oriental Solar Motif and Its Western Extension," *JNES*, XX (1961), 239-247.

Goodenough, E. R. "The Crown of Victory," *Art Bulletin*, XXVIII (1946), 139-159.

———. "The Menorah Among the Jews of the Roman World," *HUCA*, XXIII, pt. 2 (1950-51), 449-492.

———. "Pagan Symbols in Jewish Antiquity: The Vine, the Eagle, the Lion," *Commentary*, XXIII (1957), 74-80.

Güterbock, H. "The Composition of Hittite Prayers to the Sun," *Journal of the American Oriental Society*, LXXVIII (1958), 237-245.

Gutmann, J. rev. of *Israel Mosaics* in *The Reconstructionist*, XXVII (1961), 25-27.

———. "The 'Second Commandment' and the Image in Judaism," *HUCA*, XXXII (1961), 161-174.

Hanfmann, G. M. A. "The Seasons in John of Gaza's Tabuli Mundi," *Latomus*, III (1939), 111-118.

Haran, M. "The Ark and the Cherubim: Their Symbolic Significance in Biblical Ritual," *IEJ*, IX (1959), 20-38, 89-94.

———. "The Disappearance of the Ark," *IEJ*, XIII (1963), 46-58.

Herzfeld, E. E. "Der Thron des Khosrô: I. Typus des Sonnen- und Mondwagens in der sasanidischen Kunst," *Jahrbuch der preuszischen Kunstsammlungen*, XLI (1920), 105-147.

Heuzey, L. "Monuments de la Palestine," *Comptes rendus, acádemie des inscriptions et belles-lettres* (1905), 344-347.

Hollis, F. J. "The Sun-Cult and the Temple at Jerusalem," in S. H. Hooke, ed., *Myth and Ritual*. Oxford, 1933.

Holmberg, U. "Der Baum des Lebens," *Annales Academiae Scientiarum Fennicae*, ser. B, XVI (1923), 1-157.

Homès-Fredericq, D. *Hatra et ses sculptures parthes, études stylistique et iconographique*. Istanbul, 1963.

Hommel, P. "Giebel und Himmel," *Istanbuler Mitteilungen*, VII (1957), 11-55.

Hours-Miedan, M. "Les Représentations figurées sur les stèles de Carthage," *Cahiers de Byrsa*, I (1950), 15-160.

Iliffe, J. H. "A Model Shrine of Phoenician Style," *QDAP*, XI (1944), 91-92.

Ingholt, H. *Parthian Sculptures from Hatra, Memoirs of the Connecticut Academy of Arts and Sciences*, XII (1954).

Isserlin, B. S. J. "Some Recent Archaeological News from Israel," *PEQ* (1952), 42-47.

[198]

Jacobsen, T. "Parerga Sumerologica," *JNES*, II (1943), 117-121.

Kahane, P. P. "Classical and Local Elements in the Art of the Ancient Land of Israel," *Atti del settimo congresso internazionale di archeologia classica, 1958*, III (Rome, 1961), 17-25.

Katzenellenbogen, A. "The Sarcophagus in S. Ambrogio and St. Ambrose," *Art Bulletin*, XXIX (1947), 249-259.

Kitzinger, E. "Notes on Early Coptic Sculpture," *Archaeologia*, LXXXVII (1938), 181-215.

Kleiner, G. "Hellenistische Sarkophage in Kleinasien," *Istanbuler Mitteilungen*, VII (1957), 1-10.

Komoróczy, G. "Cinq cylindres-sceaux de la mésopotamie archaïque," *Bulletin du musée national hongrois des beaux-arts*, XIX (1961), 3-18.

Kon, M. "The Menorah of the Arch of Titus," *PEQ* (1950), 25-30.

Kramer, S. N. "Death and Nether World According to the Sumerian Literary Texts," *Iraq*, XXII (1960), 59-68.

Krauss, S. "Die galiläischen Synagogenruinen," *Gesellschaften für Palästinaforschung*. 3rd publ. Berlin, 1911.

———. "Nouvelles découvertes archéologiques de synagogues en Palestine," *REJ*, LXXXIX (1930), 385-413.

Kühn, H. "Die Lebensbaum und Beterschnallen der Volkerwanderungzeit," *IPEK*, XVIII (1949-53), 33-58.

Labat, R. "Elam and Western Persia," *Cambridge Ancient History*, Fasc. ii (1964), chap. XXXII. Cambridge.

Lagrange, M.-J. "Études sur les religions sémitiques," *RB*, XI (1902), 234-238.

Lambert, M. and R. Tournay. "Le Cylindre a de Gudea," *RB*, LV (1948), 402-437.

Landsberger, F. "Jewish Artists Before the Period of Emancipation," *HUCA*, XVI (1941), 321-414.

Lawrence, M. "City-Gate Sarcophagi," *Art Bulletin*, X (1927-28), 1-59.

———. "Columnar Sarcophagi in the Latin West," *Art Bulletin*, XIV (1932), 103-185.

Lechler, G. "The Tree of Life in Indo-European and Islamic Cultures," *Ars Islamica*, IV (1937), 369-416.

Legrain, L. "Seal Cylinders," *Ur Excavations*, X. Philadelphia, 1951.

Lehmann, K. "The Dome of Heaven," *Art Bulletin*, XXVII (1945), 1-27.

Lehmann-Haupt, C. F. "Materialien zur älteren Geschichte Armeniens und Mesopotamiens," *Abhandlung der königlichen Gesellschaft der Wissenschaften zu Göttingen*, n. F. IX (1907), 3-124.

Lenzen, H. *Die Entwicklung der Zikurrat*. Leipzig, 1941.

Lévi, I. "Les Morts et l'avènement de l'ère messianique," *REJ*, LXIX (1919), 122-128.

Lods, M. "Autel ou réchaud? à propos du 'brûle-parfumes' de Taanak," *Revue de l'histoire des religions*, CIX (1934), 129-147.

Loud, G. "The Hittites at Megiddo?" *Mélanges Syriens*, II (Paris, 1939), 557-558.

May, H. G. "Material Remains of the Megiddo Cult," *Oriental Institute Publications*, XXVI (Chicago, 1935).

————. "The Ark—A Miniature Temple," *American Journal of Semitic Languages and Literatures*, LII (1936), 215-234.

McEwan, C. W. "The Syrian Expedition of the Oriental Institute of the University of Chicago," *AJA*, XLI (1937), 8-16.

Meissner, B. "Altorientalische Teppiche," *Orientalia*, n.s. XVI (1947), 166-168.

von Mercklin, E. "Untersuchungen zu den antiken Bleisarkophagen," *Berytus*, III (1936), 51-75.

du Mesnil du Buisson, R. "Le Lever du soleil dans le cylindre hittite du Louvre," *Syria*, XXXVI (1959), 145-147.

Morey, C. R. *The Sarcophagus of Claudia Antonia Sabina and the Asiatic Sarcophagi. Sardis*, V, pt. 1. Princeton, 1924.

de Morgan, J. *Délégation en Perse, Mémoirs*, XII. Paris, 1911.

Morgenstern, J. "The Book of the Covenant," *HUCA*, V (1928), 1-152.

————. "The Origin of the Synagogue," *Studi orientalistici in onore di Giorgio Levi della Vida*, II (Rome, 1956), 192-201.

Müller, V. "Types of Mesopotamian Houses," *Journal of the American Oriental Society*, LX (1940), 151-180.

Müller-Karpe, H. *Vom Anfang Roms. Mitteilungen des deutschen archaeologischen Instituts, roemische Abteilung*, 5th Ergänzungsheft (1959).

Myres, J. L. "King Solomon's Temple and Other Buildings and Works of Art," *PEQ* (1948), 14-41.

Nelson, H. "Medinet Habu Reports," *Oriental Institute Reports*, X. Chicago, 1931.

————. "The Egyptian Temple," *Biblical Archaeologist Reader*. New York, 1961.

Neugebauer, O. "The History of Ancient Astronomy, Problems and Methods," *JNES*, IV (1945), 1-38.

Nielsen, E. "Some Reflections on the History of the Ark," *Vetus Testamentum, Supplement VII* (1960), 61-74.

Obermann, J. "The Divine Name *YHWH* in the Light of Recent Discoveries," *Journal of Biblical Literature*, LXVIII (1949), 301-323.

Parrot, A. *The Temple of Jerusalem*. New York, 1955.

Pering, B. "Die geflügelte Scheibe in Assyrien," *Archiv für Orientforschung*, VIII (1933), 281-296.

Perkins, J. B., and R. G. Goodchild. "The Christian Antiquities of Tripolitania," *Archaeologia*, XCV (1953), 1-82.

Perrot, N. *Les Représentations de l'arbre sacré sur les monuments de Mesopotamie. Babyloniaca*, XVII. Paris, 1937.

Pinkerfeld, J. "Two Fragments of a Marble Door from Jaffa," *'Atiqot*, I (1955), 89-94.

Porada, E. "A Lyre Player from Tarsus," in S. Weinberg, ed., *The Aegean and the Near East*. New York, 1956.

Pritchard, J. B. *The Water System of Gibeon*. Philadelphia, 1961.

Rahmani, L. Y. "Roman Tombs in Shmuel ha-Navi Street," *IEJ*, X (1960), 140-148.

———. "Jewish Rock-Cut Tombs in Jerusalem," *'Atiqot*, III (1961), 93-120.

Riefstahl, E. "A Coptic Roundel in the Brooklyn Museum," *Coptic Studies in Honor of Walter Ewing Crum*. Boston, 1950.

Ronzevalle, P. S. "Venus lugens et Adonis byblius," *Mélanges de l'université Saint-Joseph*, XV (1930), 141-204.

Rosenau, H. "Some Aspects of the Pictorial Influence of the Jewish Temple," *Palestine Exploration Fund, Quarterly Statement* (1936), 157-162.

———. "The Synagogue and the Diaspora." *PEQ* (1937), 196-202.

Rostovtzeff, M. I. "Dura and the Problem of Parthian Art," *Yale Classical Studies*, V (1935), 155-301.

Roth, C. "An Ordinance Against Images in Jerusalem, A.D. 66," *Harvard Theological Review*, XLIX (1956), 169-177.

Rowton, M. B. "The Date of the Founding of Solomon's Temple," *Bulletin of the American Schools of Oriental Research*, CXIX (1950), 20-22.

Rudenko, S. I. *The Culture of the Population of the High Altai in the Scythian Period*. Moscow, 1953. In Russian.

Salonen, A. *Die Türen des alten Mesopotamien. Annales Acadamiae Scientiarum Fennicae*, Ser. B, CXXIV (1961).

Saphrai, S. "Beth She'arim in Talmudic Literature," *Eretz-Israel*, V (1958), 206-212. In Hebrew; English summary, p. 95.

Savignac, M.-R. "Nouveaux ossuaires juif avec graffites," *RB*, XXXIV (1925), 253-266.

Sayce, A. H. "The Hieroglyphic Inscription on the Seal of Subbiluliuma," *Archiv für Orientforschung*, VII (1931), 184-185.

Schapiro, M. "The Angel with the Ram in Abraham's Sacrifice: A Parallel in Western and Islamic Art," *Ars Islamica*, X (1943), 134-147.

Schlumberger, D. "Descendants non-méditerranéens de l'art grec," *Syria*, XXXVII (1960), 131-166, 253-318.

Schmökel, H. "Ziegen am Lebensbaum," *Archiv für Orientforschung*, XVIII (1958), 373-378.

Scholem, G. "The Curious History of the Six-Pointed Star," *Commentary*, VIII (1949), 243-251.

Scott, R. B. Y. "The Pillars Jachin and Boaz," *Journal of Biblical Literature*, LVIII (1939), 143-149.

Segall, B. "Notes on the Iconography of Cosmic Kingship," *Art Bulletin*, XXXVIII (1956), 75-80.

Seyrig, H. "La Religion palmyrénienne d'après un livre récent," *Syria*, XVI (1935), 393-402.

———. "Antiquités syriennes: une idole bétylique," *Syria*, XL (1963), 17-32.

Shapley, J. "A New Reading of Old Egyptian Textiles," *Journal of Aesthetics and Art Criticism*, XX (1962), 375-388.

Sjöqvist, E. "Excavations at Morgantina (Serra Orlando) 1961: Preliminary Report VI," *AJA*, LXVI (1962), 135-143.

Smith, A. M. "The Iconography of the Sacrifice of Isaac," *AJA*, XXVI (1922), 159-173.

Smith, M. "The Image of God," *Bulletin of the John Rylands Library*, XL (1957-58), 473-512.

Sonne, I. "The Zodiac Theme in Ancient Synagogues and in Hebrew Printed Books," *Studies in Bibliography and Booklore*, I (1953), 3-13.

Soper, A. "The 'Dome of Heaven' in Asia," *Art Bulletin*, XXIX (1947), 225-248.

Sprengling, M. "A New Pahlavi Inscription," *American Journal of Semitic Languages and Literatures*, LIII (1937), 126-144.

Stern, H. "Nouvelles recherches sur les images des conciles dans l'église de la nativité à Bethléem," *Cahiers archéologiques*, III (1948), 82-105.

Strauss, H. "The History of the Seven-branched Candlestick of the Hasmonean Kings," *Journal of the Warburg and Courtauld Institutes*, XXII (1959), 6-16.

Sukenik, E. L. "Designs of the Torah Shrines in Ancient Synagogues in Palestine," *Palestine Exploration Fund, Quarterly Statement* (1931), 22-25.

———. "The Present State of Ancient Synagogue Studies," *Bull Rab*, I (1949), 8-23.

Sundwall, J. *Die italischen Hüttenurnen. Acta Academiae Aboensis Humaniora*, IV, 5. Finland, 1925.

Torge, P. *Aschera und Astarte*. Leipzig, 1902.

Trell, B. "The Naophoroi of Greek Imperial Coins," *AJA*, LXVI (1962), 200.

Urbach, E. E. "The Rabbinical Laws of Idolatry in the Second and Third Centuries in the Light of Archaeological and Historical Facts," *IEJ*, IX (1959), 149-165.

Van Buren, E. D. "The Guardians of the Gate in the Akkadian Period," *Orientalia*, n.s., XVI (1947), 312-332.

———. "Akkadian Stepped Altars," *Numen*, I (1954), 288-234.

de Vaux, R. "Les Chérubins et l'arche d'alliance," *Mélanges de l'université Saint-Joseph*, XXXVII (1960-61), 91-124.

Vincent, A. *La Religion des judéo-araméens d'Éléphantine*. Paris, 1937.

Vincent, L.-H. "Nouveaux ossuaires juifs," *RB*, XI (1902), 103-107.

———. "La Description du temple de Solomon," *RB*, XVIII (1907), 515-542.

———. "Sur la date des ossuaires juifs," *RB*, XLIII (1934), 564-567.

———. "La Notion biblique du Haut-Lieu," *RB*, LV (1948), 245-278.

Wachtsmuth, F. "Achaemenid Architecture," in A. U. Pope, ed. *Survey of Persian Art*. 6 vols. New York, 1938.

van der Waerden, B. L. "History of the Zodiac," *Archiv für Orientforschung*, XVI (1952-53), 216-230.

Waterman, L. "The Damaged 'Blueprints' of the Temple of Solomon," *JNES*, II (1943), 284-294.

Watzinger, C. "Die antiken Synagogen galiläas, neu Ausgrabungen und Forschungen," *Der Morgen*, VI (1930), 356-367.

Weidner, E. "Der Tierkreis und die Wege am Himmel," *Archiv für Orientforschung*, VII (1931), 170-178.

Wendel, C. *Der Thoraschrein im Altertum*. Halle, 1950.

Wessel, K. "Die grosse Berliner Pyxis," *Rivista di archeologia cristiana*, XXXVI (1960), 263-307.

Widengren, G. "Some Remarks on Riding Costume and Articles of Dress among Iranian Peoples in Antiquity," *Studia Ethnographica Upsaliensia*, XI (1956), 228-276.

Wiener, H. M. *The Altars of the Old Testament*. Leipzig, 1927.

Will, E. "Art parthe et art grec," *Etudes d'archéologie classique*, II (1959), 125-135.

Winlock, H. E. "A Roman Tapestry and a Roman Rug," *Bulletin, Metropolitan Museum of Art*, XXVII (1932), 157-159.

Wirgin, W. "On the Shape of the Foot of the *Menorah*," *IEJ*, XI (1961), 151-153.

―――. "The Menorah as Symbol of Judaism," *IEJ*, XII (1962), 140-142.

Wischnitzer, R. *The Messianic Theme in the Paintings of the Dura Synagogue*. Chicago, 1948.

―――. "The Beth Alpha Mosaic: A New Interpretation," *Jewish Social Studies*, XVII (1955), 133-144.

van Woerden, I. S. "The Iconography of the Sacrifice of Abraham," *Vigiliae Christianae*, XV (1961), 214-255.

Wright, G. E. "Herod's Nabataean Neighbor," *BA*, I (1938), 2-3.

―――. "The Steven's Reconstruction of the Solomonic Temple," *BA*, XVIII (1955), 41-44.

Zeitlin, S. "The Origin of the Synagogue," *Proceedings of the American Academy for Jewish Research*, II (1931), 69-81.

ANCIENT SITES

(Aegina). *Archäologischer Anzeiger*, XLVII (1932), 164-165.

―――. *RB*, XLV (1936), 462.

Albertini, E. "Fouilles d'Elche," *Bulletin Hispanique*, IX (1907), 109-127.

Andrae, W., and E. Heinrich. *Fara*. Berlin, 1931.

Avigad, N. "Excavation at Beth She'arim, 1954," *IEJ*, V (1955), 205-239.

―――. "Excavations at Beth She'arim," *Eretz-Israel*, V (1958), 61-67, 171-188. In Hebrew.

―――. "Excavations at Beth She'arim, 1958," *IEJ*, IX (1959), 205-220.

Avi-Yonah, M. "A Sixth Century Synagogue at 'Isfiya," *QDAP*, III (1933), 118-131.

―――. "The Synagogue of Caesarea," *Bull Rab*, III (1960), 44-48.

―――, and A. Negev. "Notes and News: Caesarea," *IEJ*, XIII (1963), 147-148.

Bagatti, B., and J. T. Milik. "Nuovi scavi al 'Dominus Flevit'," *Liber Annus, Studii Biblici Franciscani*, IV (1954), 246-276.

―――. *Gli scavi de "Dominus Flevit."* Jerusalem, 1958.

Bar-Adon, P. "Expedition C—The Cave of the Treasure," *IEJ*, XII (1962), 215-226.

Beyer, H. W., and H. Lietzmann. *Jüdische Denkmäler* I. *Die jüdische Katakombe der Villa Torlonia in Rom.* Berlin, 1930.

Bittel, K. *Die Felsbilder von Yazilikaya.* Bamberg, 1934.

———. "Beitrag zu Eflân-Pinar," *Bibliotheca Orientalis*, X (1953), 2-5.

Butler, H. C. *Princeton University Archaeological Expeditions to Syria.* Div. II, *Architecture, Southern Syria.* Leyden, 1919.

Clermont-Ganneau, Ch. "Découverte à Jérusalem d'une synagogue hérodienne," *Syria*, I (1920), 190-197.

Dalton, O. M. "The Tessellated Pavement of Umm Jerar," *Burlington Magazine*, XXXIV (1919), 3-10.

(Delos). *RB*, XLV (1936), 461-462.

Ferrua, A. "Il Cimitero sopra la catacombe di Domitilla," *Rivista di archeologia cristiani*, XXXVI (1960), 173-210.

Fitzgerald, G. M. *A Sixth Century Monastery at Beth-Shan.* Philadelphia, 1939.

Forrer, R. *Die frühchristlichen Alterthümer aus dem Gräberfelde von Achmimpanoplis.* Strassburg, 1893.

von Gerkan, A. "Eine synagogue in Milet," *Zeitschrift für Neuetestamentliche Wissenschaft*, XXII (1921), 177-181.

———. "Die frühchristliche Kirchenanlage von Dura," *Römische Quartalschrift*, XLII (1934), 214-232.

Ghirshman, R. "La Tour de Nourabad," *Syria*, XXIV (1944-45), 175-193.

Glueck, N. "The Nabataean Temple of Khirbet et-Tânnur," *Bulletin of the American School of Oriental Research*, LXVII (1937), 6, 25, 34.

Goodchild, R. G., and J. B. W. Perkins. "The Christian Antiquities of Tripolitania," *Archaeologia*, XCV (1953), 1-84.

Hanfmann, G. M. A. "The Fifth Campaign at Sardis," *Supplement, Annual Report of the Fogg Art Museum for 1962.* Cambridge, 1962.

Hestrin, R. "A New Aramaic Inscription from 'Alma," *Bull Rab*, III (1960), 65-67.

Holleaux, M. "Fouilles au temple d'Apollon Ptoos," *Bulletin de correspondance héllenique*, XII (1888), 380-404.

Hopkins, C. *The Excavations at Dura-Europos, Preliminary Report VI.* New Haven, 1936.

('Isfiya). "Archaeological News," *AJA*, XXXVIII (1934), 303-304.

Kahane, P. P. "Tombs at Huqoq," *'Antiqot*, III (1961), 126-147.

Kaufmann, D. "La Synagogue de Hammam-Lif," *REJ*, XIII (1886), 46-61.

Kosay, H. Z. *Alacahöyük.* Ankara, n.d.

Kraeling, C. H. *The Synagogue. The Excavations at Dura-Europos, Final Report VIII*, pt. 1. New Haven, 1956.

Lagrange, M.-J. "La Mosaïque de Chellal en Palestine," *RB*, XXVI (1917), 569-572.

Laroche, E. "Eflatun Pinar," *Anatolia*, III (1958), 43-47.

Levy, Rahmani, Hiram, Dunayevsky, Avi-Yonah, and Yeivin. "The Ancient Synagogue of Ma'on (Nirim)," *Bull Rab*, III (1960), 6-40.

Lifshitz, B. "Die Entdeckung einer alten Synagoge bei Tiberias," *Zeitschrift des deutschen Palästina-Vereins*, LXXVIII (1962), 180-184.

Maisler, B. *Excavations at Beth She'arim*. Jerusalem, 1940. In Hebrew.

Mallowan, M. E. L. "Excavations at Brak and Chagar Bazar," *Iraq*, IX (1947), 1-259.

Marmorstein, A. "The Synagogue of Claudius Tiberius Polycharnus in Stobi," *Jewish Quarterly Review*, XXVII (1936-37), 373-384.

Marquet-Krause, J. "La Deuxième campagne de fouilles à Ay," *Syria*, XVI (1935), 325-345.

Mayer, L. A., and A. Reifenberg. "The Synagogue of Eshtemo'a," *JPOS*, XIX (1941), 314-326.

(Miletus). *RB*, XXXI (1922), 472-473.

Mitten, D. G. "The Synagogue at Sardis," *AJA*, LXVII (1963), 215.

Moortgat, A. "Tell Chūēra," *Archiv für Orientforschung*, XX (1963), 225-231.

"Ostia." Anon. not., *Bollettino d'arte* (1961), 316.

"Ostia." Anon. not., *AJA*, LXVI (1962), 396.

Payne, H. *Perachora, The Sanctuaries of Hera Akraia and Limenia*. Oxford, 1940.

Perrot, J. "Une tombe à ossuaires du ive millénaire à Azor, près de Tel-Aviv," *'Atiqot*, III (1961), 1-83.

Peters, J. P., and H. Thiersch. *Painted Tombs in the Necropolis of Marisa*. London, 1905.

Plassart, A. "La Synagogue juive de Délos," *Mélanges Holleaux* (Paris, 1913), 201-215.

———. "La Synagogue juive de Délos," *RB*, XI (1914), 523-534.

Renan, E. "La Mosaïque de Hamman-Lif," *Revue archéologique*, III (1884), 273-275.

Rostovtzeff, M. I., et al. *Excavations at Dura-Europos, Preliminary Report V*. New Haven, 1934.

———. *Excavations at Dura-Europos, Preliminary Report of the Seventh and Eighth Seasons*. New Haven, 1939.

Rowe, A. *The Four Canaanite Temples of Beth-Shan*. Philadelphia, 1940.

"Sardis." Anon. not., *AJA*, LXVII (1963), 188.

Schaeffer, C. F. A. *Ugaritica*, III. Paris, 1958.

Schlumberger, D. "Le Temple de Surkh Kotal en Bactriane," *Journal asiatique*, CCXL (1952), 433-453.

———. *The Excavations at Surkh Kotal and the Problem of Hellenism in Bactria and India*. London, 1961.

Schmidt, E. F. *Persépolis, Vol. II*, Oriental Inst. Pub., LXIX (1957).

Schrader, H., and Th. Wiegand. *Priene, Ergebnisse der Ausgrabungen 1895-1898*. Berlin, 1904.

Schwabe, M. "The Synagogue of Caesarea and its Inscriptions," *Alexander Marx Jubilee Volume*. New York, 1950. In Hebrew.

Sjöqvist, E. "Excavations at Morgantina, 1961," *AJA*, LXVI (1962), 135-144.

Squarciapino, M. F. "Die Synagoge von Ostia antica," *Raggi, Zeitschrift für Kunstgeschichte und Archäologie,* IV (1962), 1-8; V (1963), 13-17.

Sukenik, E. L. *The Ancient Synagogue of Beth Alpha.* London, 1932.

————. "The Ancient Synagogue of El-Hammeh," *Journal of the Palestine Oriental Society,* XV (1935), 101-108.

————. "The Ancient Synagogue at Yafa near Nazareth, Preliminary Report," *Bull Rab,* II (1951), 6-24.

————. "Notes: A New Discovery at Beth Alpha," *Bull Rab,* II (1951), 26.

————. "More About the Ancient Synagogue of Caesarea," *Bull Rab,* II (1951), 28-30.

Trendall, A. D. *The Shellal Mosaic.* Canberra, 1942.

Tsori, N. "Notes and News: Beth Shean," *IEJ,* XIII (1963), 148-149.

Vincent, L.-H. "Le Sanctuaire juif d' 'Aïn Douq," *RB,* XXVIII (1919), 532-563.

————. "La Synagogue de Noarah," *RB,* XXX (1921), 442-443, 579-601.

————. "Vestiges d'une synagogue antique à Yafa de Galilée," *RB,* XXX (1921), 434-438.

————. "Une Ville gréco-romaine à Beit Djebrin," *RB,* XXXI (1922), 259-281.

————. "Un Sanctuaire dans la région de Jericho," *RB,* LXVIII (1961), 163-173.

Yadin, Y. "Excavations at Hazor, 1958, Preliminary Communiqué," *IEJ,* IX (1959), 74-88.

Young, R. S., "Progress at Gordion, 1951-52," *University Museum Bulletin,* XVII (1953), 3-39.

Index

Note. The general topics which are continuously treated throughout the book (e.g. mosaics, portals) are indexed according to the various headings under which they are discussed. Major documentary citations only are given for the synagogue of Beth Alpha and its artists, Marianos and Ḥanina.

Eflatun Pinar, monument at, 84-85, Fig. 8
Egg, 54
Egypt, art, 58, synagogues, 41
Elahsams, painter, 47
Elche, synagogue of, 170n.
Eleaza b. Perata, R., 146n.
Elephantine, temple, 170
El Greco, 59
El Hammeh. *See* Hammath-by-Gadara
Elijah, in Dura-Europos painting, 139
Emessa, 137, 138
Enkidu, 100, as doorkeeper, 78
Epiphany, at the portal, 73, 82; door of, 135
Erdmann, K., 129, 135
Erech, Temple of Inanna, 92
Ereshkigal, goddess of underworld, 101
er-Rafid, synagogue of, 60
Esarhaddon, his building, 73
Eschatology in ancient world, 101-103
Estan, earth deity, 84
Etchmiadzin Gospels, 140n., 159
Ethrog, 65, 66, 108, 112
Etruscan, burials, 117; urn, 120
Eucharist, 39
Eudoxius, catacomb painter, 167n.
Ezekiel, 37

Fire temples, 129-135
Fish, 53, 60, 72
Folk-art, at Beth Alpha, 154, 156-157, 162
Footstool of Yahweh, 114, 124
Frankfort, H., 74, 130
Frontality in ancient art, 156, 189n.
Fruit, 53

Gallienus, 136
Gamaliel, Rabbi, 64; tomb of, 104, Fig. 17
Garlands, 119, 122
Gates of Heaven, in Homer, 78
Gaza Strip, 50n.
Gehenna, 102, 103
Gemara, 40n., 44n.
Ghirshman, R., 129
Gilgamesh, 22, 100, 101; as doorkeeper, 78
Giotto, and Western illusionism, 158
Gizzida, as doorkeeper, 78

Glassware, 42, 58, 67-68, 108, 114, 140, Fig. 18, Photos 28, 57
Glueck, N., 138
Godard A., 130, 134
Gods and heroes, Adonis, 110; Aglibôl Shalma, 136; Ahura Mazda, 70, 81; Amon-Re, 70; Anu, 38n., 78; Artemis, 121; Asherah, 47; Assur, 58, 70; Astarte, 62, 87; Atargatis, 54; Baba, 79; Baal, 73; Baal Shamin, 47; Bel, 136n.; Dionysus, 121; Enkidu, 78, 100; Ereshkigal, 101; Estan, 84; Gilgamesh, 22, 78, 100-101; Gizzida, 78; Hadad, 54; Hathor, 86, 88; Helios, 29, 50, 138; Heracles, 61; Inanna, 22, 92, 101; Ishtar 22, 88, 93, 94n. 101; Isis, 92; Istanu, 83; Jupiter, 61, 77; Marduk, 70, 71, 75, 79; Meleager, 121; Mithra, 61; Nephthis, 92; Nergal, 70; Ningirsu, 73, 79; Ninurta, 70; Nut, 85-86; Osiris, 22; Re, 85; Selene, 63; Semea, 111; Shamash, 70, 71; Shu, 82, 86, Fig. 10; Tammuz, 78; Tanit, 87; Tiamat, 79; Tyche, 62-63, 138; Victory, 61; Wurusemu, 84; Yarhibol, 136n.; Zeus-Baal, 138
Golden Heaven, 75
Gold glass, 67-68, 114, 162, Photo 28
Goodenough, E. R., 64, 66-67, 103, 107, 113, 119, 126, 139
Good Fortune. *See* Tyche
Gournia, altar from, 97
Graeco-Roman art. *See* Classical art
Graven image, 42
Greece, synagogues, 41
Griffin, 63
Guardian figures, 54
Gudea of Lagash, temple builder, 73

Hadad, 54
Hadda, figure from, 159
Hades, 102
Haggadic manuscripts, possible source of illustrations, 152-153
Hagia Triada, sarcophagus from, 118
Haifa, Municipal Museum stone door. *See* Kefar Tamra
Hamman-Lif, synagogue of, 115, 154, 171n., Photos 59, 60
Hammath-by-Gadara (El Hammeh), 49, 172n.

PHOTOGRAPHS

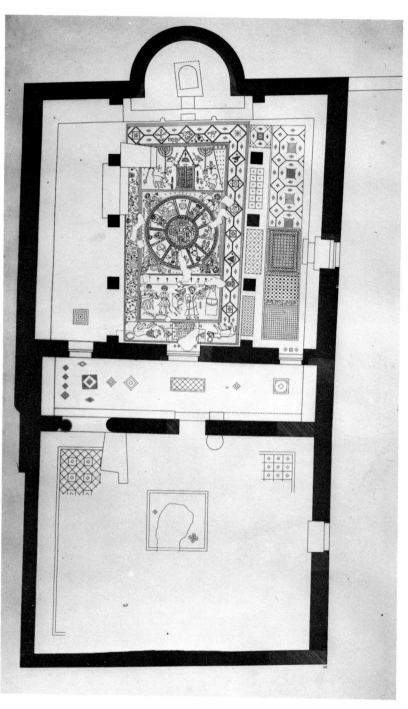

1. Beth Alpha: plan showing location of mosaics.
(Drawing: Department of Archaeology, Hebrew University)

2. Beth Alpha: view of synagogue remains looking toward the wall niche.
(Photograph: Department of Archaeology, Hebrew University)

3. Beth Alpha: view of synagogue remains looking
from niche toward stone bema.
(Photograph: Department of Archaeology, Hebrew University)

4. Beth Alpha mosaic: the Sacrifice of Isaac panel.
(Photograph: Department of Archaeology, Hebrew University)

5. Beth Alpha mosaic: the zodiac panel.
(Photograph: Department of Archaeology, Hebrew University)

6. Beth Alpha mosaic: the Sacred Portal panel.
(Photograph: Department of Archaeology, Hebrew University)

7. Beth Alpha mosaic: Greek and Aramaic inscriptions.
(Photograph: Department of Archaeology, Hebrew University)

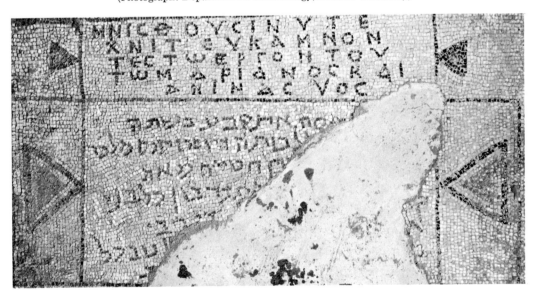

8. Beth Alpha mosaic: Bull flanking inscriptions.
(Photograph: Department of Archaeology, Hebrew University)

9. Beth Alpha mosaic: border pattern, woman holding fowl.
(Photograph: Department of Archaeology, Hebrew University)

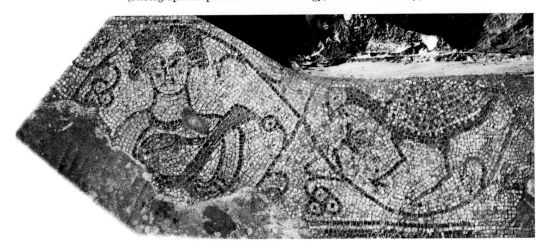

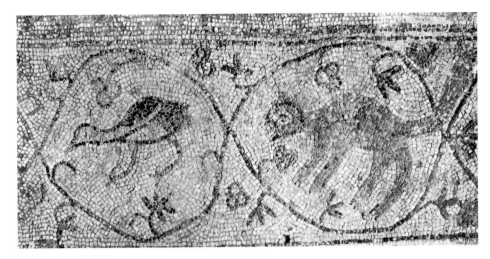

10. Beth Alpha Mosaic: border pattern, bird and animal.
(Photograph: Department of Archaeology, Hebrew University)

11. Beth Alpha Mosaic: border pattern, rabbit (?).
(Photograph: Department of Archaeology, Hebrew University)

12. Beth Alpha mosaic: border pattern, hen and chicks.
(Photograph: Department of Archaeology, Hebrew University)

13. Lead coffin from Beth She'arim: die-made design on narrow end.
(Photograph: N. Avigad, Department of Archaeology, Hebrew University)

14. Chancel screen from Ashdod.
(Oslo, Nasjonal galleriet)

15. Chancel screen from Byzantine church in vicinity of Massu'ot Itzhak.
(Israel, Department of Antiquities)

16a. Dura-Europos synagogue: painted panel over arch of Torah shrine.

16b. Christian sarcophagus with Sacrifice of Isaac (right lateral face).
5th century A.D.
(Milan, San Ambrogio Basilica: photograph: Alinari)

17. Coptic textile fragment with Sacrifice of Isaac. 6th-7th century A.D.
(New York: Cooper Union Museum)

18. Glass dish with Sacrifice of Isaac. Inscribed: VIVAS IN DEOS.
(Trier, Rheinisches Landesmuseum)

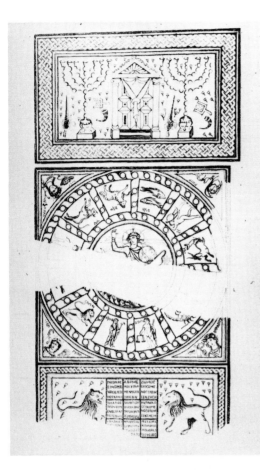

19. Tiberias: drawing of synagogue mosaic. 6th century A.D. (Photography courtesy of Dr. Asher Hiram, Jerusalem)

20a. Mithra relief from Dura-Europos. (Photograph: Dura-Europos Publications)

20b. Relief of Aion in zodiac belt.
(Modena, Museo Estense; photograph, Orlandini)

21. Barberini sarcophagus with zodiac circle.
(Washington: Dumbarton-Oaks Collection)

22a. Zodiac relief from Nabataean Khirbet et-Tannur. (Cincinnati Art Museum)

22b. Relief of Selene from Argos.
(London, Trustees of the British Museum).

23. Central mosaic from pavement of church at Hanita.
6th century A.D. (Hanita, Museum)

24. Mosaic pavement from Roman villa at Corinth.
(Corinth, Museum)

25. Byzantine silk with victorious quadriga.
(Aachen; photograph, Bredol-Lepper)

26. Coptic textile fragment with charioteer.
Late 6th, early 7th century A.D. (Brooklyn, Museum)

27. Painted arcosolium in the Torlonia catacomb:
drawn curtain reveals Torah cupboard flanked by Jewish ritual objects.

28. Jewish gold glass with
"Temple of Solomon."

29. Solar deity between open doors
with lion pivots on
Akkadian cylinder sealing.
(Boston, Museum of Fine Arts)

30. Sacred portal on Sumerian cylinder sealing.
(Boston, Museum of Fine Arts)

31. Elamite bronze plaque of "High Place" dedicated by Shilhak-Inshushinak.
(Paris, Louvre)

32. Shrine on Neo-Assyrian cylinder sealing.
(from *Corpus*, no. 694;
Collection of the Pierpont Morgan Library)

33. Achaemenian sealing showing *aedicula* formed by equestrians supporting winged disk; within, kneeling figure holds circle with portrait inside.
(Tehran, Archaeological Museum)

34. Columnar figures of water-gods on façade of the Temple of Inanna at Erech. Cassite Period.
(from Beek, *Atlas of Mesopotamia*, fig. 164)

35. *Kudurru* with altar shrines
carrying symbols of the gods,
12th century B.C.
(from Beek, *Atlas of Mesopotamia,* fig. 258)

36a. Terra-cotta shrine from Idalion, Cyprus.
(Paris: Louvre Museum)

36b. Altar-shrine with snakes and birds from Beisan (Beth-Shan).
(Philadelphia, University Museum)

37. Etruscan cinerary urn.
(Vatican, Museum; photograph, Moscioni)

38. Ceramic ossuary with door posts from Azor.
(Photo: J. Perrot, Mission archéologique française en Israel)

39. Copper "Crown" with representation of portal.
(Israel, Department of Antiquities)

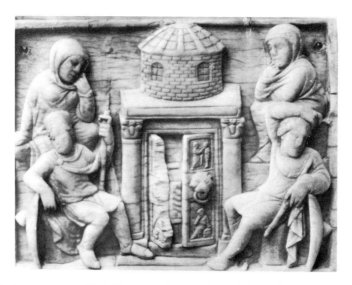

40. Ivory carving of Holy Sepulchre from early Christian casket, *circa* 400 A.D.
(London, Trustees of the British Museum)

41. Stone tomb door from Kefer Yosef.
(Paris, Louvre)

42. Stone tomb door from Ovalin.
(Israel, Department of Antiquities)

43. Hamman-Lif mosaic: panel with Jewish cult objects.
(Brooklyn, Museum)

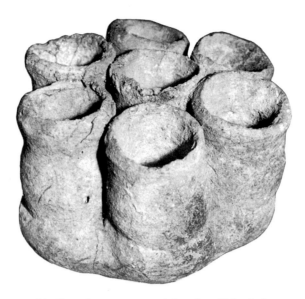

44. Ceramic seven-cup container from Nahariyah.
(Israel, Department of Antiquities)

45. Mosaic pavement from building near Hulda with
standard Jewish cult objects.
6th century A.D.
(Israel, Department of Antiquities)

46. Stone tomb portal from
Kefar Tamra, near Shefar'am.
5th-6th century A.D.
(Haifa, Municipal Museum of Ancient Art)

47. Ceramic lamp with eight nozzles
and portal enclosing lozenge.
(from *Sym.* III, fig. 282)

48. Gabled lid with antefixes from
sarcophagus at Beth She'arim.

49. Jewish ossuary with portal and rosettes.
(Photograph: N. Avigad, Department of Archaeology, Hebrew University)

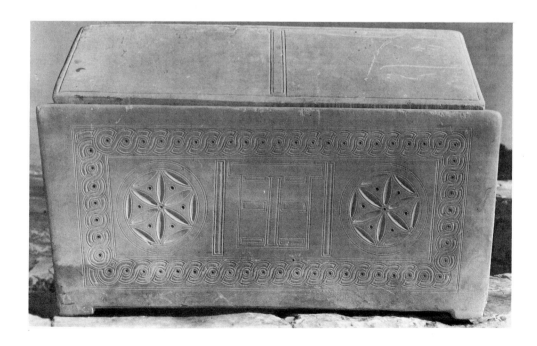

50. Columnar sarcophagus from Beth She'arim.
(Photograph: N. Avigad, Department of Archaeology, Hebrew University)

51. Stone relief from Dura-Europos of deity on camelback before horned altar.
(Photograph: Dura-Europos Publications)

52. Decorated sarcophagus from Beth She'arim.
(Photograph: Israel Exploration Society)

53. Dipinto from Dura-Europos
with eagle mounted on
horned altar within a niche.
(Photograph: Dura-Europos Publications)

54. Coin of Macrinus:
betyl on horned altar in temple enclosure.
(from Ronzevalle, "Venus lugens et
Adonis byblius," pl. xxii, no. 7)

55. Altar of *Alexandros Amrou*
from Khirbet-et-Tannur:
winged goddess in niche.
(Photograph: N. Glueck,
Hebrew Union College)

56. Altar of *Alexandros Amrou*
from Khirbet-et-Tannur:
Zeus-Baal in niche.
(Photograph: N. Glueck,
Hebrew Union College)

57. Glass chalice with Cross in sacred portal.
(Washington, Dumbarton-Oaks Collection)

58. Coptic wool textile fragment from Antinoë, Egypt.
(New York, Metropolitan Museum of Art, Rogers Fund, 1931)

59. Hamman-Lif mosaic: head of Amazon in synagogue pavement.
(Brooklyn, Museum)

60. Hamman-Lif mosaic: head of young shepherd in synagogue pavement.
(Brooklyn, Museum)